ELEMENTARY LOGIC

ELEMENTARY LOGIC

BY

ALFRED SIDGWICK

Author of *The Application of Logic*
The Use of Words in Reasoning
The Process of Argument
etc. etc.

Cambridge :
at the University Press
1914

CAMBRIDGE
UNIVERSITY PRESS

University Printing House, Cambridge CB2 8BS, United Kingdom

Cambridge University Press is part of the University of Cambridge.

It furthers the University's mission by disseminating knowledge in the pursuit of education, learning and research at the highest international levels of excellence.

www.cambridge.org
Information on this title: www.cambridge.org/9781316509692

© Cambridge University Press 1914

First published 1914
First paperback edition 2015

A catalogue record for this publication is available from the British Library

ISBN 978-1-316-50969-2 Paperback

CONTENTS

PART I

THE OLD SYSTEM

CONTENTS

PART II

THE RISKS OF REASONING

INTRODUCTION

BOOKS on Logic often begin with what professes to be a definition of the Science. And if by a definition all that is meant is a vague general statement of aim or purpose, that is easy to give; the aim of Logic, always and everywhere, is to study the difference between good and bad reasoning. Even the loftiest and least mundane kind of Logic cannot really escape from this purpose; for what interest could there be in ideally perfect truths if no one was ever in the least danger of forgetting them? It was the liability of mankind to reason badly that first called Logic into existence, and that still makes the study worth while; and to confess its lack of power to detect bad reasoning, or to boast of a lack of interest in doing this, would be fatal to its claims. The general aim of Logic, then, is clear.

But real difficulties begin as soon as we try to get the " scope and method " of the Science into its definition, for thereby we run a risk of begging the very important question whether a particular limitation of scope, or a particular method, is a help or a hindrance in achieving the aim. There is no general agreement on this point. Indeed that is a mild way of putting it, for we live in times when there is a widespread and growing revolt against certain old methods and old limitations of Logic which have come down to us by tradition. At present they still survive in the examination room, and they still have a harmful influence on some kinds of philosophy; but both in science and in ordinary life they are almost universally reckoned as out of date. At the present day we may safely admit that the best reason for knowing something about the old system is in order to see exactly why modern Logic has been driven to make certain far-reaching departures from it.

This book therefore attempts to give some account, for beginners, of both the old system and the new. Logic is here treated (1) as a carefully limited subject to get up for an elementary examination; and (2) as a free study of some of the chief risks of error in reasoning. For the former purpose we must be content to take the traditional doctrines and technicalities as obediently as we can, making light of the serious difficulties in them and treating them mainly as rules and definitions that have to be learnt with a particular end in view. On the other hand, for the latter purpose a different method is necessary. Even an elementary treatment of the real risks of reasoning will require a fundamental change of attitude towards the old Logic. Here we must rely on modern ways of thought—modern philosophy, science, and common sense; we must allow free criticism of the assumptions and the self-imposed limitations of the old Logic; and, without refusing to benefit by tradition wherever we find it helpful, we must recognise also its power of hampering and misleading the operations of our reason.

Desirable as it might be to keep these two modes of logical study separate, it is almost impossible to avoid giving some hints of the deep defects of the old doctrines and the old definitions, in the process of explaining them. But as a help against confusion of the two points of view I shall adopt the plan of spelling the traditional Logic[1]

---

[1] Also Logical, Logically, and Logician.

with a capital letter and the modern logic with a small one. This seems at any rate a less offensive mode of distinction than by giving the old Logic the doubtful dignity of inverted commas. And something can also be done to mark the distinction by separating the book into two chief Parts.

Part I will deal with those portions of the traditional doctrine which are generally reckoned as elementary. These include two main divisions known respectively as *deductive* and *inductive* Logic. Under the former come in the first place the doctrine of the *Syllogism*, and the technicalities directly accessory to it ; and in the second place the usual curious and haphazard collection of doctrines and technicalities, some (e.g. those of "Immediate Inference ") arising out of the assumptions made by the syllogistic doctrine, others concerned with problems of definition, others grammatical and concerned with the customary uses of words and forms of sentence, and others a mere survival of technicalities which once were accepted as satisfactory but have now for excellent reasons dropped out of use. In this part of the book remarks on the confusion and inconsistency from which nearly all these technicalities suffer will be much curtailed, so as to interfere as little as may be with the student's power of learning them for examination. Under the head of inductive Logic we shall for the same reason be content to accept most of the assumptions under which such writers as J. S. Mill and his many followers have attempted to lay down rules for the examination of material evidence ; but we shall have to accept them under protest.

In Part II the elementary character is more difficult to preserve. Both the grounds and the results of the new logic require a good deal of explanation. But there is nevertheless a certain amount of definite doctrine and technicality which is comparatively simple ; and there is room for a gradual extension of this part of the study as far as the reader may afterwards care to push it. In the meantime its chief interest consists in a new enquiry into the nature of *ambiguity*—a subject which Logic has always, for reasons which we shall duly notice, been exceedingly shy of treating.

A. S.

March 1914

PART I

CHAPTER I

THE "CATEGORICAL SYLLOGISM": ITS PRELIMINARIES

§ 1. *Our Starting Point.*

FROM a modern point of view the central core of Logic —the Doctrine of the Syllogism—may best be regarded as a set of rules for playing a certain kind of game with words, and a set of technicalities the function of which is partly to state the rules of the game and partly to explain the methods that have from time to time been invented for playing it successfully. The reader will understand, however, from what was said in the Introduction, that the conception of Logic as a mere game was far from the minds of its founders. Both the original purpose of the doctrine and its development throughout the Middle Ages were as serious as could be ; it was invented in order to provide a final and indisputable criticism of arguments, a *coercive* method of settling disputes, by formulating " the ideal of true knowledge and the universal form of demonstrative reasoning[1]." It may be added that there are people living even to-day to whom the conception of Logic as a game seems little short of sacrilege. It is a curious fact however that these devotees have so far hesitated to come forward to defend the old Logic against the many attacks that have lately been made upon it. Even such a thorough-going indictment of it as Dr Schiller's *Formal Logic* has

---

[1] See Dr Schiller's *Formal Logic*, p. 190.

not yet prevailed upon them to stand to their guns. In fact the usual line taken by adverse reviewers of that and similar books is to complain that attacks on the old Logic are a slaying of the slain; which is always an easy and safe thing to say, but which can only be believed by those who mean by it that Logic is no longer openly appealed to in everyday controversial writing or speaking. As Dr Schiller well shows, its influence in philosophy and its secondary influence in ordinary thought is still regrettably strong. Those who are inclined to think Logic dead had better read his Chapters XXIV., XXV.

At the present stage of this book however, there is no need to decide whether the old Logic deserves more respect than we shall here be able to give it. At any rate its details remain the same whether it is regarded as a game or as sober doctrine, so that we may take our choice which general view of it is the more suitable. Under the former view, at least, it can be easily mastered and afterwards as easily forgotten.

The reader is not asked to believe that the game is an attractive one, like bridge or chess. If he happens to think it cumbrous and dull there are few who would now disagree with him. A generation ago there used to be a good deal of discussion as to whether Logic is properly a Science or an Art; but of late years this discussion has become less fashionable, and it is reported of Jowett that he once openly declared it to be " neither a science nor an art, but a dodge." Regarded as a dodge however—a dodge in reasoning and disputing—it is in modern times anything but effective. In everyday reasoning or disputing we all ignore its restrictions when we feel inclined to do so. Any arguer who finds that its results conflict with his own can always claim—and often justly—that Logic makes assumptions which he is not forced (in the name of Reason) to grant.

The game itself is played with *syllogisms*—that is to

say, with groups of three *propositions* (statements) constructed in a manner that will presently be explained.
Two of the three propositions in a syllogism are called
the *premisses*, and the third is called the *conclusion*, and
said to be *drawn from* or *yielded by* the premisses. And
the main object of the game is to draw the *legitimate* (or
valid) conclusion—if there is one—from any two given
premisses, and to avoid drawing from them any conclusion
which is illegitimate. The examiners will require you to
perform this operation easily and securely. For instance,
the two premisses " All men are liars " and " George
Washington is a man " yield the legitimate conclusion
that " George Washington is a liar " ; for the legitimacy of
a conclusion is not the same as its truth ; and the two
premisses " All bad workmen complain of their tools " and
" Thomas complains of his tools " do not yield the legitimate conclusion that " Thomas is a bad workman." He
may as a matter of fact be an idle bungler, but the two
premisses just given do not throw any light at all on the
question—from a strict Logical point of view.

Further, the examiners will require you not only to see
at a glance the illegitimacy of a faulty conclusion but to
give the name of the fault correctly. There are certain
technical names for all the faults that any syllogism (or
apparent syllogism) can have, and you may be asked to
say which of these " fallacies " a given invalid syllogism
illustrates. The fallacies in question are few in number
and easily learnt, but in order to explain them we must
first get to know certain other technicalities. It is here
that we begin to make acquaintance in detail with the
Rules of the Game.

§ 2.   *Subject and Predicate.*

Syllogisms, we saw just now, are—from this point of
view—constructions made of three " propositions," and a

proposition is, roughly speaking, the same as what is generally called a statement[1]. I say roughly speaking, because only a small proportion of actual statements come before us, in real life, in the shape in which Logic can accept them as propositions ready for use in a syllogism. They often have to be first translated into *Logical Form*. This notion of a " Logical Form " of propositions arose out of the supposition that all statements are best understood as cases of *predication*[2]—a supposition which does apply naturally to a good many statements, and which by a little forcing—and a little inattention to actual meanings or purposes—can be made to seem applicable to all. Grammarians also have adopted this notion. In Grammar you are supposed to be able to look at any ordinary statement and discover in it (1) " That which is spoken about "; this you call the *Subject*; and (2) " That which is said about the Subject "; and this you call the *Predicate*. But what Grammar calls the Predicate Logic regards as a combination of Predicate and *Copula*. To take the simplest kind of example, the sentence " John is a bachelor " would be analysed by Grammar into: Subject " John," Predicate " is a bachelor." Logic would agree in regarding " John " as Subject, but would divide the rest of the sentence into: Copula " is," and Predicate " a bachelor." We need not here trouble ourselves with the enquiry how there came to be this difference between Logic and Grammar. All that matters from our present point of view is that the division into Subject, Copula and Predicate, is one of the rules we have to abide by. In order to get material for playing the game, propositions must be regarded as made up of two

[1] The difference between a " proposition," an " assertion," a " statement " and a " judgment " are here of no importance. But see p. 226.

[2] Some beginners may need to be warned that predication has nothing to do with prediction. The fact that is asserted in a predication may be either past, present, or future.

"terms" (Subject term and Predicate term) *connected by a copula*. It is assumed that there are in existence a large number of words unattached, whether ranged in order as in a dictionary or floating about casually in our minds. You can take any two of them and join them together with a copula—i.e. you insert between them the word "is" (or "is not" or "are" or "are not") and then you have got a proposition, whether true or not. Out of propositions so obtained you can then proceed to construct syllogisms by following certain further rules to be presently explained. To analyse an ordinary sentence and express it so as to show its two terms and its copula is called "putting it into Logical Form" or "showing its Logical character," and in § 4 we shall have to consider this operation a little more closely.

Here again it may be well to notice that this conception of "Logical Form" was not consciously invented as part of a game. That is only our modern way of regarding it now that we can see its defects when considered as part of a theory of reasoning. But historically it dates from a time when men's view of the nature of *classes* was much more rigid and simple than is now generally possible. Perhaps there never was a time when it was believed strictly and universally that if a thing belongs to a class A, then A it must be called in every context and for every purpose. But the further back we look within the last few centuries the greater tendency we find to regard accepted classes as beyond the reach of criticism. Not only was Mathematics, with its clear and sharp and permanent divisions, regarded as the type of knowledge, but classes of all kinds—even the obviously artificial classes of society—were habitually thought of as unalterable facts of Nature; indeed, within the memory of the present generation it used to be taken almost as an axiom that a thing could not be in a class A and also outside it. The notion that a thing can be A *for one purpose* and not-A for another has won its way only slowly and partially into general acceptance, and would still shock and displease those of us who are incurably Logical. Classes, it used to be supposed, exist in Nature ready made, and individual things are either inside or outside them, either belong to them or do not, and there is an end of the matter. That classes are only our human way of grouping things, to suit our own purposes, which are liable to change and vary, is one of the troublesome modern notions that are still resented by the kind of thought that only asks to be let alone. The active thought of the present day is far more concerned with causes than with classes; we are more interested in knowing how things behave and work than in knowing how they have been traditionally named and classified.

This subject will occupy us at greater length in Part II, and here it is only referred to for the sake of noting that Logic is in this respect extremely simple-minded and inactive. That is why it takes as its most general type of proposition statements about the relation of an individual case to a class (e.g. "John is a bachelor"), or of a smaller class to a larger one (e.g. "Bats are not birds"). Both these kinds of statement are still often made, and there will always be a use for them. Only they are much less representative than they formerly were of thought as a whole; and to a great extent they are now used with a clear remembrance that the justification of a class is convenience merely, and that the notion of a class must take into account a possible *variety of purposes*, which is ignored by Logic. One of the fundamental rules of the Logical game is that if a thing is inside the class A it cannot also be outside it. And another fundamental rule is that it must be either inside or outside. In the material with which the game is to be played Logic allows no sitting on the fence, and no speculation about doubtful margins.

§ 3. *The Laws of Thought.*

In many text books of Elementary Logic the fundamental rules just mentioned are set out in the form of
three "Laws of Thought," and at first sight they seem to
be a harmless formulation of truths which everybody admits
and of which we hardly need to be reminded. In Part II
we shall have to criticise this view of them, but for the
present we may take them simply as rules of the game.

The first is called the *Law of Identity*, and says that
"A is A"; or that if we have admitted that a particular
thing or class (S)[1] deserves the predicate A, then in
drawing inferences from that statement we are bound by
that admission. In other words "What I have said, I have
said."

The second is called the *Law of Contradiction*[2], and
says that "A is not not-A," or that S cannot both be and
not be A. In other words "Two negatives make an
affirmative," or "If you contradict yourself you save me
the trouble of contradicting you." A statement that S is
both A and not-A is called "a contradiction in terms."

The third is called the *Law of Excluded Middle*, and
says that "Everything must be either A or not-A," or that
S must either be or not be A. In other words, every
question whether S is A, if answered at all, must be
answered either "yes" or "no." We all know how freely
this principle is appealed to by cross-examining Counsel
in the Law Courts.

When the "Laws of Thought" are regarded as rules
of a game, most of the difficult questions that have from
time to time been raised about them become irrelevant.
From our present point of view therefore it does not matter

---

[1] The symbol S is commonly used in Logic to stand for any Subject that
happens to be spoken of.

[2] By Krug, Hamilton, and others it is called the *Law of Non-contradiction*.

whether they give us information about Things, or about Thought, or about nothing; nor, if they do give any information, whether it is true or false. The point that here concerns us is that Logic assumes that breaches of them are possible, and that when such breaches are committed they disqualify the player. They are postulates that have to be accepted before the "reasoning" operation can begin.

Though we must reserve our fuller criticism of them we may at once notice one thing that is involved in their acceptance. What they postulate is that the terms used in a syllogism must be taken as perfectly unambiguous, and the distinction between every term and its "contradictory" (i.e. between A and not-A) as perfectly sharp and clear. That is to say, they ignore any difficulty there may be in making sure that the terms we use *are* of this extremely satisfactory type. It is true that the Laws do not altogether ignore the possibility of such difficulties arising; for, in the case of the Law of Contradiction at least, certain cautionary clauses are at times included in the statement; e.g. "S cannot be both A and not-A *at the same time*, and *the same place*, and *in the same respect*"; thus recognising (theoretically) that trouble may arise through the gradual change of A into not-A, through S being A in one part and not-A in another, and even through S being A for one purpose and not for another. But since we can only apply the Law of Contradiction on the assumption that these troubles of interpretation have been somehow removed, it cannot be taken as a *rule*, with recognisable breaches, so long as our terms are allowed to be in the smallest degree indefinite. However many qualifying clauses therefore we may add to the bare statement of the Law, the difficulties are supposed to be over and done with before the Law comes into operation; that is to say, before "reasoning" begins.

§ 4. *Quality and Quantity.*

To return now to the Logical Form of propositions. The basis of this we have seen to be Subject, Copula, Predicate; and the typical form is "*S is P.*" But since the kind of statements considered were those about *inclusion in* or *exclusion from* a class, it was natural to recognise a difference of copula as *affirmative* or *negative.* "S is P" was called an affirmative proposition, and "S is not P" a negative one. This is technically called a difference in the *quality* of propositions. Equally natural was it to notice the difference between speaking of the *whole* of a class and only an indefinite *part* of it. Our acquaintance with the members of any class—except a few specially limited ones like "the contents of my pocket" or "the books on that shelf"—is always more or less imperfect; we cannot make a personal inspection of *all* members of a kind of animal, vegetable, or mineral; and when we are clearly aware of this limitation of our knowledge we may hesitate to assert that *all* the S's are P, keeping to the safer and less definite statement that *some* are so. Hence arose a division in what was called the *quantity* of propositions; the statement about the whole of the class S being called a *universal* proposition, and that about an indefinite part ("some") being called a *particular* proposition. And, in order to guard against an obvious uncertainty of meaning, the rule was laid down that the "some" in a particular proposition should always be interpreted as "some, and possibly all" instead of as "some, but not all." For instance, a proposition like "Some truths are useful" must not be interpreted as implying that any truths are not so.

These two divisions, of quality and quantity, are independent of each other and therefore give us altogether four "Logical forms of proposition[1]":

[1] In this chapter we are concerned only with "categorical" propositions. The distinction between them and other kinds is discussed in § 15.

Universal Affirmative (e.g. *All wasps are insects*).

Universal Negative (e.g. *No women are voters*).

Particular Affirmative (e.g. *Some scholars are clergy-men*).

Particular Negative (e.g. *Some roses are not scented flowers*).

For convenience in referring to these kinds of proposition shortly and distinctively it is usual to express them by means of the letters A, E, I and O, putting A for the universal affirmative, E for the universal negative, I for the particular affirmative, and O for the particular negative. These letters and their meaning have to become perfectly familiar to us ; and a help in remembering them at first is that A and I are the two first vowels in the word *affirmo*, while E and O are the two vowels in the word *nego*. If we are to play the game of Logic at all, we had better get rid of any shame we may feel in " reasoning " by means of artificial aids to memory.

It should be noted also that where the Subject is an individual thing (e.g. *John, America, this pencil, the highest mountain in the world*) the proposition is called *singular*, but ranks as "universal" for Logical purposes. For instance, " John is a bachelor " would be treated as an A form, and " this pencil is not sharp " as an E form, though both would be described as singular propositions. This rule may seem strange at first, but the reason for it will be understood when we come to the syllogistic rules about " distribution " of terms (pp. 17—19).

We are not here[1] concerned with the whole subject of the difficulty of translation from ordinary language into Logical Form. The old Logic treats it lightly, and at present we must do the same. Still, some of the more obvious difficulties are usually noticed in the textbooks, and questions may be asked about them.

[1] More is said about it in § 13, and again at pp. 165—7.

There is, for example, the question how to translate sentences which are technically called *pre-indesignate* (in contrast to *predesignate*). That means, sentences in which the "quantity" is not expressly stated: e.g. "Cats are quadrupeds." If this were expressed "All cats are quadrupeds" it would be called predesignate and we should recognise it as a universal affirmative. But as long as the "All" is not expressly stated there is a theoretical possibility of either "some only" or "some at least" being intended.

Logicians are not agreed as to the best way of treating sentences of this type. Some have tried to lay down the rule that they must be understood as "particular" propositions—on the ground that every statement should be interpreted as taking the line of least risk, and as intending only the minimum of its possible meaning. Others have allowed themselves to recognise that very often—as in "Cats are quadrupeds"—the actually intended meaning is universal, and their common sense has rebelled against leaving the intended meaning out of account. It is clear that the sentence-form "Y is Z" is actually used in both ways and that our interpretation of the speaker's intention is influenced by our knowledge of the matter asserted. No one would suspect a speaker of meaning that anything short of *all* cats are quadrupeds; but if he said that "barristers are clever," no one would suspect him of meaning literally *all*. The most one can say therefore is that if a question of this sort is met with in an examination the safest course is to give "Some Y are Z" as the strict formal answer, but to mention the practical doubt.

Much the same applies to the cases where, instead of "all" or "some," the sentence speaks of Most, or Many, or Few. We may here adopt Prof. Carveth Read's statement that these are generally interpreted to mean "some"; but that as *Most* signifies that exceptions are known, and *Few* that the exceptions are the more numerous, propositions thus predesignate are in fact exponibles[1], amounting to "some are, and some are not." He adds that "if to work with both forms is too cumbrous, so that we must choose one, apparently *few are* should be treated as *some are not*. The scientific course to adopt with propositions predesignate by *most* or *few* is to collect statistics and determine the percentage[2]."

A somewhat similar question applies to "Only Y are Z" or "None but Y are Z." Here, if we decline to speculate about the speaker's actual intention, and assume that he is taking the least risk of possible error, both these sentences are universal negatives of the form "No *non-Y* are Z," and therefore do not assert anything at all about *Y*, —not even that Some Y are Z. If I said, for instance, "None but the brave deserve the fair," I might possibly not want to take the risk of asserting that anyone, whether brave or not, does deserve the fair, but only to express the opinion that cowards at any rate do not.

In practice, however, sentences of this form very often are intended to convey an assertion about Y as well as about non-Y, and sometimes to assert that *all* Y are Z. For instance, "Only material bodies have weight" is obviously intended to imply that all material bodies have weight ; and "No roses but hybrid teas thrive in Cornwall" seems to imply that at least *some* roses are suited to the Cornish climate. As soon as we allow ourselves to think about the speaker's actual intention all sorts of questions become relevant which Logic generally avoids considering except under strong compulsion from common sense. In cases where sentences of this form are taken to make an assertion about Y as well as about non-Y, Logic would regard them as "exponible."

[1] A compound of two or more propositions is technically called "exponible."
[2] *Logic, Deductive and Inductive*, p. 53.

But the truth is that the question how far the assertor's probable real intention is to be taken into account has never been seriously considered by the old Logic, and the only rule that comes within its limited scope is that a sentence should be translated into Logical Form in the way that will make it least assertive. Cases where the difficulty of translation is not met by this rule must either be settled by common sense as well as it can, or else—as in modern logic—we must frankly recognise that only the assertor can decisively say what his own meaning is. Anyhow the syllogistic operation, as Logic understands it, cannot begin till these difficulties are at least supposed to be settled.

In speaking of forms of sentence and their Logical meaning we must briefly notice the *Quantification of the Predicate*. Sir William Hamilton[1] is responsible for this additional burden on the student's memory. By "Quantification of the Predicate" is meant affixing a mark of Quantity to both the Subject and the Predicate, so as to make eight forms instead of the ordinary four. The letters A E I O are retained for half of them, and the letters U, Y, η and ω are employed for the remainder. The complete list is as follows:

    U. All Y is all Z.
    A. All Y is some Z.
    Y. Some Y is all Z.
    I. Some Y is some Z.
    E. No Y is any Z.
    η. No Y is some Z.
    O. Some Y is no Z.
    ω. Some Y is not some Z.

[1] Mr Macleane (*Reason, Thought, and Language*, p. 311) says that some Logicians at the end of the Scholastic period played with the quantifying of predicates, and Hamilton allows that the ancients who rejected the idea placed it distinctly before their minds. He adds that Bentham has also been claimed as its pioneer, and that another school of predicate-quantifiers was headed by De Morgan. The tendency of recent Logicians is to treat the process as unimportant.

The suggestion served to occupy the minds of Logicians for a time, but they now generally recognise its futility. Mr Joseph objects to it on the ground that "the predicate of a proposition is not thought of in extension"—i.e. that the function of the predicate is not to say anything about the *number of other things* to which the same predicate may be applied. Others object to it on the ground that, of the four additional forms, U is reducible to two A propositions, Y is in effect an A proposition written with its Subject and Predicate transposed, η is in effect O similarly reversed, and ω is truistic and therefore useless[1]. Others again have pointed out[2] that the strict Logical "some" makes no difference in the propositions quantified, except to introduce a useless awkwardness of expression, and that Hamilton himself used "some" partly in this sense and partly in the sense of "some only." On the whole the most that can be said for the scheme is that it can be made some use of in "Equational Logic"—a subject with which the reader need not here be troubled.

§ 5. *Some Minor Points.*

Another grammatical question which has been much discussed is whether the copula asserts the "existence" of the Subject. The simple answer that this depends on the intention of the assertor would at once end the discussion, which arises only in the Logic which tries to make general rules for interpreting sentences, and which fails to see that no such rules can have more than a *primâ facie* value. That "existence" is an extremely indefinite word, most Logicians understand, and that some kinds of existence are beyond question *not* asserted in a statement like "Mr Hyde

---

[1] See Mr Boyce Gibson's *Problem of Logic*, p. 161. For a fuller account of the objections to the scheme see also Mr Joseph's *Introduction to Logic*, pp. 198—204.

[2] See Dr Keynes's *Formal Logic*, Part III. chap. ix.

is an impossible character." And so they make use of the phrase *Universe of discourse*[1] (or of *diction*) to mark the limited kind of existence that must be—and that is all that need be—claimed for any Subject. The copula, they say, asserts existence *within a universe of diction*, or *suppositio*. On this Dr Schiller[2] remarks " Agreement therefore on the *suppositio* is essential to understanding, and is by no means easy. In default of it, discussion is at cross-purposes, and comes to nothing." Starting with the attempt to make a general rule for interpreting statements, Logic here ends by giving us a phrase that tells us no more than that there is always a prior question to settle. To those who did not already know this—to those who did not already know that "the meaning" of a statement is just what it is meant and taken to mean—such a phrase will convey information.

But if Logic should ever succeed in grasping the fact that *meaning always depends upon a person who means*, or that the average or usual meaning is not necessarily the actual one, all these grammatical discussions would sink down to their proper level. The utmost that they can do for anyone is to give him some rough rules by which to accomplish the translation from ordinary language into Logical Form. They are possibly a help towards this, at least for those whose knowledge of ordinary forms of speech is slight, but they become misleading as soon as they are taken for decisive, or trustworthy. No verbal form of statement carries its correct interpretation (as intended by the assertor) unmistakably on its face.

But even when the grammatical part of Logic is made the most of, and even in those cases where the rough average method of interpreting a sentence does not mislead us, it carries us a very little way towards solving the whole problem of translating from ordinary language into Logical

[1] See also p. 105.
[2] *Formal Logic*, p. 108.

Form.   Such difficulties as that of saying what exactly is
the Subject, and what the Predicate, of an actual assertion,
or even whether it is truly a case of predication at all[1], are
scarcely touched upon by the textbooks.   The textbooks
notice, indeed, that there are such things as Subject-less
propositions—sometimes called *impersonal*—and that in
certain cases a single word is used to convey an assertion
(e.g. *Fire!*); but they give us no idea of the real extent to
which ordinary modern language leaves uncertain the
correct analysis of a given statement into its Logical parts.

CHAPTER II

THE "CATEGORICAL SYLLOGISM": ITS WORKING

§ 6.   *The Rules of the Syllogism.*

There is a set of traditional Rules for distinguishing
between valid and invalid forms of syllogism.   The first
two of these are:

(1)   *A syllogism contains three propositions, and no more.*

(2)   *The three propositions of any syllogism contain
between them three terms, and no more.*

These two rules, it is evident, define the difference
between a syllogism (whether valid or invalid) and a
combination of propositions which is not to be called
a syllogism at all.   The first rule requires no further
explanation—for the purposes of Logic—now that we
know what a "proposition" is.   But the second introduces
a special feature of syllogisms which is worth notice.

Take the eight terms used on p. 10 in illustrating the

[1] See p. 73.

forms of proposition: *wasps, insects, scholars, clergymen, women, voters, roses, scented flowers.* So long as we are speaking of propositions independently of the question whether they are true or false, fairly disputable, or obviously absurd, any two of these terms may be joined together by a copula and called a proposition: for example *All scholars are insects*, or *No women are wasps* or *Some voters are scented flowers.* But these three propositions do not make a syllogism, because between them they contain six terms instead of only three. If a combination of three propositions is to contain three terms only, while each proposition contains two, it is arithmetically evident (1) that from each of the three propositions one of the three terms is absent; and (2) that each of the three terms must occur once in two of the propositions. That is, in fact, what strings the three propositions together and makes them a syllogism. Each of the three propositions is connected with one of the others by means of a term common to both. For instance, the three propositions *Some scholars are insects, Some insects are voters, Some voters are not scholars* would pass these two rules and so be called a syllogism, though we shall presently see that there is another rule which they would not pass, and therefore they do not make a "valid" syllogism. And the three propositions *All women are roses, Some women are insects, Some roses are insects* would pass all the rules if we take the last of them as the conclusion, but otherwise not. The obvious absurdity of a proposition, whether a valid conclusion or not, is, as noted above, irrelevant to the game.

(3) The third of the Rules is that *No term must be "distributed" in the conclusion unless it is distributed in the premisses.* And in order to understand what this means we have to explain the technicality "distribution of a term," and also the structure of the syllogism as containing premisses and conclusion.

For the "distribution" of a term it is difficult to find a definition which shall be at once concise and easily understood, though for examination purposes it would be sufficient to say[1] that "a term is said to be distributed (within a proposition) when it is used in its whole extent; i.e. when there is either an explicitly stated or a logically implied reference to all the individuals contained in the class for which it stands." But for the purpose of knowing beyond any doubt which terms in a syllogism are distributed and which are not, a simpler method than that of trying to interpret this definition will suffice. Since every proposition in any syllogism must be one of the four kinds A, E, I, or O, all we need remember is that the *only* distributed terms are :—

> In the A proposition, the Subject
> In the E proposition, both Subject and Predicate
> In the O proposition, the Predicate ;

and the reason is that in the universal affirmative (all Y are Z) *every part* of the class Y is spoken of[2], but no assertion is made that every part of the class Z coincides with it; in the universal negative *every part* of Y, and in the particular negative *some part* of Y, is said to lie outside *any part* of Z ; while in the particular affirmative (I) some part of Y is said to coincide with some part of Z, but nothing is said or implied about the whole of either class. The propositions "All rats are vermin," "No Britons are slaves," "Some historians are prigs," "Some soldiers are not heroes" may here serve better than Y and Z for illustration.

Or we may sum up the matter in another way :—

[1] See Boyce Gibson's *Problem of Logic*, p. 148.

[2] From this we see why the singular proposition (see p. 10) is counted as universal. The Subject of a singular proposition, being indivisible, is necessarily spoken of as a whole.

In both kinds of universal the Subject is distributed ;

In both kinds of particular the Subject is undistributed ;

In both kinds of negative the Predicate is distributed ;

In both kinds of affirmative the Predicate is undistributed.

These details have to be remembered perfectly, but are easily learnt.

Next as to premisses and conclusion. In any syllogism —in any combination of three propositions which satisfies Rules 1 and 2—any one of the three propositions may conceivably be intended as the conclusion, the other two being the premisses. Having decided which the conclusion is, we can then find which of the two other propositions is the *major* premiss and which the *minor* ; also which is the *middle term* of the syllogism. It will be remembered that each of the three propositions contains one term in com- mon with each of the other two ; also that each of the three propositions necessarily omits one of the three terms. Now the rule is that the proposition which contains the predicate term of the conclusion is the major premiss—the predicate term of the conclusion being called the *major term*—the proposition which contains the subject term of the con- clusion is consequently the minor premiss ; and the middle term is that one of the three terms which is absent from the conclusion. And when we have found not only the conclusion but also the major and minor premisses, it is usual and convenient to write the major premiss first in order, the minor premiss second, and the conclusion last.

An example will serve to show these points, and also the operation of Rule 3. Let us imagine the following three propositions given :—

> All liberals are socialists,
> Some home-rulers are not liberals,
> Some home-rulers are not socialists.

(*a*) If the first of these three be taken as the conclusion, then the third would be the major premiss and the second the minor. The syllogism would then be written :—

> Some home-rulers are not socialists,
> Some home-rulers are not liberals,
> Therefore, All liberals are socialists ;

and though this conclusion would not be valid it would not break the rule we are here discussing—Rule 3.

(*b*) If the second be taken as the conclusion, then the first would be the major premiss and the third the minor ; and the syllogism would be written :—

> All liberals are socialists,
> Some home-rulers are not socialists,
> Therefore, Some home-rulers are not liberals ;

and this conclusion would be valid.

(*c*) If the third be taken as the conclusion, then the first would be the major premiss and the second the minor ; the syllogism would be written as it stands, and would be invalid. For the term *socialists* is undistributed in the major premiss and distributed in the conclusion.

The technical name for the breach of this rule is *Illicit Process* ; and it is usual to specify whether it occurs in the major or the minor term. Thus the instance just given would illustrate *illicit process of the major term.*

(4) The fourth of the Rules is that *the middle term must be distributed once at least in the premisses.* The reader now knows how to discover, in any given syllogism, whether the rule is broken. He would see, for instance, that the defect in question is exemplified in case (*a*) above ; or again in the syllogism :—

> All conservatives are unionists,
> Jones is a unionist,
> Therefore, Jones is a conservative.

This rule has the merit of being easily justified by common sense. For, so long as we know only that Jones and the conservatives respectively correspond to "some" unionists, we have no guarantee that the two statements refer to the same part of that class; they may or may not, and therefore no conclusion can be drawn. If they happen not to, then "unionist" is *in effect* a word with two meanings, so that the syllogism suffers from "ambiguity in its middle term[1]." The class "unionists" may, for anything that is said in the premisses, extend beyond the class "conservatives"; i.e. *all* conservatives and also *some* liberals may belong to the unionist party, and Jones may be a liberal unionist. How then are we to "conclude" from such premisses that he is necessarily a conservative?

This may also be shown in a diagram, where circles are made to represent classes and a black spot to represent Jones.

For all that the premisses tell us, he may be in either of the two positions indicated. The technical name for the breach of this rule is "undistributed middle."

(5) The fifth of the Rules is that *from two negative premisses no conclusion can be drawn.* This defect also is exemplified in the syllogism (*a*) on p. 20. It needs no other technical name than "negative premisses."

(6) The sixth Rule is that *if one premiss be negative, the conclusion must also be negative; and that to prove a negative conclusion one premiss must be negative.* No special name has been invented for the breach of this rule.

---

[1] See pp. 163–4, § 32.

Lastly there are some corollaries which follow from Rules 3, 4, 5 and 6 taken together :—

(i) *Two particular premisses yield no conclusion.*

(ii) *If one premiss is particular, so is the conclusion.*

These are sometimes called Rules 7 and 8 respectively, and we will here adopt that numbering. A third, which I have not seen elsewhere given[1], and which we will call Rule 9 is that *if one premiss is negative and the major term is undistributed in its premiss, there is no conclusion.*

With these Rules at our fingers' ends we are fully equipped for discriminating (though rather slowly) between valid and invalid syllogisms ; and also for discovering, when a conclusion and one premiss only are given, what the other premiss must be in order to make the conclusion legitimate. But for performing these operations more quickly and easily another, more mechanical, method has been invented which will be explained presently.

———————

So far, our examples of the syllogistic process have been expressed in words. But it is easy, and often convenient, to use for this purpose letters of the alphabet instead of words; for instance the letters X Y Z, or the letters S M P. The convention is that X (or S) shall represent the minor term of the syllogism, Y (or M) the middle term, and Z (or P) the major term. Thus, for the purpose of seeing

---

[1] Prof. Carveth Read (*Logic, Deductive and Inductive*, p. 110) gives as a third corollary "*From a particular major premiss and a negative minor premiss, nothing can be inferred.*" Taking Z as major term, this corollary disposes of the premisses $\begin{cases} \text{Some Y is Z} \\ \text{No X is Y} \end{cases}$ $\begin{cases} \text{Some Z is Y} \\ \text{No X is Y} \end{cases}$ $\begin{cases} \text{Some Y is Z} \\ \text{No Y is X} \end{cases}$ $\begin{cases} \text{Some Z is Y} \\ \text{No Y is X} \end{cases}$; but leaves us with no direct means of discarding the premisses $\begin{cases} \text{All Y is Z} \\ \text{No X is Y} \\ \text{Some Z is not Y} \\ \text{All Y is X} \end{cases}$ $\begin{cases} \text{All Y is Z} \\ \text{Some X is not Y} \end{cases}$ $\begin{cases} \text{All Y is Z} \\ \text{No Y is X} \end{cases}$ $\begin{cases} \text{All Y is Z} \\ \text{Some Y is not X} \end{cases}$ $\begin{cases} \text{Some Z is not Y} \\ \text{All X is Y} \end{cases}$

whether the conclusions are correct, the syllogism (*c*) given on p. 20 might be expressed as follows :—

> All liberals are socialists—All Y is Z (or All M is P),
> Some home-rulers are not liberals—Some X is not Y (or Some S is not M),

∴ Some home-rulers are not socialists—Some X is not Z (or Some S is not P).

And, generally speaking, where a difficulty is felt in saying whether, in a syllogism expressed in words, the conclusion is legitimate, some of the difficulty will be removed by translating the syllogism into letters ; always remembering to put X (or S) for the term which is Subject in the conclusion, Z (or P) for the term which is Predicate in the conclusion, and Y (or M) for the term which is present in the premisses but absent from the conclusion. In the rest of this chapter we will use letter symbols instead of words for expressing all syllogisms. They are shorter and clearer, and they help to disguise the absurdity which attaches to so many of the syllogistic forms when we try to find words to fit them.

§ 7. *Exercises.*

The most rudimentary exercise on the application of the Rules is where two premisses are given, without a conclusion, and the problem is to say whether they allow any conclusion or not. It is evident that, since there are four forms of proposition possible for each premiss, there are in the first place sixteen variations even if we suppose the order of the terms in each proposition to remain the same. But if we suppose this also to be variable, so that the Subject and Predicate in any premiss among these sixteen varieties may change places, we get a further source of variation which brings the total number up to sixty-four.

Now the simplest application of the Rules is where we use Rules 4, 5, 7, and 9 to discard at once any pairs of premisses that give no conclusion at all. There are altogether, among the sixty-four possible combinations, no less than forty-five of this nature; and the first three of the Rules just mentioned enable us to discard thirty-five of them at a glance. The remaining ten couples[1] (for which Rule 9 is required) are perhaps a little less obvious.

Exercise 1. Take the following pairs of premisses, and say which of them allow of no conclusion about X. Also in each such case say which Rule is referred to.

1 { All Z is Y / All X is Y }   2 { All Y is Z / Some Y is X }

3 { All Y is Z / No Y is X }   4 { No Z is Y / Some X is not Y }

5 { No Z is Y / Some X is Y }   6 { Some Z is Y / Some X is not Y }

7 { No Y is Z / Some Y is X }   8 { Some Y is not Z / All X is Y }

9 { Some Y is not Z / Some X is not Y }   10 { Some Z is not Y / All X is Y }

11 { Some Z is Y / All Y is X }   12 { All Z is Y / Some Y is X }

13 { Some Z is not Y / No X is Y }   14 { No Z is Y / Some X is not Y }

15 { No Z is Y / All Y is X }   16 { Some Y is not Z / All Y is X }

[*Answers:* Nos. 1, 3, 4, 6, 8, 9, 10, 12, 13, 14, allow no conclusion; No. 1 by Rule 4; No. 3 by Rule 9; No. 4 by Rule 5; No. 6 by Rule 7; No. 8 by Rule 4; No. 9 by Rule 5; No. 10 by Rule 9; No. 12 by Rule 4; Nos. 13 and 14 by Rule 5.]

[1] These are given in the footnote on p. 22.

Besides enabling us to say whether a given pair of premisses yield any conclusion, the Rules may be used for saying whether the premisses will allow a *given* conclusion ; and thus indirectly for saying *what* conclusion they allow.

Exercise 2.   Criticise the following syllogisms :—

1
$\begin{cases} \text{All Y is Z} \\ \underline{\text{All Y is X}} \\ \therefore \text{ All X is Z} \end{cases}$

2
$\begin{cases} \text{All Y is Z} \\ \underline{\text{Some X is not Y}} \\ \therefore \text{ Some X is not Z} \end{cases}$

3
$\begin{cases} \text{No Y is Z} \\ \underline{\text{All Y is X}} \\ \therefore \text{ Some X is not Z} \end{cases}$

4
$\begin{cases} \text{All Z is Y} \\ \underline{\text{All X is Y}} \\ \therefore \text{ Some X is Z} \end{cases}$

5
$\begin{cases} \text{All Z is Y} \\ \underline{\text{Some Y is not X}} \\ \therefore \text{ Some X is Z} \end{cases}$

6
$\begin{cases} \text{All Z is Y} \\ \underline{\text{No Y is X}} \\ \therefore \text{ No X is Z} \end{cases}$

7
$\begin{cases} \text{No Y is Z} \\ \underline{\text{All X is Y}} \\ \therefore \text{ Some X is not Z} \end{cases}$

[*Answers :* No. 1 illustrates illicit process of the minor term (Rule 3). Both premisses being affirmative, the conclusion must be affirmative also (Rule 6). As we have seen, it cannot be universal. But the conclusion "Some X is Z" would break no rule.

No. 2 illustrates illicit process of the major term (Rule 3). With these premisses there cannot be any conclusion (Rule 9).

No. 3 breaks no rule, and is therefore valid.

No. 4 illustrates undistributed middle (Rule 4). Any conclusion from these premisses would be invalid.

No. 5 lies open to the same objection ; but it also breaks Rules 6 and 9.

No. 6 breaks no rule, and is therefore valid.

No. 7 breaks no rule ; but the wider conclusion "No X is Z" may be drawn from these premisses.]

When asked to say *what* conclusion a given pair of premisses allow (when they allow any) note first whether both premisses are affirmative. If so, the choice of a conclusion is restricted to the affirmative ones. If not, it is restricted to the negative ones. Then see whether the universal conclusion is possible; for this purpose it is only necessary to see whether such a conclusion breaks Rule 3. If the universal conclusion is not valid, then the particular must be. For example if the given premisses be :—

$$\begin{cases} \text{No} \quad \text{Z is Y} \\ \text{Some Y is X} \end{cases}$$

We see at once that the conclusion must be negative. But if it were " No X is Z " there would be an illicit process of the minor. Therefore " Some X is not Z " is the correct conclusion.

A third operation that may be performed by the Rules is that of saying, when a conclusion and one premiss are given, what the other premiss must be in order to make the proof complete.

Exercise 3. Take the following examples :

1. Some X is Z ; for All Y is Z.
2. No X is Z ; for All X is Y.
3. Some X is not Z ; for Some X is not Y.
4. All X is Z ; for Some Z is not Y.
5. All X is Z ; for All Z is Y.
6. Some X is not Z ; for No Y is Z.

[*Answers:* In No. 1 the middle term, Y, is given distributed and therefore need not be distributed in the missing minor premiss (Rule 4). The minor term, X, is undistributed in the conclusion, and therefore need not be distributed in its premiss (Rule 3). Since the conclusion is affirmative, both premisses must be affirmative (Rule 6). Therefore either " Some X is Y " or " Some Y is X " will serve the purpose.

In No. 2, Y is undistributed in the given minor premiss, and therefore must be distributed in the missing major premiss (Rule 4). Z is distributed in the conclusion and therefore must be distributed in the major premiss (Rule 3). The universal negative is the only form that distributes both its terms. Therefore either " No Y is Z " or " No Z is Y " will serve.

In No. 3, Y is distributed in the given minor premiss, and therefore need not be distributed in the missing major premiss (Rule 4). Z is distributed in the conclusion, and therefore must be distributed in its premiss (Rule 3). The given premiss is negative, and therefore the missing one must be affirmative (Rule 5). Therefore " All Z is Y " is the only form that suffices.

In No. 4, we have a negative premiss given, with an affirmative conclusion. By Rule 6 this is not allowed. Therefore no possible other premiss would here suffice.

In No. 5, Y is undistributed in the given major premiss, and therefore must be distributed in the minor (Rule 4). X is distributed in the conclusion, and therefore must be distributed in its premiss (Rule 3). But since the conclusion is affirmative both premisses must also be affirmative (Rule 6), and an affirmative proposition cannot distribute both its terms. Therefore no other premiss would here suffice.

In No. 6, Y is distributed in the given major premiss, and therefore need not be distributed in the minor (Rule 4). X is undistributed in the conclusion and therefore need not be distributed in its premiss (Rule 3). Therefore either " Some X is Y " or " Some Y is X " would suffice.]

Exercise 4. Rules 7, 8 and 9 were said to be corollaries from Rules 3, 4, 5 and 6. Explain this.

(For Rule 7.) If both premisses are negative, Rule 5 is broken. If one premiss is negative and both premisses particular, the premisses between them contain only one distributed term. But since, by Rule 6, the conclusion must in this case be negative, and therefore its predicate (the major term) distributed, the middle term must be undistributed and Rule 4 broken. If both premisses are affirmative and particular all their terms are undistributed, and Rule 4 broken.

(For Rule 8.) If both premisses are negative, Rule 5 is broken. If one premiss is negative and one particular, only two terms can be distributed. By Rule 4, one of these must be the middle term ; the other, since by Rule 6 the conclusion must be negative, must be the major term. Therefore the minor term is undistributed and the conclusion particular. Lastly, if both premisses are affirmative and one particular, only one term is distributed, and by Rule 4 this must be the middle term. The minor term is therefore undistributed and the conclusion particular.

(For Rule 9.) By rule 6 the conclusion must be negative and so distribute the major term. Any conclusion therefore would break either Rule 3 or Rule 6.

§ 8.   *Mood and Figure.*

We now come to the quicker and more mechanical method of discriminating between valid and invalid syllogisms, and also of discovering what conclusion a given pair of premisses allow, and what further premiss is required when a conclusion and one premiss are given.

It was noticed above that the sixteen different ways in which the four forms of proposition can be combined in two premisses become sixty-four when we are allowed to take account of the further different combinations that are got by turning any one of the propositions round so that its Subject becomes its Predicate—an operation which is technically called *conversion*. We "convert" the proposition "No X is Y" when we write "No Y is X" in place of it. In the case of two of the four forms of proposition, such conversion does not affect the distribution of the terms; namely (1) where both terms are already distributed, as they are in the E form, and (2) where neither term is so, as in the I form. In the A and O forms however, this is not the case; if we convert " All X is Y " into " All Y is X " we change Y into a distributed term; and if we convert " Some X is not Y " into " Some Y is not X " we change the distribution of both terms. We shall see in § 10 why such conversion is not allowed.

The differences between the four different sets of the sixteen original combinations of premisses are technically called differences of *Figure*; the figures being distinguished as First, Second, Third, and Fourth. Under the usual custom of writing the major premiss before the minor:

In the   first   figure the order of the terms is $\begin{cases} YZ \\ XY \end{cases}$

  „ second   „   „   „ $\begin{cases} ZY \\ XY \end{cases}$

  „ third   „   „   „ $\begin{cases} YZ \\ YX \end{cases}$

  „ fourth   „   „   „ $\begin{cases} ZY \\ YX \end{cases}$

It is necessary to know these differences so perfectly that we can say at a glance which figure any given syllogism is in. A convenient way of remembering the figures is by means of the position of the *middle* term (Y) in each. Imagine four squares, side by side, with the above pairs of premisses set out in them in their proper order, and Y in thicker type than X and Z. We get:

Fig. 1	Fig. 2	Fig. 3	Fig. 4
Y Z X **Y**	Z **Y** X **Y**	**Y** Z **Y** X	Z **Y** **Y** X

So that "First Figure" should call up an image of a line slanting down from left to right; and the other figures similar distinctive mental pictures.

We next come to the differences of *Mood*. In each figure there are, as we have seen, sixteen possible moods. Now it is clear that different combinations of *three* propositions (i.e. complete syllogisms in different moods and figures) must, since there are four kinds of proposition, be exactly four times as numerous as different combinations of the two premisses only. That is to say, there are 256 of them, instead of 64[1].

Fortunately, however, 45 out of the 64 possible pairs of premisses are, as we saw at p. 24, easily discarded as allowing of *no* conclusion; which reduces the number of doubtful moods to 76 (i.e. 19 × 4). Out of these, we shall find, only 24 escape condemnation by the rules; and out of the 24, five show a smaller conclusion than is allowable— a particular conclusion where a universal may be drawn— thus leaving nineteen recognised "valid moods of the Syllogism." The five just mentioned are usually reckoned as unimportant; they are called *subaltern*[2] moods, or moods with *weakened conclusions*.

To some ingenious person long ago[3] it occurred that a shorter way than applying the Rules to a given mood, in order to discover whether it is valid, would be to have at our fingers' ends a list of the nineteen valid moods so designated that we could easily discover whether a given mood is one of them or not. So he invented a simple

---

[1] Writing the syllogisms in the regular order (major, minor, and conclusion) we get *in each figure* A A A, A A E, A A I, A A O; A E A, A E E, A E I, A E O; and so on till the 64 are complete.

[2] The reason of this name will be understood by consulting the "square of opposition" on p. 86.

[3] Said by some to be Petrus Hispanus (13th century). Mr Joseph, however (*Introduction to Logic*, p. 261 *n.*), mentions that he has not been able to trace the verses, in their present form, further back than to Aldrich (1691).

memoria technica which tells you this almost at a glance.
He found that in the first figure the moods A A A, E A E,
A I I, and E I O are the only ones that escape condemnation by the rules ; and similarly certain moods in the other
three figures ; and he hit on the plan of stringing together
artificial words containing three vowels each, so as to show
which moods in each figure are valid. These were arranged
in hexameter verses as follows :

> *Barbara, Celarent, Darii, Ferio*que, prioris ;
> *Cesare, Camestres, Festino, Baroko,* secundæ ;
> Tertia, *Darapti, Disamis, Datisi, Felapton,*
> *Bokardo, Ferison,* habet ; Quarta insuper addit
> *Bramantip, Camenes, Dimaris, Fesapo, Fresison.*

§ 9. *Exercises.*

Armed with these verses, and with a knowledge of the
figures, any one can easily solve the following types of
problem :

(1) Given any two premisses and a conclusion, is the
conclusion valid ?

(2) Given any conclusion and one premiss, what must
be the other premiss in order to make the conclusion valid?

(3) Given any two premisses, what conclusion legitimately follows from them ?

Exercise 5.

Given the syllogisms :

(1) All Y is Z
No X is Y
∴ No X is Z

(2) All Z is Y
All X is Y
∴ All X is Z

(3) No Z is Y
Some Y is Z
∴ Some X is not Z

(4) No Y is Z
Some Y is X
∴ No X is Z

Say which figure they belong to; which are valid; which Rules the invalid ones break; and what is the technical name of the fallacy.

[*Answers:* (1) is in the first figure. Its formula is A E E; and in that figure no such mood is allowed (see the first line of the verses). The syllogism is therefore invalid. It breaks Rule 3, since the term Z is distributed in the conclusion but not in the major premiss. It therefore exemplifies "illicit process of the major term."

(2) is in the second figure, and its formula is A A A. The verses show that in that figure no such mood is allowed. The conclusion therefore is illegitimate. It breaks Rule 4, since the middle term (Y) is undistributed in both premisses. "Undistributed middle."

(3) is in the fourth figure, and its formula is E I O. The verses show in that figure the mood *Fresison.* The conclusion is therefore legitimate.

(4) is in the third figure, and its formula is E I E. There is no such valid mood in any figure (by Rule 8). It also breaks Rule 3, since the term X is distributed in the conclusion but not in the minor premiss; and so there is an "illicit process of the minor."]

Exercise 6.

(*a*) Given the conclusion "*All X is Z*" and the premiss "*All X is Y,*" what other premiss is required?

[*Answer:* The given premiss is the minor. The verses show that *Barbara* is the only valid mood with A for a conclusion. Therefore the missing premiss is "All Y is Z."]

(*b*) Given the conclusion "*Some X is not Z*" and the premiss "*All Z is Y*" what other premiss is required?

[*Answer:* The verses show that there are valid moods with conclusion in O in all four figures; but here, since the

major premiss is of the form Z Y, we are restricted to the
second and fourth. The verses show that the only mood
in these two figures with A for its major premiss is *Baroko*
(fig. 2). Therefore the minor premiss must be " Some X is
not Y."[1]]

(c) *Given the conclusion " Some X is Z" and the premiss*
" No X is Y," what further premiss is required ?

[*Answer:* A search through the verses will show no
conclusion in I with either premiss in E. But here we
might more easily arrive at this result by remembering
Rule 6.]

(d) *Given the conclusion " Some X is not Z" and the*
premiss " No Y is Z," what other premiss is required ?

[*Answer:* The verses show no less than six valid moods
with major premiss in E and conclusion in O. The form
of the given major premiss here restricts us to figures 1 and
3. Therefore it is indifferent whether the minor is " Some
X is Y " (*Ferio*), or " Some Y is X " (*Ferison*), or " All Y is
X " (*Felapton*). Any one of these three minor premisses
will suffice for the conclusion.]

Exercise 7.

Given the following pairs of premisses, what conclusion
follows :

1 { No   Z is Y   2 {Some Z is not Y
  { All Y is X   { All Y is X

3 {Some Y is not Z   4 { All Z is Y
  { All Y is X   { No   Y is X

[*Answers:* In (1) we have E A in the fourth figure.
Therefore the conclusion is " Some X is not Z " (*Fesapo*).

In (2) we have O A in the fourth figure ; and there is no
such valid mood, and therefore no conclusion.

---

[1] See example (*b*) on p. 20.

In (3) we have O A in the third figure. Therefore the conclusion is "Some X is not Z" (*Bokardo*).

In (4) we have A E in the fourth figure. Therefore the conclusion is "No X is Z" (*Camenes*).]

In addition to the mnemonic lines, and as sometimes providing a convenient way of discarding invalid syllogisms, the following rules, applicable to the separate figures, are worth remembering:

In Fig. 1, the major premiss must be universal,
    the minor premiss must be affirmative;
In Fig. 2, one premiss (and therefore also the conclusion) must be negative,
    the major premiss must be universal;
In Fig. 3, the minor premiss must be affirmative,
    the conclusion must be particular;
In Fig. 4, when the major premiss is affirmative, the minor must be universal,
    when the minor premiss is affirmative, the conclusion must be particular,
    when the major premiss is particular, both premisses must be affirmative.

The reader may find it useful to work out the connexion between these special rules and the general rules of the Syllogism. They seem perhaps a little difficult to remember, but that is chiefly a matter of practice.

It appears, then, that there are three different methods of working syllogistic problems: (1) by applying the general Rules of the Syllogism; (2) by means of the mnemonic lines; and (3) by the special rules of the separate figures. The last, however, is of narrower scope than the other two, either of which is sufficient to solve any of the types of problem above mentioned.

Some account should also here be given of the method of expressing syllogisms by means of what are known as

"Euler's[1] circles." We have already made use of a figure of this sort to illustrate a case of undistributed middle (p. 21). Such circles can be used to express any actual relation of two classes to each other, or of an individual to a class.

There are altogether five possible relations between the classes X and Z. Any two classes may be:

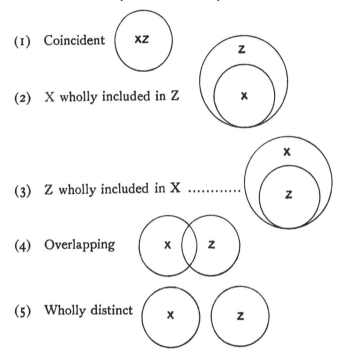

(1) Coincident

(2) X wholly included in Z

(3) Z wholly included in X ....

(4) Overlapping

(5) Wholly distinct

So that if we know what the actual relation is, we can always express it by a single one of these figures. But only one of the A E I O forms expresses the relation between X and Z definitely, namely the E proposition. The others leave the actual relation vague, because they

---

[1] Euler was a Swiss Logician of the 18th century, who lectured for a time in Berlin.

allow two or more alternative possibilities. For instance, A leaves it uncertain whether No. 1 or No. 2 is the actual relation; O leaves a choice between Nos. 3, 4, and 5; and I leaves all the relations possible except No. 5.

In spite of the fact, however, that the E form is the only one which makes a definite choice, these circles can be used for observing *why* a given conclusion is legitimate or not, or *why* no conclusion is possible. Each premiss gives at least negative information about the relation between the middle term and one of the others; it *excludes* some of the five possible alternatives.

Take a major premiss in the vaguest of the forms, I: "Some Y is Z" or "Some Z is Y." What this tells us is that the classes Y and Z are *not* wholly distinct from each other. It thus bars out the fifth of the possible relations given above. Now let us see what results when we join to this a minor premiss of A form, in different figures.

Take first the A form in the first and second figures, namely "All X is Y." The circle X, that is to say, cannot get even partly outside the circle Y. It may be coincident with it, or wholly included, with a margin of Y which is not X.

The major premiss has told us only that Y and Z are not wholly distinct from each other. Now, if we definitely knew that X and Y were coincident, we could infer that X, like Y, is not wholly distinct from Z. But, since there *may* be a portion of Y that is not X, Z may be wholly inside such portion. On the other hand it may be either wholly or partly inside X. Thus any one of the five relations between X and Z is possible. And since each of the A E I O forms bars out at least one of the five relations, this means that no statement about X and Z can be drawn as a conclusion.

Take next as minor premiss the A form in the third and fourth figures; "All Y is X," which says that no part of Y can be outside the circle X. Now since we know, from the major premiss, that Z and Y are not wholly distinct from each other, it is clear that since Y is either coincident with X or included in it, some part at least of Z must be in the same predicament. Therefore the situation that the premisses declare to be *impossible* between X and Z is No. 5 of the alternatives, the E proposition. And to say that E is false is the same as to say that I is true[1]. Hence, with the premisses:

$$\begin{cases} \text{Some Y is Z (or Some Z is Y)} \\ \text{All Y is X} \end{cases}$$

we can draw the conclusion "Some X is Z" (*Disamis* or *Dimaris*). Or, if we take the same premisses and change their order, making "All Y is X" the major premiss, we can draw the conclusion "Some Z is X" (*Datisi*, or *Darii*).

When we get E as major premiss, the result of adding an A or I minor premiss is very simple. The major tells us definitely that Y and Z are wholly distinct from each other. Then if the minor premiss tells us that X is even partly within the circle Y, we see at once that at least part of X must be *outside* Z.

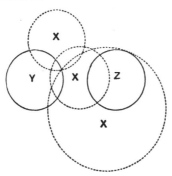

That is why the premisses E A and E I give a con-clusion in all the four figures.

[1] See p. 87.

§ 10. *Reduction.*

We have not yet exhausted all the potted information given by the mnemonic lines. Besides enabling us to solve any problem of the types already discussed, they tell us how to " reduce " any valid, mood in the second, third, or fourth figures to one of the four moods that are valid in the first figure. Why we should want to do this, however, requires some explanation.

The desire arose out of the old belief that Logic was not merely a game, but a theory of reasoning. As Dr Schiller[1] says, Aristotle believed that the syllogisms of the first figure rested on the self-evident principle known as the *Dictum de Omni et Nullo*, and that their truth—i.e. their Formal validity—was indisputable. This he did not hold to be equally the case with the other figures. The *dictum* referred to is commonly[2] quoted in several slightly different forms, and the pith of it is that "Whatever is predicated (affirmed or denied) of a whole class is predicated of any part of it."

This notion that in order to show the truth of a belief— e.g. of the belief that a valid syllogistic conclusion follows necessarily from its premisses—you must be able to deduce it from some wider principle which is " self-evident," was in Aristotle's time and for many centuries afterwards accepted without question[3]. And the *dictum de omni et nullo* evidently did cover all the valid moods in the first figure, though it was not so easily applicable to the other figures. Hence it was thought that by " reducing " moods in these

---

[1] *Formal Logic*, p. 184.

[2] Some Latin forms of it are given by Mr Joseph (*Introduction to Logic*, p. 274), and also a reference to the passage in Aristotle from which it was derived.

[3] The modern distrust of it arises out of the difficulty of finding principles which are at once evidently true and free from doubt as to their *application*. This subject is discussed at some length in Part II.

other figures to a corresponding valid mood in the first figure—i.e. by showing them to be *equivalent* to it—we give to them also the protection of this axiomatic principle.

We have seen that the difference between the various figures consists in the arrangement of the terms in the premisses. Therefore "conversion" (p. 28) must be the process by which we take a syllogism in one figure and express it in another. For instance, in the second figure the middle term is predicate in both premisses, while in the first figure it is predicate in the minor premiss only. Hence, in order to reduce a mood in the second figure—e.g. the mood *Cesare*—to the corresponding mood in the first, we have to convert its major premiss. Thus:

$$\left.\begin{array}{l}\text{No Z is Y} \\ \text{All X is Y}\end{array}\right\} \text{ becomes } \left\{\begin{array}{l}\text{No Y is Z} \\ \text{All X is Y}\end{array}\right.$$

which gives us the valid mood *Celarent*.

But in speaking of conversion above it was noticed that only in the E and I forms of proposition does simple transposition of the terms give us equivalent meaning. If we "simply convert" an A proposition, writing "All Y is X" for "All X is Y" we are asserting something that "All X is Y" gives us no warrant for[1]. To say that "All sleeping animals are breathing" is not the same as to say that "All breathing animals are asleep"; and to say that "All cats are quadrupeds" is not the same as to say that "All quadrupeds are cats." Hence, whenever an A proposition occurs in one of the three last figures we must be careful

---

[1] It sometimes happens that the "simple converse" of an A proposition is *true*. But we can only become aware of this through our knowledge of the "matter" (see pp. 163—7), and therefore its truth requires to be independently asserted, and cannot Logically be inferred. On the other hand in the case where "X is Y" is given as an answer to the question "How am I to know an X when I see it?" (and so is, in effect, a *definition* of "X"), the simple converse is asserted in the proposition itself. See Boyce Gibson's *Problem of Logic*, p. 197, No. 10. The case where X and Y are two proper names for the same person, place, or thing, is noticed at p. 195 *n.*

not to convert it into an A proposition in the first. "All X is Y" allows us to say "*Some* Y is X"—this is called conversion *per accidens*, or conversion *by limitation*, as contrasted with *simple* conversion—but we are not allowed to turn an undistributed term into a distributed one and suppose that we are making no larger assertion than before.

For instance, take the mood *Felapton*:

No Y is Z

All Y is X
_____

∴ Some X is not Z

If we simply converted the minor premiss we should illegitimately get the mood *Celarent* and infer that No X is Z. All that we are in fact entitled to is:

No　Y is Z

Some X is Y
_____

∴ Some X is not Z

and so we get the mood *Ferio*.

Similarly with the O proposition. If we change "Some X is not Y" into "Some Y is not X" we change the undistributed subject term X into the distributed predicate term of a negative proposition. Clearly we have no right to change (e.g.) "Some quadrupeds are not cats" into "Some cats are not quadrupeds" as meaning the same thing. How the O proposition is actually dealt with in the process of "reduction" we shall presently see.

It was said above that the mnemonic lines contain information about the right way of reducing any mood to a corresponding mood in the first figure. They do this by means of some of the consonants in the words. On looking at the lines we see, in the first place, that the initial consonants of the valid moods in the first figure are repeated in the other figures. There is no mood in any figure which begins with any other letter than B, C, D, or F. This is meant to show which mood in the first figure any other will reduce to. For instance, *Bramantip* reduces to *Barbara*, *Dimaris* to *Darii*, and so on throughout. But further the consonants *s* and *p* perform the function of telling us which proposition needs converting, and how. One of these letters coming *after* a vowel representing one of the premisses—as in *Fesapo* they come respectively after E and A—shows the process that has to be performed on that premiss; *s* means "convert *simply*," and *p* means "convert *per accidens*." In order therefore to reduce *Fesapo* to *Ferio*, we proceed as follows :—

(*Fesapo*)   (*Ferio*)

No Z is Y ... *s* ... No Y is Z

All Y is X ... *p* ... Some X is Y

∴ Some X is not Z

The letter *m* means "change the order of the premisses." Thus in reducing *Camenes* to *Celarent* we proceed as follows :—

(*Camenes*)   (*Celarent*)

All Z is Y ⟶ No Y is X

No Y is X ⟶ All Z is Y

∴ No X is Z ... *s* ... ∴ No Z is X

A reference to the verses will show that every mood that has *m* in its name has either *s* or *p* after its conclusion. This is because if we transpose the premisses, making the minor premiss the major, we must also convert the conclusion, so that its predicate shall be the new major term and its subject the new minor. Now since simple conversion does not involve any loss of meaning, we may safely translate *s* at the end of a mood as "simply convert the conclusion *of that mood*." For example, simply convert "No X is Z" in *Camenes*, and the corresponding syllogism in *Celarent* has a conclusion equivalent to it. But in the one mood that ends in *p* (*Bramantip*) this explanation does not suffice. We cannot perform conversion *per accidens* on an I proposition, because it is already particular. What the letter *p* here means therefore is that the conclusion of *Bramantip* is itself the "converse *per accidens*" of the conclusion A which the premisses when reduced to *Barbara* would allow. Thus :—

(*Bramantip*)   (*Barbara*)
All Z is Y ⟍ ⟋ All Y is X
All Y is X ⟋ ⟍ All Z is Y
∴ Some X is Z ⟵ All Z is X

One more indicatory letter remains to have its meaning explained—the letter *k* (sometimes written *c*). This occurs only in the two moods *Baroko* and *Bokardo*, and means that these two moods admit only of "indirect" reduction (or *reductio ad impossibile*) as contrasted with the processes just noticed—where the reduction is technically called *ostensive*. Indirect reduction consists in showing that if the conclusion in O were supposed *not* to follow from the given premisses, then it could be proved (in *Barbara*) that one of the premisses is false; whereas, by hypothesis, they are true. Here another technicality comes in, namely *contradictory* propositions. By this is meant a pair of propositions such that the truth of either implies the falsity of the other, while the falsity of either also implies the truth of the other. A moment's reflection shows that A and O are a pair of contradictories, and similarly E and I.

Take, then, *Baroko* :—

All Z is Y
Some X is not Y
∴ Some X is not Z

Since this conclusion is in O, its falsity would mean

that the corresponding A proposition "All X is Z" is true. Now if we make this the minor premiss of a new syllogism in which the other premiss (given true) is major, we get the premisses of *Barbara* :—

All Z is Y
All X is Z

and these necessitate the conclusion that "All X is Y." But this is the contradictory of the original minor premiss which was given true. Hence we find that if the premisses of *Baroko* do not yield the O conclusion the mood *Barbara* is invalid; which in the eyes of a Logician is impossible.

This indirect process of reduction, however, dates from the time before the processes known as *obversion* (or *permutation*) and *contraposition*[1] were recognised. Obversion consists in altering the "quality" of a proposition by either taking the negation out of the copula and regarding it as part of the predicate, or regarding the affirmative copula as a doubled negative. Thus by obversion :—

All X is Y is taken as equivalent to No X is non-Y
No X is Y as equivalent to All X is non-Y
Some X is Y as equivalent to Some X is not non-Y
Some X is not Y as equivalent to Some X is non-Y.

Now since we can thus get an E proposition out of an A, and an I proposition out of an O, it is obvious that the old difficulty of converting A and O propositions disappears; if not they, at least their equivalents, can now be converted *simply*. In other words the contrapositive[2] equivalent of

[1] Contraposition is said to have been first definitely invented by Boethius, about A.D. 500.

[2] This is sometimes called the *converse by negation*, and the name *contrapositive* reserved for the equivalent form "All non-Y is non-X." See p. 88. Though the contrapositives of E and I are never needed, it is conceivable that they might be asked for in an examination. The contrapositive of E would have to be "*Some* non-Y are X"; and since I when obverted becomes "Some X are *not* non-Y" it does not admit of contraposition at all.

"All X is Y" is "No non-Y is X" and that of "Some X is not Y" is "Some non-Y is X."

Now let us apply this method to the reduction of *Bokardo*:—

$$
\begin{array}{ll}
\text{Some Y is not Z} = & \text{Some non-Z is Y} \\
\underline{\text{All Y is X}} & \underline{\text{All Y is X}} \\
\therefore \text{ Some X is not Z} = \therefore & \text{Some X is non-Z}
\end{array}
$$

Thus, by contrapositing the major premiss of *Bokardo* we get the obverse equivalent of its conclusion in *Dimaris*; which is "ostensively" reducible to *Darii*.

Obversion and contraposition are useful not only in reducing to the first figure, but also sometimes in finding what conclusion follows from two propositions which *apparently* contain between them more than three terms. Suppose, for instance, we are asked to draw a conclusion from

$$
\left\{
\begin{array}{l}
\text{No non-Z is Y} \\
\text{No non-Y is X.}
\end{array}
\right.
$$

Here, on the face of it, there are two negative propositions (breaking Rule 5) with four terms between them (breaking Rule 2). But by obverting the first of these propositions we correct both defects. "No non-Z is Y" becomes by obversion "All non-Z is non-Y"; and by making this the minor premiss, with "No non-Y is X" as major, we have the premisses of *Celarent* and can draw the conclusion "No non-Z is X" (equivalent to "All X is Z")[1].

Again, from the premisses—

$$
\left\{
\begin{array}{l}
\text{All Z is Y} \\
\text{All X is non-Y}
\end{array}
\right.
$$

---

[1] Or, if we like to obvert both premisses and transpose them we get:—
All non-Y is non-X ⎫
All non-Z is non-Y ⎬ which give us (in *Barbara*) the conclusion "All non-Z is
non-X"; which is also equivalent to "All X is Z."

which also contain four terms, we can either get, by changing the first of them into "All non-Y is non-Z," a syllogism in *Barbara* with the conclusion "All X is non-Z" (equivalent to "No X is Z"); or, if we prefer it, we can be content with obverting "All X is non-Y" into "No X is Y" and then we can draw the conclusion "No X is Z" in *Camestres*.

We have now finished our review of the Categorical Syllogism and of the technicalities directly accessory to it. With the materials before him the reader is fully equipped for playing the game and solving any of its technical problems.   But questions of this kind are not the only ones to be met with even in an elementary examination. Logic has had a long history, in the course of which all sorts of supplementary issues have been raised—partly through a natural desire to justify the supposed connexion between Logic and real reasoning, and partly because one enquiry so often suggests another.   In the next chapter we shall discuss some of these various departures from the main line of mechanical reasoning operations, sufficiently at least to show their general direction and to acquaint the reader with some further scraps of logical knowledge useful in the examination room.

§ 11.   *Tables:* of possible pairs of premisses, showing

    (1)   What conclusions, if any, they allow ;

    (2)   What Rule forbids the drawing of any con-
          clusion.

(Where more than one Rule is broken, only the first in order is given.)

FIRST FIGURE.

All Y is Z All X is Y ∴ All X is Z (*Barbara*)	All Y is Z No X is Y (Rule 9)	All Y is Z Some X is Y ∴ Some X is Z (*Darii*)	All Y is Z Some X is not Y (Rule 9)
No Y is Z All X is Y ∴ No X is Z (*Celarent*)	No Y is Z No X is Y (Rule 5)	No Y is Z Some X is Y ∴ Some X is not Z (*Ferio*)	No Y is Z Some X is not Y (Rule 5)
Some Y is Z All X is Y (Rule 4)	Some Y is Z No X is Y (Rule 9)	Some Y is Z Some X is Y (Rule 4)	Some Y is Z Some X is not Y (Rule 7)
Some Y is not Z All X is Y (Rule 4)	Some Y is not Z No X is Y (Rule 5)	Some Y is not Z Some X is Y (Rule 4)	Some Y is not Z Some X is not Y (Rule 5)

SECOND FIGURE.

All Z is Y All X is Y (Rule 4)	All Z is Y No X is Y ∴ No X is Z (*Camestres*)	All Z is Y Some X is Y (Rule 4)	All Z is Y Some X is not Y ∴ Some X is not Z (*Baroko*)
No Z is Y All X is Y ∴ No X is Z (*Cesare*)	No Z is Y No X is Y (Rule 5)	No Z is Y Some X is Y ∴ Some X is not Z (*Festino*)	No Z is Y Some X is not Y (Rule 5)
Some Z is Y All X is Y (Rule 4)	Some Z is Y No X is Y (Rule 9)	Some Z is Y Some X is Y (Rule 4)	Some Z is Y Some X is not Y (Rule 7)
Some Z is not Y All X is Y (Rule 9)	Some Z is not Y No X is Y (Rule 5)	Some Z is not Y Some X is Y (Rule 7)	Some Z is not Y Some X is not Y (Rule 5)

THIRD FIGURE.

All Y is Z All Y is X ∴ Some X is Z (*Darapti*)	All Y is Z No Y is X (Rule 9)	All Y is Z Some Y is X ∴ Some X is Z (*Datisi*)	All Y is Z Some Y is not X (Rule 9)
No Y is Z All Y is X ∴ Some X is not Z (*Felapton*)	No Y is Z No Y is X (Rule 5)	No Y is Z Some Y is X ∴ Some X is not Z (*Ferison*)	No Y is Z Some Y is not X (Rule 5)
Some Y is Z All Y is X ∴ Some X is Z (*Disamis*)	Some Y is Z No Y is X (Rule 9)	Some Y is Z Some Y is X (Rule 4)	Some Y is Z Some Y is not X (Rule 4)
Some Y is not Z All Y is X ∴ Some X is not Z (*Bokardo*)	Some Y is not Z No Y is X (Rule 5)	Some Y is not Z Some Y is X (Rule 4)	Some Y is not Z Some Y is not X (Rule 4)

FOURTH FIGURE.

All Z is Y All Y is X ∴ Some X is Z (*Bramantip*)	All Z is Y No Y is X ∴ No X is Z (*Camenes*)	All Z is Y Some Y is X (Rule 4)	All Z is Y Some Y is not X (Rule 4)
No Z is Y All Y is X ∴ Some X is not Z (*Fesapo*)	No Z is Y No Y is X (Rule 5)	No Z is Y Some Y is X ∴ Some X is not Z (*Fresison*)	No Z is Y Some Y is not X (Rule 5)
Some Z is Y All Y is X ∴ Some X is Z (*Dimaris*)	Some Z is Y No Y is X (Rule 9)	Some Z is Y Some Y is X (Rule 4)	Some Z is Y Some Y is not X (Rule 4)
Some Z is not Y All Y is X (Rule 9)	Some Z is not Y No Y is X (Rule 5)	Some Z is not Y Some Y is X (Rule 7)	Some Z is not Y Some Y is not X (Rule 5)

§ 12. *Examination Questions*[1].

I. *On Conversion, Obversion, and the Distribution of Terms.*

(1) *Explain how the Logical Conversion of a proposition depends on the distribution of its terms.*

"Conversion" means turning a proposition round, so that its Subject and Predicate change places (p. 28). If we do this without paying attention to the character (as A, E, I or O) of the proposition, we should in certain cases get a larger assertion than we are entitled to as the converse. Thus in the proposition "All X is Y," Y is undistributed (p. 18); to convert it "simply" into "All Y is X" is therefore to say more than we have warrant for. We must convert it into "Some Y is X" (called "conversion *per accidens*," p. 40). If however we wish to get another universal from it, we can do this by "contraposition,"—i.e. by converting its "obverse" (p. 43). The obverse of "All X is Y" is "No X is non-Y," and since that is an E proposition we may convert it simply, getting "No non-Y is X."

Both E and I may be converted simply; E because both its terms are distributed, and I because neither of them is so.

O has its Subject undistributed and its Predicate distributed. Therefore if it were simply converted—if we changed "Some X is not Y" into "Some Y is not X"— X would be undistributed in the original proposition and distributed in the supposed converse. The contrapositive of "Some X is not Y" is "Some non-Y is X."

---

[1] Nearly all of these, both here and in § 19, are taken from papers set for the Previous Examination at Cambridge.

(2) *Determine whether the Subject or the Predicate is distributed or undistributed in each of the following propositions:*

(a) *A triangle is a three-sided figure.*

This distributes its Subject only. But a *definition* of a triangle—e.g. " A triangle is *the* figure contained by three *straight* lines "—would distribute both terms.

(b) *Only adults are legally responsible.*

If this is taken as meaning no more than " No non-adults are legally responsible " (p. 12) it distributes both its terms; if it is also taken to imply that " All adults are legally responsible," this latter proposition distributes its Subject only.

(c) *Few dishonest persons thrive.*

If taken as meaning " Less than fifty per cent. of dishonest persons thrive," it is exponible (p. 12) into " Some dishonest persons thrive, but most do not," in the first of these neither term is distributed, in the second the Predicate only.

(d) *An Englishman was the first to fly across the Channel and back.*

If this is taken as meaning " The first man who &c. &c. was English," the proposition is singular, and therefore its Subject is distributed (pp. 10, 18) and its Predicate undistributed.

(3) *Give, where possible, the converse, and the converse of the obverse of:*

(a) *All S is P.*
(b) *No S is P.*
(c) *Not all S is P.*
(d) *Some S is P.*

	Converse	Converse of the obverse
(a)	Some P is S	No non-P is non-S
(b)	No P is S	None (see note 2 on p. 43)
(c)	None	Some non-P is S
(d)	Some P is S	None (see note 2 on p. 43)

(4) *Convert the following propositions:*

(a) *All that glitters is not gold.*

This means " Not all that glitters is gold," and therefore becomes, in logical form, " Some glittering things are not gold." It does not admit of conversion, but by contraposition it becomes " Some things which are not gold are glittering."

(b) *Anyone must be diligent who is to succeed.*

This may be taken as " All successful persons are diligent " and either converted *per accidens* into " Some diligent persons are successful," or contraposited into " None who are not diligent are successful."

(c) *None but graduates are eligible.*

Taken as " No non-graduates are eligible " its converse would be " No eligible persons are non-graduates."

II. On the Categorical Syllogism and its Rules.

(1) *Examine, with the aid of diagrams, the validity or invalidity of the following syllogisms:*

(a) *All M is S; No P is M; therefore Some S is not P.*

Since all M is S, some S is M ; and since M and P are wholly distinct from each other, whatever part of S is M must be outside P.   Hence the conclusion is valid.

If S and M are coincident, P must be wholly outside them

If there is any part of S outside M, then P may be either wholly inside such part, or partly inside and partly outside, or wholly outside it.

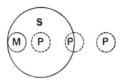

(*b*)　*All S is M; Some P is not M; therefore Some S is not P.*

In the diagram these premisses are satisfied, and yet all S is P. The given syllogism therefore is not valid.

(2)　*Given* (*a*) *a valid, and* (*b*) *an invalid argument in the second figure of the syllogism, show how the validity of the former and the invalidity of the latter can be proved by reduction to the first figure.*

(*a*)　The syllogism:

> No　Z is Y
> Some X is Y
> ∴ Some X is not Z

is valid in the second figure. Reduced to the first figure it becomes:

> No　Y is Z
> Some X is Y
> ∴ Some X is not Z

which is also valid.

(*b*)　The syllogism:

> All　Z is Y
> All　X is Y
> ∴ Some X is Z

is invalid in the second figure.   Reduced to the first figure
by converting its major premiss, it becomes :

$$\begin{array}{c} \text{Some Y is Z} \\ \underline{\text{All   X is Y}} \\ \therefore \text{ Some X is Z} \end{array}$$

which has an undistributed middle term and is therefore
invalid.   Or if we contraposit the major premiss into "All
non-Y is non-Z," and obvert the minor into "No X is
non-Y," we have one negative premiss and an undistributed major term (non-Z); which, according to Rule 9
(p. 22), allow of no conclusion.

(3)   *Find out, from the general Rules of the Syllogism,
in what figures the moods AEE and IAI are valid.*

Set out in full these moods are :

AEE

Fig. 1	Fig. 2
All Y is Z	All Z is Y
No X is Y	No X is Y
No X is Z	No X is Z

Fig. 3	Fig. 4
All Y is Z	All Z is Y
No Y is X	No Y is X
No X is Z	No X is Z

IAI

Fig. 1	Fig. 2
Some Y is Z	Some Z is Y
All X is Y	All X is Y
Some X is Z	Some X is Z

Fig. 3	Fig. 4
Some Y is Z	Some Z is Y
All Y is X	All Y is X
Some X is Z	Some X is Z

Taking these one by one we find:

AEE in fig. 1 has illicit process of the major (Rule 3)

   ,,   ,,   2 is valid

   ,,   ,,   3 has illicit process of the major (Rule 3)

   ,,   ,,   4 is valid

IAI   ,,   1 has an undistributed middle (Rule 4)

   ,,   ,,   2   ditto

   ,,   ,,   3 is valid

   ,,   ,,   4 ditto

(4) *Determine, from the Rules of the Syllogism relating to quality or distribution (without reference to the corollaries relating to quantity), the fallacies involved in the following syllogisms:*

(a) *AEE in the first figure*

> All Y is Z
> No X is Y
> ———————
> No X is Z

Illicit process of the major (Rule 3).

(b) *AAA in the second figure*

> All Z is Y
> All X is Y
> ———————
> All X is Z

Undistributed middle (Rule 4).

(c) *OAE in the third figure*

> Some Y is not Z
> All Y is X
> ———————
> No X is Z

Illicit process of the minor (Rule 3).

(d) *IEO in the fourth figure*

> Some Z is Y
> No Y is X
> ———————
> Some X is not Z

Illicit process of the major (Rule 3).

(5) *Give two ways of reducing to the first figure the moods AEE in the second figure and OAO in the third.*

AEE in the second figure is:

> All Z is Y
> No X is Y
> ――――――
> No X is Z

Change the order of the premisses and convert the minor, getting

> No Y is X
> All Z is Y
> ――――――
> No Z is X = No X is Z

Or, secondly,

> "All Z is Y" has for its contrapositive "All non-Y is non-Z."
> "No X is Y" has for its obverse "All X is non-Y."

The latter pair of premisses, with non-Y as middle term, give the conclusion (in *Barbara*) "All X is non-Z"; the obverse of which is "No X is Z."

OAO in the third figure is:

> Some Y is not Z
> All Y is X
> ――――――
> Some X is not Z

If this conclusion is false, then "All X is Z" (its contradictory) is true. And if "All X is Z" is true, and also "All Y is X" (which was given true), we may infer from these premisses in *Barbara* that "All Y is Z." But "Some Y is not Z" was given true. Therefore either a conclusion in *Barbara* is invalid or the conclusion *O* from the original premisses is valid.

A second way of reducing this syllogism (*Bokardo*) is given at p. 44.

(6) *Explain fully why the conclusions in the second figure must be negative, and in the third figure particular.*

In the second figure, since the middle term is predicate in both premisses, it would be undistributed (and Rule 4 broken) unless one premiss is negative ; and if one premiss is negative, so must the conclusion be (Rule 6).

In the third figure, if there were an affirmative minor premiss and a universal conclusion there would be an illicit process of the minor term, X. But in this figure the minor premiss must be affirmative ; for if it were negative the major premiss must (by Rule 5) be affirmative, and so have an undistributed predicate, Z ; while (by Rule 6) the conclusion must be negative, and so have its predicate, Z, distributed. Thus, in the third figure, if the minor premiss is negative, there is illicit process of the major ; while if it is affirmative, then, in order to avoid illicit process of the minor, the conclusion must be particular.

(7) *Show what syllogistic rules would be broken in the different cases in which the conclusion is universal and one premiss particular.*

There are eight possible different cases :

1.	Conclusion A,	major	I
2.	„	A „	O
3.	„	E „	I
4.	„	E „	O
5.	„	A, minor	I
6.	„	A „	O
7.	„	E „	I
8.	„	E „	O

In 1, by Rule 6 the minor premiss must be affirmative, and therefore in the first and second figures the middle term would be undistributed, and Rule 4 broken ; while in the third and fourth figures there would be an illicit process of the minor, and Rule 3 broken.

2. In any figure this would break Rule 6.

3. In any figure there would be an illicit process of the major term and Rule 3 broken.

4. By Rule 5 the minor premiss must be affirmative. Therefore in the first figure there would be an undistributed middle, and Rule 4 broken; in the second figure there would be an illicit process of the major, and Rule 3 broken; in the third figure there would be an illicit process of the minor, and Rule 3 broken; and in the fourth figure there would be an illicit process of both terms.

5. In any figure there would be an illicit process of the minor.

6. In any figure this would break Rule 6.

7. In any figure there would be an illicit process of the minor.

8. By Rule 5 the major premiss must be affirmative, and therefore in the first and third figures there would be an illicit process of the major, in the first and second figures an illicit process of the minor, and in the fourth figure an undistributed middle.

[A less detailed way of answering this question is the deduction of Rule 8 from Rules 3—6, at p. 28.]

(8) *Reduce the following pairs of premisses to the first figure; and draw the conclusion, if any, which follows from each pair:*

(a) {No X is Y
      {All Y is Z

Convert the first of these into "No Y is X" and the second into "Some Z is Y"; and we get the conclusion "Some Z is not X" (in *Ferio*).

If we merely alter the *order* of the given premisses, making the second the major premiss, we can draw no conclusion about X. Such premisses would break Rule 9.

(*b*) $\begin{cases} \text{No X is Y} \\ \text{All Z is Y} \end{cases}$

Convert the first into " No Y is X," leave the second as it is, and we can draw the conclusion " No Z is X " (in *Celarent*).

[Here, simple alteration of the order of the premisses would give us *Camestres*, with the conclusion " No X is Z."]

(*c*) $\begin{cases} \text{All Y is X} \\ \text{All Y is Z} \end{cases}$

Leave the first as it is, convert the second into " Some Z is Y " and we can draw the conclusion " Some Z is X " (in *Darii*).

[Here, simple alteration of the order of the premisses gives us *Darapti*, with the conclusion " Some X is Z."]

(9) *Test the following syllogisms, and reduce them to the first figure*:

(*a*)   No Z is Y

             No X is not-Y

        ∴ All X is not-Z

As it stands, this argument has five terms, as well as both premisses negative. But by obverting the minor premiss we get :

              No Z is Y

              All X is Y

        ∴ No X is Z

which is a valid conclusion in *Cesare*. Convert its major premiss and we get *Celarent*.

(*b*)   All Z is Y

             All X is not-Y

        ∴ No X is Z

Obvert the minor into " No X is Y " and the conclusion follows in *Camestres*. Convert " No X is Y " into " No Y is X "; make this the major premiss, keep " All Z is Y " as minor, and we can draw " No Z is X " in *Celarent*.

> (c)   No not-Y is X
> <u>All not-Y is Z</u>
>
> ∴ Some X is not-Z

Convert the second premiss into " Some Z is not-Y," and the premisses are those of *Ferio*, giving as conclusion " Some Z is not X." But from this the given conclusion " Some X is not-Z " is *not* deducible.

If we change the order of the premisses and convert the minor, the premisses allow of no conclusion (Rule 9).

III.   On simple arguments expressed in words.

Examine technically the following arguments:

(a) *If you were innocent you would not refuse to answer my question. I therefore presume you are guilty.*

This is an enthymeme (see p. 90). It is a hypothetical syllogism (see p. 74) with one premiss missing. That premiss should be the denial of the consequent—i.e. " You do refuse to answer my question."

(b)   *This is not a rose; for it has no smell.*

Also an enthymeme. It is a categorical syllogism with its major premiss missing. That premiss should be "All roses have smell," which makes a syllogism in *Camestres*.

(c) *Hume was a good historian but a bad philosopher. Therefore a man may be good and bad at the same time.*

Taken as a syllogism (and neglecting the past tense) we have the premisses

> { Hume is a good historian
> { Hume is a bad philosopher

from which the conclusion "Some good historians are bad philosophers" follows correctly in *Darapti*. But there is no warrant for altering this into "Some good *men* are bad *men*."

(*d*) *With regard to the different forms in which men work, it may be said that all of them are either remunerative or enjoyable, while none of them are at the same time both remunerative and physically injurious; hence, if any of them are physically injurious they must be enjoyable.*

Let I stand for "physically injurious forms of work."
  „ E   „   "enjoyable forms of work."
  „ R   „   "remunerative forms of work."

We are given[1]:
  (1) All not-R are E.
  (2) All not-E are R.
  (3) All R are not-I = No R are I.
  (4) All I are not-R = No I are R.

(2) and (3) are irrelevant to the conclusion "All I are E" but for this conclusion (1) and (4) are respectively major and minor premisses in *Barbara*. The conclusion is therefore valid.

(*e*) *It is impossible to maintain at the same time that some desires are harmless, that all desires are liable to excess, and that no things liable to excess are harmless.*

Put   D for desires,
             H for harmless,
             L for liable to excess.

Then the three propositions are:
  (1) Some D is H.
  (2) All D is L.
  (3) No   L is H.

[1] See pp. 76, 77.

From (1) and (2) as premisses, the valid conclusion (in *Disamis*) is

"Some L is H," the contradictory of (3).

From (1) and (3) as premisses, the valid conclusion (in *Festino*) is

"Some D is not L," the contradictory of (2).

From (2) and (3) as premisses, the valid conclusion (in *Celarent*) is

"No D is H," the contradictory of (1).

(*f*) *A man who is out of work must be either a scamp or an invalid; and he cannot be both a simpleton and a scamp; therefore if he is a simpleton he must be an invalid.*

If we take the universe of discourse (p. 105) as "men out of work," we are given :—

All non-scamps are invalids,
All simpletons are non-scamps,

from which we can draw (in *Barbara*) the conclusion

All simpletons are invalids.

The argument therefore is valid.

(*g*) *Some voters are ignorant, for all householders are voters.*

This is an enthymeme, with its major premiss missing. Its given minor premiss is

"All householders are voters"

and its conclusion is

"Some voters are ignorant."

The added major premiss

"Some householders are ignorant"

would give this conclusion in *Disamis* and

"Some ignorant people are householders"

would give it in *Dimaris*.

(*h*) *No one that is truly disinterested would pursue ambitious ends; therefore no one who pursues ambitious ends can be regarded as a patriot.*

This also is an enthymeme. If we shorten it into :—

> No one disinterested is ambitious
> Therefore no one ambitious is a patriot

we have a conclusion and a minor premiss given, and the major missing. Since the minor is negative and the conclusion universal, the major must (Rule 5) be affirmative and (Rule 8) universal.

It must therefore be either

> "All who are disinterested are patriots"
or   "All patriots are disinterested."

If it were the former there would be an illicit process of the major, but with the latter as major premiss, the syllogism is valid (in *Camenes*).

IV. On arguments of doubtful interpretation.

(*a*) *Whatever is to be regarded as desirable must be something that is desired by someone; now pain is not desired by anyone; therefore in no circumstances can pain be regarded as desirable.*

Put   Z for "regarded as desirable,"
         Y for "desired by someone,"
         X for "pain."

The difference between "desired by someone" and "desired by anyone" may probably be taken as grammatical only, but it is not quite clear whether in the minor premiss "pain in all circumstances" is spoken of, or only "some pain." In the conclusion "pain in no circumstances" may probably be taken as "no pain."

The given major premiss is "All Z is Y." If we may take the minor as saying "No X is Y," the conclusion is

valid (in *Camestres*). But if we may only take it as
"Some X is not Y," there would be an illicit process of
the minor.

(*b*) *Whatever is desired by someone must be in itself
desirable; now pleasure is desired by everyone; therefore
pleasure is in itself desirable.*

Here the same doubt attaches to "pleasure," but as it
belongs equally to the minor premiss and the conclusion
it does not affect the validity of the argument.

May we tacitly assume that if pleasure is desired by
everyone it is desired by someone? If so,

Put   Y for "desired by someone,"
             Z for "in itself desirable,"
             X for "pleasure."

We are given "All Y is Z" and "All X is Y" and the
conclusion follows in *Barbara*.

(*c*) *Whatever is not desired by everybody cannot be
intrinsically desirable; now B's pleasure is not always
desired by A; therefore B's pleasure cannot be intrinsically
desirable.*

By the use of a fourth term, W, and a second syllogism
the difficulties of interpretation can here be resolved.

Put   W for "desired by everybody,"
             Z for "intrinsically desirable,"
             Y for "desired by A,"
             X for "B's pleasure."

We are given :—

                    (1) All not-W is not-Z.
                    (2) Some X is not-Y.

If we also assume

                    (3) All W is Y,

then the contrapositive of this, "All not-Y is not-W," together with (1), allows us to infer, in *Barbara* "All not-Y is not-Z."

Taking this conclusion along with (2) we can infer "Some X is not-Z," but to infer "All X is not-Z" (equivalent to "No X is Z") would involve an illicit process of the minor.

(*d*) *In all circumstances honesty would be the best policy; therefore the wise man is always honest.*

Here "the best policy" is not a general term (as "good policy" would be), but singular. Hence "Honesty is the best policy" is convertible simply in spite of its A form[1]. If so, the argument might be translated: "All wise conduct is honest conduct; therefore all of a wise man's conduct is honest." Then all that is needed to complete the proof would be an assurance that a wise man's conduct is at all times wise.

To express this syllogistically, put

> Y for "wise,"
> Z for "honest,"
> X for "of a wise man"
> (the universe of discourse being "conduct").

And if we are allowed to assume that all X is Y the argument is in *Barbara*.

(*e*) *No man is always wise; and as wisdom would lead to the adoption of the best policy, all men are sometimes dishonest.*

Here, to get from "All men are sometimes-unwise" to "All men are sometimes-dishonest," we need a major premiss universally connecting occasional unwisdom with occasional dishonesty. All that we are given for this purpose is an assurance that "wisdom would lead to the

---

[1] See note, p. 39.

adoption of the best policy." Possibly this might be meant to imply that *only when* a man is wise does he adopt the best policy. If we then identify the best policy with honesty we may infer that *only when* a man is wise, is he sure to be honest ; and hence that if he is sometimes unwise he is sometimes dishonest.

(*f*)   *The wise man is sometimes dishonest, and the wise man of course always adopts the best policy.*

If we take this to mean :—

>   All wise men are sometimes-dishonest (D)
>   All wise men are always-best-policy-men (B)

we may infer, in *Darapti*, that some B are D ; which perhaps admits of being re-translated into " There is nothing to prevent a man who always adopts the best policy from being sometimes dishonest."

But in all these questions under head IV we have examples of the difficulty of forcing ordinary language into the requisite forms in such a way as to satisfy everybody.

CHAPTER III

OTHER FORMS OF DEDUCTIVE INFERENCE

§ 13.   *Form and Matter of Reasoning.*

It must often strike a beginner in Logic as unsatisfactory that as soon as he has mastered the intricacies of the Categorical Syllogism, and has learnt that all assertion can be expressed in the A E I O forms, he is forthwith introduced to another form of assertion and another kind of syllogism with a different set of rules. The custom is, however, so firmly established that we must here follow it. And though the existence of a double set of syllogistic forms cannot strictly be justified there is some interest in the enquiry how it arose; an enquiry which incidentally throws a fresh light on the nature of syllogistic reasoning in general.

The creation of a class of propositions called *conditional* (including *hypothetical* and *disjunctive*) may be traced to the fact that the analysis of propositions into Subject, Copula, and Predicate has some serious defects when supposed to be applicable to assertions generally. Just so long as our assertions are restricted to the relations of inclusion or exclusion between a pair of classes, or between an individual S and a class P, no difficulty arises about the copula; it is then merely a sign showing whether inclusion or exclusion is the relation asserted. But even in early times, when assertion in general was more concerned than now with putting Subjects into their proper classes, it was obvious that some assertions—" Cain killed Abel," for instance—had really nothing to do with the relation between classes. We *can*, of course, force this assertion into the form Cain (S) is in the class "people who killed Abel" (P); but would anyone seriously put this forward as a satisfactory explanation of its meaning? And generally speaking assertions about events of any kind have a way of looking ridiculous when forced into the A E I O forms. The question they answer is "What happened?" and not "How are the classes S and P related to each other?"

In §§ 4 and 5 something was said about the difficulties of translating ordinary statements into Logical Form—a difficulty which Logic treats as lightly as common sense will permit, so that only an unusually inquisitive reader of the textbooks ever gains an insight into the real extent of it. But at this point we are forced to make acquaintance with some further difficulties which have been found troublesome and reluctantly dealt with in a patchwork manner.

In speaking, however, of Logic's reluctance to press enquiries it is easy to do an injustice to Logicians. We must not suppose that the attempt to minimise Logical difficulties is a case of simply shirking trouble. In this instance, at any rate, it is one result of a fundamental assumption made by Logic in good faith—the assumption that it is possible to separate the *form* from the *matter* of reasoning ; and the belief that when we insist on trying to do so we are pursuing a useful and not a mistaken ideal, and taking an important step towards understanding the risks of error in reasoning. By the separability of form and matter Logicians mean nothing more recondite than the fact that the "Logical character" of two different propositions may be the same, and that any syllogistic mood may be exemplified in different subject-matter ; its terms may differ, but their arrangement remains the same. Thus the two propositions " All men are mortal" and " London is huge" are both in the form A, though their matter is different ; and the same with any two different syllogisms of a given mood.

But simple as this idea is, the application of it to Logical theory in general is full of unexpected traps and difficulties, some of which we shall notice in due course. The difficulty of applying it consistently is a source of much confusion to Logicians and we shall often have to refer to it. Its intention is excellent, and at first sight the notion of separating the form from the matter, and of dealing with one of them at a time, looks sensible and practical enough. It looks like learning to walk before we try to run, or like a preliminary clearing of the jungle before the permanent road is made. And if in reasoning we never did anything but compare the relation of two classes to each other (or of an individual to a class) by means of a third class to which both are related, the separation would not only be consistently feasible but might also be

of some use. As things are, however, we can no longer
be content with it. We are finding out that this assumption, which looks at first like a useful piece of method,
has the vice that trouble-saving methods so often have of
encouraging a false security and directing attention away
from matters of more importance. The recognised forms
are too few and too simple to represent well the complexity and variety of the assertions we meet with in real
life. On that account they often fail to fit the actually
intended meaning of the sentences they profess to translate.
And so far as Logic is to be not merely a game but a real
help in distinguishing between good and bad reasoning it
cannot afford to ignore the problem of translating from
ordinary language into the forms; an enquiry which
involves some consideration of the "matter" asserted, and
therefore of the intended meaning. It cannot altogether
ignore this problem, but it can and does feel reluctance in
pressing the enquiry. To ignore it altogether would be to
confess its own inapplicability to actual reasonings; to
pursue the enquiry is to depart from its own fundamental
assumptions; and so it steers a middle course, neglecting
the difficulties just so far as common sense can be per-
suaded that they are negligible. This is a position of
unstable equilibrium, and the inevitable fall has already
begun.

§ 14. *Tense and Modality.*

At a very early date some of the difficulties about
the copula began to force themselves upon the notice
of Logicians. There was, for instance, the question how
to deal with past and future tenses of the verb "to be."
Shall we say "Jones *was* found drowned" or "Jones *is*
a-person-who-was-found-drowned"? Shall we say "The
sun *will* soon rise" or "The sun *is* one of a class of
things-that-will-soon-rise"? These may seem trivial points,

but at least they are one indication among many others of the fact that to translate from ordinary language into correct Logical Form is not the simple matter it is sometimes assumed to be. As regards this particular difficulty all that need here be said is that there is no general agreement among Logicians on the point, but that a considerable number are in favour of taking the function of the copula to be in all cases merely that of a sign that the two terms are connected as Subject and Predicate. Those who take this view regard tense-modifications as part of the predicate, not of the copula, and restrict the copula itself to the present tense.

Some other difficulties about the copula arise in connexion with the distinctions of *Modality*. These were formerly thought to be of considerable importance—for example, by Aristotle himself—but are now seldom heard of except in the textbooks. Shall we regard phrases like "must be," "cannot be," "may be," as differences of copula, or as altering the predicate, or as compelling us to recognise other kinds of proposition besides the simple AEIO? It is easy to find names for the different kinds of "modal" propositions, and so far as these differences are still thought worth referring to, the old names have remained: *apodeictic* for "must be" or "cannot be," *problematic* for "may be," and *assertoric* for the simple "is." The question whether the modality belongs to the copula or to the predicate or to the proposition as a whole, has also not been settled by general agreement; it is difficult to ignore the fact that every proposition claims to be assertoric in the sense of asserting *something* definitely, and also the fact that the *claim* to be apodeictic (or not problematic) still leaves us enquiring whether the proposition is *true*. And if we regard all assertions as assertoric, modal assertions look like "assertions about assertions"—e.g. "That the earth is round is probably true"—and so may be viewed as

compound instead of simple; yet the question what constitutes simplicity (or singleness) in a proposition is barred by
the hesitation of Logic to allow any such difficult point to
be seriously considered. As a rule, in the textbooks, we
find that the distinction between a simple and a compound proposition is assumed to be applicable without
any trouble; which means in practice that it is decided
sometimes by consideration of the matter asserted, and
sometimes by the verbal or grammatical construction of
the sentence. Thus Mr Joseph[1] decides that "The last
rose of summer is over and fled" is *one* judgment; his
knowledge of the matter suggests to him that the "and"
does not here couple two different predicates, since a rose
can hardly be "over" without also being "fled." On the
other hand Prof. Read[2] thinks that "Tobacco is injurious,
but not when used in moderation" is a compound of two
propositions, apparently because it happens to be expressed
in this form instead of in the simpler sentence "immoderate
smoking is injurious." Evidently there is not and cannot
be any consistent rule to follow in such a matter. Any
statement admits of being viewed as a compound if we can
admit part of it without admitting the whole, and many
of the shortest possible statements—e.g. "Jones is mad"—
are capable of being split up into true and false or doubtful
portions, or of being true in one sense and false in another.
Wherever ambiguity is possible—and we shall see later
how wide that possibility is—"S is P" may be split up
into the two statements "S is P when P means Q," "but
not when it means R." And generally speaking the
apparent simplicity which hides a real complexity in an
assertion is one of the chief sources of error. On what
ground except a merely verbal one is *any* proposition
to be called simple? Its terms may be single words,

[1] *Introduction to Logic*, p. 145.
[2] *Logic, Deductive and Inductive*, p. 17.

certainly, as in "Cats are quadrupeds"; but when we remember that under the process of definition recognised by Logic itself each word breaks up into two[1] what real value has such simplicity? But questions of this kind are not encouraged by Logic; they lead to dissatisfaction with its whole method.

An instructive example of the treatment that the puzzles of Modality receive from Logicians may be taken from Mr Joseph's account of them[2]. "It is clear," he writes, "that the modality of the judgment whose Subject and Predicate are X and Y does not in any way affect or modify the predicate Y." Naturally, *when* we have decided that X and Y are the terms of the proposition and that nothing shall persuade us to reconsider this decision, then the question whether the modality belongs to the predicate is settled; we can make an end of any enquiry, any difficulty, by this method. Similarly no one can deny that these modal propositions *may* be regarded as compounds—as reflections upon the truth or the grounds of the proposition "X is Y"; but that again is because we have chosen to think of X and Y as the terms. If on the other hand we choose to translate (e.g.) "X must be Y" into "The proposition 'X is Y' is necessarily true" we have got an assertoric proposition, of the A form, only its terms are no longer X and Y; we have merely discovered the assertoric meaning which was always there.

The truth about the distinctions of Modality seems to be that their preservation in Logic is partly due to their venerable antiquity and partly to the fact that they represent verbal forms that are still in use though with meanings in some respect altered. Dr Schiller[3] mentions that "Originally it was thought (by Plato and Aristotle) that

---

[1] *Genus* and *Differentia.* See §§ 21 and 22.

[2] *Introduction to Logic*, p. 169.

[3] *Formal Logic*, p. 147.

the logical nature of a judgment depended on the onto-logical nature of the object judged about....Necessary judgments therefore were simply judgments about 'neces-sary beings' (God, the stars, and mathematics); possible judgments, judgments about contingent beings (everything sublunary); impossible judgments, judgments about im-possibilities." In modern times we do not so airily decide what is possible and what is not. And further, as Dr Schiller says, when we say "X *must* be Y" we are usually trying to banish a shade of doubt from our own minds— doubt whether X in fact *is* Y. Also, we mostly under-stand that no proposition can, after all, be more than *true*; that no piling up of adverbs like "certainly" or "necessarily" will intimidate the actual facts; nor will it guard our notions of God, the stars, or even mathematics, against all risk of error.

§ 15. *Categorical and Hypothetical Propositions.*

It is a similar difficulty about the copula on which the distinction between categorical and other propositions is based. Under the head of "other" the usual[1] practice is to include *hypothetical* and *disjunctive* propositions as two varieties of the *conditional*; as if there were something non-categorical in asserting that "If (or when, or where) X is Z, X is Y," or that "X is either Y or Z." It is quite true that in propositions of this kind *something* is asserted not categorically but under a condition. The hypothetical as a whole consists of two clauses, an "antecedent" clause and a "consequent," and *the latter* is asserted under a con-dition. But why should we confuse the proposition as

[1] Dr Keynes prefers to reserve the name "conditional" for those proposi-tions, with antecedent and consequent clauses, which "affirm a connexion between phenomena"; and "hypothetical" for those which express "not a connexion between phenomena, but a relation of dependence between two truths." His reasons are given in Part II. chap. ix. of his *Formal Logic*.

a whole with its own consequent clause? The proposition as a whole, whatever name we call it by, is made up of its two clauses taken together. If we choose to say that every proposition as a whole is divisible into two terms, then the terms of a hypothetical are its clauses, and a peculiar relation is categorically asserted between them: Given the antecedent, the consequent *may be inferred*. On this account they are sometimes, even by Logicians[1], called *Inferential* propositions.

The confusion is traceable partly to the same source as in Modals generally—a determination to make X and Y the terms—and partly to the assumption that a "simple" proposition is easily distinguishable from a compound one. On what grounds are we to say that "If corn is scarce, it is dear" is compound, while "scarce corn is dear" is simple? Or if "bachelor" be defined as an "unmarried man," why should we say that the proposition "If a man is unmarried, he is usually selfish" is any more compound than "Bachelors are usually selfish"? The difference is merely verbal, and depends on the accidental form of the sentence used.

That the distinction between hypothetical and categorical propositions has some purpose to serve may be readily granted. Even differences of verbal form are seldom wholly out of relation to purpose. And some Logicians have now begun to understand what the purpose of the distinction between hypothetical and categorical is. Mr Joseph[2], for instance, sees that "The distinction rests upon the difference between asserting a dependence of a consequent upon conditions, and asserting an attribute of a Subject." He sees also that this involves a consideration of the matter asserted, and so "shows the impossibility of making Logic a *purely* formal science."

[1] E.g. Miss E. E. C. Jones, *Introduction to General Logic*, p. 42.
[2] *Introduction to Logic*, p. 165.

A point that he has not seen, and that Logic cannot see without becoming logic, is that *always* the purpose which a given assertion is intended to serve is the distinctive mark of the "kind" of assertion; and that consequently a proposition is made hypothetical or categorical by its *function in a syllogism*; the major premiss, as such, being hypothetical, and the minor premiss, as such, categorical.

As regards the *Disjunctive* (X is either Y or Z) the source of the difficulty is the same, for if we make up our minds that X and Y are the terms, then Y is not asserted categorically. Only there is no compulsion on us to say that X and Y are the terms. Suppose a general name W is intended to cover the two kinds Y and Z; then the apparently compound statement that X is either Y or Z may be expressed in the simpler form "X is W." And since all predicates are general[1], so that P always contains an indefinite number of alternatives, every predicate may thus be split up, and the predication regarded as a disjunctive. It is probably through a vision of this fact that Mr Boyce Gibson[2] says "the essential function of the disjunctive proposition is to develop a given categorical basis, of a more or less general and indeterminate character, by specifying the alternative possibilities which the predicate of the given categorical presents." In other words, it is a step towards the often much needed *definition* of a predicate term.

However, considerations of this sort are outside the traditional Logic. That system is in practice content to take the form of sentence as at least the chief guide, if not the only one, in deciding which propositions are categorical, hypothetical and disjunctive respectively. And having so decided it proceeds to use these forms in a separate department of syllogistic doctrine, with special rules and technicalities of its own, which have to be learnt for examinations.

---

[1] See p. 195.   [2] *The Problem of Logic*, p. 131.

§ 16. *The Conditional Syllogism.*

When once hypothetical and disjunctive propositions are allowed to be non-categorical, the question naturally arises how they come into the reasoning operation. It was found necessary to recognise another branch of Syllogism, usually called "conditional," comprising two varieties, called respectively the hypothetical and the disjunctive syllogisms. In the former the major premiss is a hypothetical proposition; in the later it is a disjunctive proposition; and in both kinds the minor premiss and the conclusion are categoricals[1].

After the intricacies of the categorical syllogism, the simplicity of these forms, and of the rules for distinguishing between legitimate and illegitimate conclusions, will come to the reader as a relief. Each kind of conditional syllogism has only two moods, and in the hypothetical syllogism there are only two kinds of formal fallacy, while in the disjunctive there is only one fallacy, and that not formal. Taking the hypothetical syllogism first, its two moods are called respectively the *modus ponens* and the *modus tollens*; or, in English, the mood in which the minor premiss *affirms the antecedent* and the mood in which it *denies the consequent*, of the major premiss.

Thus, in the syllogism :

(*Modus ponens*) If X is Y, S is P,
                            X is Y.
        Therefore   S is P,

the minor premiss "affirms the antecedent." It asserts as a fact that the hypothetical case of X being Y, which

---

[1] Dr Keynes (*Formal Logic*, 2nd ed. p. 265) prefers to reserve the names "conditional" and "hypothetical" syllogisms for the cases where all three propositions are expressed in conditional or hypothetical form; and he gives the name "hypothetico-categorical" to the ordinary hypothetical syllogism. He does not, however, show any purpose in the distinction.

if it were true would allow the inference " S is P," *is true*, here and now.   On the other hand, in the syllogism :

(*Modus tollens*)   If S is P, X is Y,
                              X is not Y.
       Therefore   S is not P,

the minor premiss *denies the consequent* of the major, and thus allows us to draw the conclusion that the antecedent of the major must also be denied.

Corresponding to these two valid moods are two possible fallacies, of equal simplicity : (1) *Denying the antecedent* and (2) *Affirming the consequent.*   Thus, in the syllogism :

" If in doubt, play a trump.
You are not in doubt,
Therefore do not play a trump,"

the conclusion is illegitimate ; and similarly in the syllogism :

" If in doubt, play a trump.
You play a trump,
Therefore you are in doubt."

Coming now to the disjunctive syllogism, we have the two forms *Modus tollendo ponens* and *Modus ponendo tollens.* Here we are not—on the surface at least—concerned with affirming or denying an antecedent or a consequent, but with a different operation ; namely that of arriving at a definite conclusion by means of a fact which removes some of the indefiniteness from the disjunctive major premiss.   Thus if we know that X is either Y or Z, and afterwards discover (minor premiss) that X is not Y, we can always infer (*tollendo ponens*) that it *is* Z ; or again, from the fact that it is not Z, we can infer that it is Y.   And sometimes, though not always, the disjunction asserted is such that we can infer (*ponendo tollens*) from the fact that X *is* Y that it is *not* Z, or from the fact that it is Z that it is not Y.   The rule is that we can only do this legitimately when the alternatives Y and Z are asserted to be *exclusive* of each other.

Logicians sometimes debate, as if it were a question admitting of settlement, whether in saying that "X is either Y or Z" we *must* mean the alternatives to be exclusive. This is called a dispute about *the* meaning of the word "or," as if it must have one and only one correct meaning. Of course the rules of a game are just what we choose to make them, and Logicians have as much right to declare that "*Or*" always (or never) expresses exclusive disjunction as to declare that "some" always expresses "some at least" and never "some only." The prevailing opinion at present among Logicians seems to be that it is best to interpret disjunctives as *not* exclusive, at least when—from a consideration of the matter asserted—there can be any doubt. This follows the principle, referred to at p. 11, of taking every statement as intending only the minimum of its possible meaning. The disjunctive syllogism is, on account of this uncertainty in the meaning of its major premiss, one of many inevitable anomalies in a Logic which professes to deal with Form only and to neglect the Matter. The *form* of a disjunctive proposition is the same whether the alternatives are exclusive or not. If they are not so, then the argument in the *modus ponendo tollens* is fallacious; otherwise both moods are valid. So that it is only through a knowledge of the "matter" that we can decide in given cases whether the argument is fallacious or not.

On the surface, as noted above, the disjunctive syllogism differs from the hypothetical syllogism in the fact that there is no question of antecedent and consequent and their affirmation or denial. This difference however, like so many other differences in Logic, is purely one of verbal form. For whenever it is supposed to be true that X is either Y or Z, that meaning may just as well be expressed in the two propositions " If X is not Y, it is Z " and " If X is not Z, it is Y "; and (where Y and Z are mutually exclusive) in the two additional propositions " If X is Y, it is not Z " and " If X is Z, it is not Y." And when the " single " disjunctive proposition is thus expanded and regarded as compound, any syllogism which makes use of it as major premiss becomes a hypothetical syllogism of the ordinary type, with a major premiss containing some irrelevant information.

It is much more important to notice the deep underlying connexion between the hypothetical syllogism and the categorical. Nearly all Logicians point out that the former can always be translated into the latter if we do not mind using clumsy verbal forms. The *modus ponens* becomes *Barbara* when we write, instead of " If X is Y, S is P," " All cases of X being Y are cases of S being P "; and for the minor premiss " This is a case of X being Y." Similarly the *modus tollens* becomes *Camestres*. It is also often pointed out that the fallacy of " affirming the consequent " corresponds to the invalid mood AAA in the second figure ; while that of " denying the antecedent " corresponds to the invalid mood AEE in the first figure.

But though many Logicians admit so much connexion as this between hypothetical and categorical syllogisms, and thus in effect regard the former as a special case of the latter, they fail to see another aspect of this admission[1]. To them it looks merely as if the hypothetical syllogism, apart from its verbal form, represents two out of the nineteen valid moods. But *it is equally open to us—and far more instructive—to view the nineteen moods as an unnecessary complication of the two*. By a little reflection upon the real meaning of the Syllogism, as independent of its merely verbal intricacies of form, we may easily see

[1] Readers who wish to keep strictly to the old Logic are warned that the remainder of § 16 will not interest them.

the hypothetical syllogism as the fundamental type of all syllogistic reasoning.   And by doing so we not only simplify enormously the problem of distinguishing between valid and invalid forms, but we take a long step towards freedom from the thoughtless verbalism which has for centuries been the curse of Logic.

The key to this view is the recognition that all syllogising consists of *the application of a general rule to a particular case*.   That one of the two premisses of any syllogism must be a "universal" proposition follows from Rule 7.   Now a universal proposition is nothing but the statement of a general rule; that is its meaning, its purpose.   Look where you will, you will never find a general rule which is not intended to be applied in particular cases[1].   If we were to be presented with a supposed general rule "All cases of Y are Z," and at the same time assured that it could never have any application, we should ask Why call it a *rule* if no judgment of ours is to be ruled by it?   A form of words only expresses a rule when it can be taken as a guide to judgment in particular cases (i.e. as *applicable*), and so as a *ground of inference*—an "inferential" proposition.

In *Barbara* we have the typical form: Rule, Case, Inference.   Armed with the rule that All Y is Z we know what to infer when we also know that Every X is a case of Y.   In *Celarent* again, our rule is that No Y is Z, which means that if we meet with a case of Y we may infer that it is *not* Z.   We find "All X" to be cases of Y, and we draw the inference accordingly.   In *Darii* our rule is the same as for *Barbara*, but instead of "All X" being our group of cases, "Some X" is so.   We know of "Some X" that they are Y, and so we infer of the same limited Subject that they are Z.   Lastly, *Ferio* is related in exactly

---

[1] This is a very important point, to which we shall often have to refer. See especially pp. 169, 185, 229—31.

the same way to *Celarent*. The first figure thus proceeds throughout by affirming the antecedent of the Rule. If instead of writing the major premiss " All Y is Z " we express it in the hypothetical form " If anything is Y it is Z " (or, for shortness, " If Y, then Z ") any possible difficulty in admitting this will be seen to be merely verbal.

In the second figure the process is, throughout, that of denying the consequent. With " All Z is Y " as our rule, if we find of " All X " (*Camestres*) or of "Some X " (*Baroko*) that they are not Y, we infer that they are not Z. With "No Z is Y " as our rule—interpreted as " All Z is non-Y " by obversion—the predication of Y in the case of "All X " (*Cesare*) or of "Some X" (*Festino*) is the denial of the consequent and gives the required negative conclusion with the predicate Z.

In the third figure the fundamental structure of the Syllogism is a good deal disguised, partly because what is *called* the major premiss in the categorical syllogism need not here be universal, and partly because X is not ostensively the Subject in the minor premiss. In this figure only *Darapti, Datisi, Felapton* and *Ferison* have the major premiss universal. In *Disamis* and *Bokardo* it is the so-called minor premiss which states the rule whose application gives the conclusion. But when we remember that the distinctions of figure are not based on differences of meaning, but merely represent the various ways in which the order of the terms can be varied when we treat them as counters devoid of meaning, there is nothing in these facts to interfere with what we are now doing. It is the essential *meaning* of the Syllogism that we are here considering, and neither the order of the premisses nor the order of the terms in them and in the conclusion can affect that. By reducing any of these moods to the first figure we see them at once as the application of a rule to a case. The same applies to the

moods in the fourth figure. These, as they stand, represent
no natural form of reasoning. They were not recognised
by Aristotle, and were only invented for the sake of ringing
the verbal changes exhaustively.

In calling this the "essential" meaning of the Syllogism
I mean that it is essential for the purpose of simplifying
the discrimination of valid from invalid forms; which
happens to be our purpose at present. The fact that we
can reduce the third figure to the first does not prevent
our also admitting that—where simplification of theory is
not our object—the third figure may[1] be regarded as having
a different explanation, peculiar to itself; namely as the
finding of examples which break down a false generalisation. Its conclusions, as we have seen, are all "particular"
propositions and so deny the opposite universals[2]; and in
every case they do this by producing an instance, or set
of instances, in conflict with the universal denied. For
example, is it true that No X is Z? Not if what we
know about Y, in relation to X and to Z respectively,
contradicts this suggested rule. If, for instance, Some Y
is X, and All Y is Z, how can X be totally cut off from
Z? (*Datisi*). Or, is it true that All X is Z? Not if No Y
is Z and yet All Y is X (*Felapton*). Nothing is gained
by denying that this way of arguing represents a real process of thought; yet we can judge the validity of a given
syllogism more simply by looking for the Rule and Application which, if it be valid, will always be found in it. For
instance, in *Datisi*, "Some X is Y" (equivalent to "Some
Y is X") applies the rule "All Y is Z"; and in *Felapton*

---

[1] For instance Lambert, in his *Neues Organon* (1764), suggested separate
dicta for the second, third, and fourth figures: the dicta *de diverso*, *de exemplo*,
and *de reciproco* respectively. He viewed the second figure as suited to the
proof of differences between things, and the third as suited to the production
of instances and exceptions.

[2] See the "Square of Opposition," p. 86.

"Some X is Y" (implied in " All Y is X") applies the rule "No Y is Z."

To sum up: Since there is no difficulty in regarding the valid moods of the first figure as examples of the application of a rule to a case (or set of cases, whether definitely or indefinitely specified), nor in reducing any of the valid moods of any other figure to some corresponding mood in the first, it follows that all the nineteen valid moods may be regarded in this light and thus shown to be essentially the same in meaning as the hypothetical syllogism.

And we need not distinguish between the *modus ponens* and the *modus tollens* if we admit that a pair of contra-positive forms are equivalent in meaning. The contra-positive, as we saw at p. 43, is got by converting the obverse; and the obverse is got by viewing the difference between the affirmative and the negative copula as a difference of predicate. Our view of this as a legitimate operation depends on whether we accept the Law of Excluded Middle[1] in the form "X must be either Y or non-Y," and the Law of Contradiction in the form " X cannot be both Y and non-Y." For then we have an exclusive disjunction, and can infer:

By the *modus tollendo ponens*

> If X is not Y, it is non-Y
> If X is not non-Y, it is Y,

and by the *modus ponendo tollens*

> If X is Y, it is not non-Y
> If X is non-Y, it is not Y.

On the other hand, suppose we take the Law of Excluded Middle in Aristotle's formulation of it, as saying that "Of each Subject each Predicate must be affirmed or denied," then nothing is said about negative predicates,

[1] See p. 7.

and we leave ourselves free to maintain—if we want to—
that a negative predicate is "a mere figment of Logic,"
and that since non-Y is not the name of a definite class, in
the way that Y is, it "has no meaning." It is amusing
to see Logicians suddenly concerned about avoiding fig-
ments, but we can hardly help reflecting that the whole
difficulty arises out of another figment which Logic has
overlooked in its own procedure ; namely in its assumption
that propositions are the result of joining together two
terms each of which has "a meaning" independently of
the proposition in which it occurs[1]. When we take the
more modern view that the meaning which words have
when merely ranged side by side in a dictionary is
exactly as much a figment as any *average* is, and that
words get their actual (as contrasted with their average)
meaning *when they are used in asserting*, so that terms—as
distinct from words in a dictionary—arise out of the proposition instead of the proposition arising out of them ;
then we see that the vagueness of a negative proposition
as compared with an affirmative one remains unaltered by
any juggling with a hyphen, or removal of the word "not"
from the copula to the predicate. The *assertion* that X is
not-Y has no less (and no more) meaning than the assertion
that X is-not Y. If either of them means anything they
both mean the same thing. What the suddenly awakened
Logical conscience has been struck by is not really any
lack of meaning in the negative *predicate*, when used as
a predicate, but the lack of meaning which the negative
word would have if it were to be used as a Subject term.
Why not wait till someone proposes so to use it?

Now if it be allowed that "All Z is Y" means the
same as "No Z is non-Y," then since the latter is an
E form and therefore admits of simple conversion, it follows
that "All Z is Y" means the same as "No non-Y is Z."

---

[1] This point is referred to again at p. 168.

But, it may be objected, here we have used non-Y as a Subject term. The answer is, Yes *if* we insist on regarding the proposition " No non-Y is Z " as a case of predication; but not otherwise. And there is no compulsion on us so to regard it, nor any gain but rather a loss in doing so. Certainly, so long as we are unable to free ourselves from the verbalism of making the distinction between categorical and hypothetical propositions turn on the form of sentence and not on the *use* that is made of the proposition, so long no doubt we must call non-Y the Subject term of the above sentence. But suppose the proposition is *used* as a major premiss, and is therefore equally well expressible in the form " If X is not Y, then it is not Z," the whole objection vanishes. There is here no question of using non-Y as a Subject term, but only as part of the antecedent in a major premiss. Since contraposition of the major premiss of a syllogism does not affect its truth, to every major premiss of the A form there corresponds an equivalent E form in which *both the terms are negated.* Thus :

All scarlet fever patients have sore throats,
No one without a sore throat has scarlet fever,
If one has scarlet fever one has a sore throat,
If one has not a sore throat, one has not scarlet fever,

are all equivalent forms for major premiss purposes. And instead of saying that the (hypothetical or categorical) Syllogism has two moods, we may equally well say that there is only one mood, which may be called either affirming the antecedent or denying the consequent (according to the accidental form of the major premiss) ; and one fallacy, which may be indifferently called denying the antecedent or affirming the consequent.

In this way we get a short and convenient formula for expressing the general meaning and purpose of rules, as contrasted with their accidental verbal statement. When any statement is *used as a major premiss*, along with a given minor, or even when it is regarded as capable of such use when a suitable minor shall be found for it, then, whether it be stated in categorical or in hypothetical form, it consists essentially of an antecedent clause and a consequent clause so related that given the former the latter may be inferred. That is what, because it is a *rule*, it always intends to say. But since contrapositives are equivalent, every rule, as such, has two different modes of application; two *different predicates* in the minor premiss will enable the rule to be *used* for inference, though not, of course, for inferring the same conclusion. If we choose to generalise the above various categorical and hypothetical forms under the one form " Y ⟶ Z " (where the symbol ⟶ means "indicates"), this may be taken as saying that either the presence in a given case of the attribute Y (or the truth of the statement Y) or on the other hand the absence (or untruth) of Z, will enable us to use the rule by drawing an inference from it. From the presence (or truth) of Y we may infer the presence (or truth) of Z, and from the absence (or untruth) of Z we may infer the absence (or untruth) of Y. There is thus a double chance[1] of inference from every rule; and that is the practical meaning and value of the contraposition of A.

It is necessary to remember however that though this is a step away from *verbalism* it does nothing to take us outside *formalism*. We are still considering only valid and

---

[1] What is here meant by a "chance" of being used in either way is only that *if* anyone wants to use it so, there is nothing to prevent him. But very often one of the terms Y or non-Z is much more easily identified than the other, and inference naturally proceeds from the more to the less obvious fact. For instance it is easier to diagnose the presence or absence of a sore throat than that of scarlet fever, and therefore of the four forms of rule given on the preceding page, the second and fourth are much more likely to be used. But take, e.g., the rule "Every definition may be simply converted," and the two minor premisses "This cannot be simply converted" and "This is a definition" are about equally useful.

invalid inferences from a form considered apart from possible differences of matter. There is, if not as much difficulty, at least as much risk of error in translating from the every-day forms of language into "Y —→ Z" as in translating into AEIO propositions. All that we have so far done is to cut away some of the confusing verbal trivialities of Logic and to simplify the purely formal operation. We understand better than before the real framework of deductive reasoning, in the abstract, but we have still left unsolved the problem of understanding the relation between ordinary forms of speech and the simplified "Logical Form" into which they have to be translated before inference can begin.

§ 17. *Immediate Inference.*

Just as Logic has to minimise the difficulty of distinguishing between the "simple" and the compound proposition so it has to deal lightly with the distinction between one proposition and "another"; and therefore it takes difference of form, rather than of meaning, as the test of "otherness." That is why Logic holds that (e.g.) the legitimate converse of any proposition is "another" proposition, and so an *inference* from it, even when the two propositions are admitted to be equivalent in meaning. Instead of having two premisses from which a conclusion is drawn, we have here one proposition alone as starting point, and "another" proposition got by reflection upon it. As Mr Joseph says[1] "This is called *immediate* inference, etymologically because (in contrast with syllogism) it proceeds without the use of a middle term; but, to put it more generally, because we seem to proceed from a given judgment to another, without anything being required as a *means* of passing to the conclusion."

It is true that even among Logicians there are at the

1 *Introduction to Logic*, p. 209.

present day some who are not quite content with thus calling translation "inference,"—translation from one form of words into another. Mr Joseph, I gather, may be one of them. But here we must try to put ourselves at the point of view of the others—the more confirmed verbalists—since otherwise the various traditional processes of Immediate Inference could not be recognised as such. I assume that the reader at present wants to know what processes are traditionally called Immediate Inference, apart from the question whether the name is satisfactory.

In general they may be described as *the processes of translation which are still possible after Logical Form has been reached.* Such re-wording, for example, as from "Great is Diana" to "Diana is great" would not be classed as immediate inference but as translation into Logical Form. It is only when we have already got a proposition in one of the AEIO forms that "immediate inference" comes into play. There are two chief branches of it: the inferences tabulated in the *Square of Opposition*; and those forms of *Conversion, Obversion,* and *Contraposition* which are legitimate. Besides these, a few less satisfactory modes are occasionally recognised—such as *Inference by Added Determinant.*

The following diagram shows what is called the Square of Opposition:

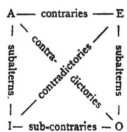

and we find in it four different relations specified as existing between AEIO propositions: the relations of *contrariety* (between A and E), mutual *contradiction* (between A and O, E and I), *subalternation* (I to A and O to E), and *sub-contrariety* (between I and O). This last technicality seems to have been invented merely to fill up the square, as it is never put to any use. And the rules explaining these relations, so far as regards immediate inference, are as follows:

Given A true, we may infer I true, E and O false
    „   E   „   „   O   „ , A and I   „
    „   I   „   „   E false
    „   O   „   „   A   „
    „   A false „   „   O true
    „   E   „   „   I   „
    „   I   „   „   E and O true, A false
    „   O   „   „   A and I   „   E   „

From this table it is evident that the truth of a universal, or (what is the same thing) the falsity of a particular proposition, gives a good deal more information than can be got from the falsity of a universal, or (what is the same thing) the truth of a particular proposition.

Conversion, Obversion, and Contraposition have been already explained, but a table of the inferences allowable by means of them may here be of use:

Given	we may infer			
	by simple conversion	by conversion *per accidens*	by obversion	by contraposition
All Y is Z		Some Z is Y	No Y is non-Z	No non-Z is Y
No Y is Z	No Z is Y		All Y is non-Z	
Some Y is Z	Some Z is Y		Some Y is not non-Z	
Some Y is not Z			Some Y is non-Z	Some non-Z is Y

It should however be remembered that (as noticed on p. 43 *n.* 2) some Logicians prefer to call what is here given as the "contrapositive" of A and O the *converse by negation*, reserving the name "contrapositive" for the forms respectively "All non-Z is non-Y" and "Some non-Z is not non-Y," but they do not suggest any use for this distinction. The unchecked impulse to make distinctions not because they are useful but because the differences happen to be observed, or even for the sake of completing a table of possibilities—e.g. "sub-contraries" in the Square of Opposition, and the fourth figure of the Syllogism—is responsible for much of the tiresome triviality of Logic.

All these "inferences" may be verified and explained by Euler's circles. At p. 35 it was shown that there are only five possible relations that two classes, X and Z, can bear to one another as regards inclusion and exclusion. They may be:

1. Coincident,
2. X wholly included in Z,
3. Z wholly included in X,
4. Overlapping,
5. Wholly distinct.

We also saw that E is the only form which represents definitely one of these relations, namely No. 5. Its contradictory, the I form, may therefore represent any one of the four remaining relations. The A form may represent either No. 1 or No. 2, and therefore its contradictory, the O form, any one of the remaining three. The reason for any of the inferences by conversion, obversion, or contraposition can now be clearly seen. For instance:

"All X is Z" cannot be simply converted because, though No. 1 may be the real relation, so also may be No. 2. On the other hand it can be converted *per accidens* because No. 5 cannot be the real relation. Similarly, it can be contraposited because neither 3 nor 4 nor 5 can be the real relation.

Again "Some X is not Z" cannot be simply converted because No. 3 may be the real relation. And it can be contraposited because neither 1 nor 2 can be the real relation.

It remains to notice briefly what is called *Inference by Added Determinant*,—another case where the attempted separation of Form from Matter leads to vacancy of result. By a "determinant" is here meant an express limitation of the extent of a class. For instance, when we speak of an isosceles triangle, "isosceles" is a determinant added to the class-name "triangle." And when we are dealing only with the extent of classes, and when all our terms are perfectly free from ambiguity, it no doubt holds true that to apply the same limitation to both terms of a proposition does not affect its truth. For instance, if it be true that cats are quadrupeds, it is equally true that black cats are black quadrupeds; and if we reckon conversion as inference we have at least as good a right to reckon this process inference also. But owing to the fact that many terms *are* ambiguous this mode of proceeding from one statement to another cannot be trusted; and since (as we shall see in Part II) Logic avoids all but the most superficial discussion of the nature of ambiguity, and is indeed forced to do so by its own fundamental assumptions, Logic can give us little help in discriminating the misleading inferences by added determinant from those which are trustworthy. The most it ever does, or can do, is to point out this or that obvious instance of its untrustworthiness; as, for example, that we cannot infer from "cats are quadrupeds" that "large cats are large quadrupeds." It has no means of recognising the risk of this kind of error generally, and when it meets with a difficult case it can only say that the difficulty "belongs to the

Matter, not to the Form," and is therefore outside its scope and jurisdiction.

§ 18. *Abbreviated and Compound Arguments.*

In this section we have to make acquaintance with some more technicalities which, although most of them are seldom or never used in modern argument, are reckoned as belonging to Logic: namely the *Enthymeme*, the *Polysyllogism*, the *Episyllogism*, the *Epicheirema*, the *Sorites*, and the *Dilemma*.

Of the first of these Prof. Read's account may be taken as sufficient. "The Enthymeme," he says[1], "according to Aristotle, is the Syllogism of probable reasoning about practical affairs and matters of opinion, in contrast with the Syllogism of theoretical demonstration upon necessary grounds. But, as now commonly treated, it is an argument with one of its elements omitted; a Categorical Syllogism, having one or other of its premisses, or else its conclusion, suppressed. If the major premiss is suppressed it is called an Enthymeme of the First Order; if the minor premiss is wanting, it is said to be of the Second Order; if the conclusion is left to be understood, there is an Enthymeme of the Third Order." These simple distinctions hardly need illustrating, but it may be noticed that some of the examination questions in § 12 have to do with Enthymemes. For instance, on p. 58, (*b*) is an enthymeme of the first order; (*a*) of the second order; and any pairs of premisses given without a conclusion—such as those on p. 56 under head (8)—are enthymemes of the third order.

A *Polysyllogism* (or chain of syllogisms) is a construction in which the conclusion of one syllogism becomes a premiss in another; and it may be of any length we like. Prof. Read adds that in any polysyllogism, a syllogism whose conclusion is used as the premiss of another is called

---

[1] *Logic, Deductive and Inductive*, p. 134.

in relation to that other a *Prosyllogism*; whilst a syllogism, one of whose premisses is the conclusion of another syllogism, is in relation to that other an *Episyllogism*.

The *Epicheirema* is a syllogism with reasons expressly given for one or both of the premisses: as for instance:

> All Y is Z, for All Y is W
> All X is Y, for All V is Y

Therefore   All X is Z

It may be more completely defined as "an abbreviated polysyllogism, comprising an episyllogism with one or two enthymematic prosyllogisms." A definition like this ought to satisfy the most ardent lover of technicalities for their own sake.

The *Sorites*, on the other hand, is a chain of syllogisms with the intermediate conclusions omitted; it may also be described as a syllogism with many middle terms. The earliest form of it was:

> A is B
> B is C
> C is D
> ∴ A is D

and there is no fixed limit to its length.

There was a certain Goclenius of Marburg, about the end of the 16th century, who achieved lasting fame in our present Logical textbooks by a very simple performance. Before his time it had been customary to write a Sorites with its minor term first, as in the form above given. To him, however, it occurred to begin the other way round and to write the Sorites:

> C is D
> B is C
> A is B
> ∴ A is D

The distinction between this "Goclenian Sorites" and the earlier form[1] is still occasionally asked for in examinations.

The term *Sorites* is derived from σωρός, a heap, and appears to refer to the way in which, by successive small steps, we may be led on to an unexpected conclusion. This explanation of the name at any rate fits the well-known old puzzle, called the *Sorites*[2], in which the successive addition of grains of sand converts into a "heap" what at first cannot be called so. The puzzle is the familiar one of "drawing the line," about which we shall have more to say in § 37.

Lastly, the *Dilemma*. Those who love technicalities may say, if they like, that a dilemma is "a compound conditional syllogism, having for its major premiss two hypothetical propositions, and for its minor premiss a disjunctive proposition whose alternative terms either affirm the antecedents or deny the consequents of the two hypothetical propositions forming the major premiss." But for any reader who prefers simpler language a dilemma may be described as an argument which offers to an opponent two or more alternatives (called the "horns of the dilemma") such that whichever he chooses, the choice displeases or contradicts him. A classical instance runs as follows:

If Æschines joined in the public rejoicings he is inconsistent; If he did not he is unpatriotic.

But he either joined or did not join; Therefore, he is either inconsistent or unpatriotic.

The dilemma, in a less fully expressed form than this, is still one of the commonest modes of argument; and

[1] The earlier form is usually called "Aristotelian," though the name "Sorites" was of later date than Aristotle.

[2] See p. 151.

owing to the use which it enables a trickster to make of an unnoticed ambiguity it has a good deal of importance. Its real force depends not in any way on its form, but on the mutual exclusiveness of the alternatives, just as in the case of the disjunctive argument. As a rule both the minor premiss and the conclusion of a dilemma are in modern times left unexpressed, since a statement of the major premiss often suggests all that is needed : e.g. " If you don't accept the challenge you are a coward, and if you do accept it you are a fool." Here the alternative *antecedent* clauses may safely be taken as exclusive. An instance where some doubt of their exclusiveness may be felt is the argument that agreeable and interesting conversation between two people, A and B, is impossible ; because any topic must be either (1) familiar to A and unfamiliar to B—in which case B can say nothing about it which will interest A, while A can only priggishly instruct B ; or else (2) equally familiar or unfamiliar to both of them, in which case neither of them is justified in saying anything about it to the other[1].

§ 19. *Examination Questions.*

1. *Discuss the argument :*

" *If a substance has inertia, it has gravity ; if it does not resist, it has no inertia ; therefore if a substance does not resist, it has no gravity.*"

[*Answer :* This may be expressed either in (*a*) categorical or (*b*) hypothetical form.

---

[1] This argument was invented by Mr H. G. Wells, with intentional whimsicality ; but Zeno's argument to prove the impossibility of motion made some pretence of being serious. It was based on the assumption that " If a body is to move, it must move either where it is, or where it is not ; both of which alternatives are impossible." It is the vice of "abstraction" of thought generally to overlook intermediate alternatives.

(*a*)   Put Y for "substance with inertia."

        Z for "substance with gravity."

        X for "substance that does not resist."

The argument then becomes :—All Y is Z

                        No X is Y

                  ∴ No X is Z

(AEE in the first figure.   Illicit process of the major.)

(*b*)   If a substance has inertia (antecedent) it has gravity (consequent).

      Non-resisting substances have not inertia.

      Therefore non-resisting substances have not gravity.

This argument is invalid because it proceeds by "denying the antecedent."]

2. *Find the relations of opposition between the following propositions; and determine in the case of each proposition whether the term S and the term P is distributed or undistributed.*

(*a*) *There is no S that is P.*

(*b*) *There is at least one S that is not P.*

(*c*) *There is at least one S that is P.*

(*d*) *There is no S that is not P.*

[*Answer:* These must first be put in Logical form, as follows :—

(*a*) No S is P,

(*b*) Some S is not P,

(*c*) Some S is P,

(*d*) All S is P.

By consulting the square of opposition (p. 86) we see that they may be arranged as follows :—

Therefore (*a*) and (*d*) are contraries, (*a*) and (*c*) are
contradictories, and also (*b*) and (*d*),

(*b*) is subaltern to (*a*) ; and (*c*) to (*d*)

(*b*) and (*c*) are subcontraries.

In (*a*) both terms are distributed ; in (*b*) only the
predicate ; in (*c*) neither term ; and in (*d*) only the
subject.]

3. *In what cases may a proposition be inferred* (*a*) *from
its converse,* (*b*) *from its contrapositive.*

[*Answer :* A cannot be inferred from its converse, but
can from its contrapositive.

E and I can be inferred from their converse, and
therefore do not need a contrapositive. There cannot be any contrapositive of I, because the obverse
of I is in the form O, which cannot be converted.
As for E, if its contrapositive were worth recognising it would be a particular proposition ; from
No S is P, we could only get by conversion of the
obverse *Some* non-P is S. If this is to be called
E's contrapositive, then E cannot be inferred from
it. (See p. 43 *n.* 2.)

O has no converse, but can be inferred from its
contrapositive.]

4. *Taking the following propositions in pairs in all
possible ways, show in what cases the truth or falsity of one
proposition can be inferred from the truth or from the falsity
of the other :*

a. *Every S is P.*

b. *Not every S is P.*

c. *Some S is non-P.*

d. *Every non-P is non-S.*

[*Answer*:

    a and *b* are contradictories.

    b and *c* are each the obverse of the other.

    ⎧ *c* is the obverse of the contradictory of the contraposi-
    ⎪   tive of *d*.
    ⎨
    ⎪ *d* is the contrapositive of the contradictory of the
    ⎩   obverse of *c*.

    ⎧ *a* is the contradictory of the obverse of *c*.
    ⎨
    ⎩ *c* is the obverse of the contradictory of *a*.

    a and *d* are each the contrapositive of the other.

    b is the contradictory of the contrapositive of *d*.

    d is the contrapositive of the contradictory of *b*.

Therefore, given *a* true, *b* is false ; given *a* false, *b* is true.

c is false ;	*c* is true.
d is true ;	*d* is false.
b true, *a* is false ;	*b* false, *a* is true.
c is true ;	*c* is false.
d is false ;	*d* is true.
c true, *a* is false ;	*c* false, *a* is true.
b is true ;	*b* is false.
d is false ;	*d* is true.
d true, *a* is true ;	*d* false, *a* is false.
b is false ;	*b* is true.
c is false ;	*c* is true.]

    5. *Discuss the argument:* " *A is to the right of B ; B is to the right of C ; therefore A is to the right of C.*"

    [*Answer*: This may be regarded as an enthymeme, requiring a major premiss which is least inconveniently expressed in hypothetical form. Let us assume that " If there are three points, such that the first is to the right of the second, while the second is to the right of the third, then the first is to the right of the third." We are given that A, B, and C, are three such points respectively ; which affirms the antecedent of the above hypothetical and so allows us to draw the consequent as conclusion.

This example helps to show the comparative convenience of the hypothetical form in syllogising, in cases where the expression of a missing major premiss in categorical form would be more than usually cumbrous.

It has been argued by some Logicians that reasoning of this sort is non-syllogistic because no one has till this moment seen *expressed in words* the major premiss as given above. But why should the character of the reasoning be supposed to depend on the major premiss being expressed in words at all, quite apart from the question whether the expression is familiarly known? We may tacitly accept a rule as true, and apply it in a given case, while yet we find it difficult to express in a compact literary form. And very often we refrain from *expressing* the rules we apply, for an even simpler reason—namely, because we assume (rightly or wrongly) that everyone accepts them as a matter of course.]

CHAPTER IV

FURTHER TECHNICALITIES

§ 20. *Kinds of Term.*

A considerable part of what is usually taught as
Elementary Logic has no direct connexion either with
formal syllogistic reasoning or with "immediate inference,"
but may be described as a legacy from early philosophies,
slightly modified by more recent common sense, of technicalities and doctrines intended to have some bearing upon
the wider question how actual arguments can be guarded
against error.   True to this its original and main purpose,
Logic does what it can—without too obviously departing
from its own limiting assumptions—to survey the nature
of language and the kinds of word that are in use.   In this
part of Logic we must not expect any depth of insight,
and must make up our minds not to trouble much about
inconsistencies.   The task of pursuing a real enquiry into
language, while hampered by the fundamental assumptions
of Logic, has been valiantly attacked by a number of
ingenious and careful writers, and the result is a series
of compromises between depth and shallowness, mostly
inclining towards the latter, but nevertheless conveying
some rough elementary information of a quasi-grammatical
sort and often touching on subjects of real interest and
importance.   As our present object is merely that of getting
to know what the technicalities are usually taken to mean,
we need not elaborately distinguish between the better and
worse ones, nor say much in criticism of the latter.   Some
are never met with except in the examination room and
yet their meaning has to be known.

For instance, a typical example of the more useless
kind of technicality is the distinction between *categorematic*

and *syncategorematic* words ; i.e. between words which are capable and those which are incapable (e.g. prepositions[1] and the like) of being terms. Logic, having invented these imposing technicalities, and having explained their meaning, never afterwards has occasion to mention them. We shall presently meet with a few other distinctions of a similarly useless kind.

The more important of the distinctions are those which refer to the different ways in which words possess *meaning*. Of these the chief one is the distinction between the *general* and the *proper* name. The typical general names are nouns, adjectives and verbs ; and the two important features of these are (1) that they may be applied to any number of individual members of a class, and (2) that they belong to such individual cases not by accident or arbitrarily, but on the ground of some quality which the cases possess. Things that are called "white," for instance, must possess the quality—otherwise called the *class-attribute*—"whiteness," else they do not deserve the name. Proper names, on the other hand, are independent of this need. They are usually given without any reference to qualities—for instance, a baby may be christened Peter not because of any firmness of character but merely because that happens to be his uncle's name ; and even when (as with nicknames, or with surnames like Smith or Butcher) they were originally given on account of a peculiarity, they are not dependent on its continuance. The original Smith's descendant may, for example, be a bookseller without losing the right to his name of Smith.

The technical name for this character of general names

---

[1] It should be noted however that any word, even a preposition, can become a Subject term of a proposition when it is spoken of *as a word*. Thus if I say " 'forever' is a single word " or " 'unto' is an archaic expression," the words thus spoken of become categorematic through what is called *suppositio materialis*.

is that they possess *connotation*, as well as *denotation*; a general name *denotes* the things or cases it refers to, the individual members of the class which owns the name; and these, taken together, constitute the name's "denotation." It also *connotes* the qualities (class-attributes) through the possession of which any individual thing or case deserves the name; and the sum total of such qualities constitutes the name's "connotation." On the other hand a proper name denotes the individual thing or person it belongs to, but connotes nothing.

By some Logicians a name's denotation has been called its *extension*, and its connotation the *intension*, or *comprehension*, of the name. The word "comprehension" is seldom now used for this purpose, but "extension" and "intension" are still found convenient for describing the different ways in which a given word may be taken. For instance it is sometimes said that the Subject term of a proposition is "taken in extension" while the Predicate term is "taken in intension[1]." These respective pairs of names—Connotation and Denotation, Intension and Extension—are generally treated as equivalent, but Dr Keynes has suggested making a difference between them by defining "comprehension" as the sum total of qualities possessed by all the things or cases denoted, whether these qualities are known to us or not; "Intension" (or "subjective intension") as the qualities which the name happens to suggest to our minds; and "connotation" as the qualities necessarily implied by the name—i.e. the name's *definition*.

It is sometimes said that the extension and the intension of a word "vary inversely," so that the more (or less)

---

[1] This is however only a loose generalisation. In some assertions both the Subject and the Predicate are taken in extension—e.g. "The class 'cats' is part of the class 'quadrupeds'"; in others, both are taken in intension—e.g. "The virtuous are happy." Sometimes, that is, we are interested in placing one class within another, and sometimes in noting the connexion between different qualities. See Schiller's *Formal Logic*, p. 105.

there is of the one the less (or more) there is of the other. This expression is liable to be misunderstood. In the first place, as Dr Keynes points out[1], it is not true that whenever the number of attributes in the connotation is doubled (or halved) the number of individual cases in the denotation will be exactly halved (or doubled). Nor again is it true that to give a fuller account of the connotation of the word X need affect its denotation. All that the doctrine amounts to, in short, is that any sub-class (*species*) is smaller in extent than the class (*genus*) out of which it is carved, while its connotation is larger by the *specific difference*,—e.g. there are fewer "steamships" than "ships[2]." The difficulty is to imagine that anyone is likely to overlook this obvious truth, or to benefit by having it expressed in the form of a " law."

A less important distinction than that between the general and the proper name is between the general and the *singular* name, based on the difference that the general name applies to (denotes) many cases while the singular name denotes only one. A singular name need not be " proper " since it may be made up of several general ones —e.g. "the largest city in the world"—each of which, because it is general, is connotative.

The distinction between *abstract* and *concrete* names is still by some people thought important ; and if the puzzles to which it gives rise had more reality in them its value might perhaps appear. The usual account that is given of it is that " a concrete name is the name of a *thing*, while an abstract name is the name of a *quality* of a thing." As a rough

[1] *Formal Logic*, 2nd ed. p. 33.

[2] Mr Macleane (*Reason, Thought, and Language*, p. 147) puts this in a slightly different way—"'All that the inverse variation of Intension and Extension means is that if you 'enlarge your conception' of a term (diminish its intension) you necessarily allow more objects to come under it, whereas if you narrow your conception (add to the meaning you put upon a name) you necessarily exclude objects from it which otherwise would be included."

guide this may serve, but we must not press the enquiry what exactly is to be meant by a "thing." Another rough guide is that abstract names are those that are formed from adjectives by adding "ness" or "ity" or other well-known terminations: e.g. white, whiteness; absurd, absurdity; long, length; high, height; extended, extension.

Two trivial but often-debated puzzles arise out of this distinction. First, are abstract names general or singular? We commonly speak of "the same" quality existing in different things, and thus we are tempted to think of every quality as possessing a unity of its own, and its name therefore as singular. "The adjective 'red,'" says Jevons[1], "is the name of red objects, but it implies the possession by them of the quality *redness*; but this latter term has one single meaning—the quality alone. Thus it arises that abstract terms are incapable of number or plurality. Red objects are numerically distinct each from each, and there are a multitude of such objects; but redness is a single existence which runs through all those objects, and is the same in one as it is in another." Then what about different kinds, or shades, of redness? May they not be viewed as different *rednesses* and therefore as different members of a class? Not only is there no reason why we should not so view them, but, as we shall presently see, there is a very good reason why we should. Jevons's assertion that "Redness, so far as it is redness merely, is one and the same everywhere" raises the question when *is* any quality perfectly pure? That is one of the many real difficulties which Logic prefers not to notice.

But this puzzle about the "singularity" of abstract names is best understood in connexion with another. Are abstract names, like general names, connotative; do they possess connotation? Here Mill fell into unnecessary confusion, and many Logicians have followed him. He

[1] *Principles of Science*, ch. 2, § 3.

thought that abstract names are not connotative except in the rare instances—as he supposed them to be—where instead of denoting " one " attribute they denote a class of attributes. The example he gives is the word " fault "; " equivalent to *bad* or *hurtful quality*.... This word is a name common to many attributes and connotes hurtfulness, an attribute of those various attributes[1]." Although what he meant, on the whole, by " connotative" was " descriptive" (and therefore " capable of definition ")[2], he failed to see the inconsistency involved in saying that they are not connotative. He seems to have been partly misled by an unfortunate phrase which he had happened to use in defining a " connotative " term, and partly by the natural inclination to suppose that unless the more doubtful kinds or degrees of an attribute happen to have well-recognised names they may be ignored. The unfortunate phrase just referred to was " a connotative term is one which denotes a subject and implies an attribute." Hence when an attribute is what is denoted there seemed to be nothing left for the name to connote. If he had happened to say —what was evidently the gist of the distinction as he conceived it—that a connotative term is one which, unlike a proper name, is capable of definition and gets its value from this capability, it is probable that the " singleness " of attributes would have been seen by him as merely verbal singleness, on a level with the singleness of any general name. The fact that any attribute is subject to variations of degree, and is liable to be submerged by other attributes opposed to it, and that the question how much (or what preponderance) of that attribute—e.g. " redness "— must be present in a given case in order that it shall

---

[1] *System of Logic* (8th ed.), p. 33.

[2] *Ibid.* p. 154, "As we define a concrete name by enumerating the attributes which it connotes, and as the attributes connoted by a concrete name form the entire signification of the' corresponding abstract name, the same enumeration will serve for both."

deserve the name ; these facts are what constitute the need of definition for abstract names just as for concrete ones. And since to define any word is to give its connotation, to refuse connotation to abstract names is to declare them indefinable. No doubt it may be disconcerting to be asked what exactly you have in view when you are talking of some abstraction like Justice or Virtue or Truth, and if it could be maintained that abstract names, as such, are indefinable, the stump orator and the windbag would escape criticism. But to enable them to do so seems hardly to be part of the business of Logic.

However, as Prof. Read wisely remarks, the whole difficulty about abstract names and their connotativeness may be avoided by making it a rule to translate—when a question as to their meaning arises—all abstract names into their corresponding general ones. For instance, whether we allow that the abstract term "nobility" has connotation or not, no one denies that the adjective "noble" is a connotative word.

The distinction between *positive* and *negative* names has more to be said for it, at least in connexion with that between pairs of *contrary* terms and pairs of *contradictory* ones. A positive name is one which implies the presence, while a negative name implies the absence, of a quality. "Equal" and "unequal" are simple instances. The distinction has no application to proper names, since, as we have seen, they do not imply either the presence or the absence of a quality.

For rough purposes we can often see at a glance, from the form of a word, which of these two classes, positive or negative, it belongs to ; especially when it is one of a well-recognised pair. Negative prefixes, such as "in," "un," "non," "a," are among the commonest devices of language. But there are many cases where it is less easy to class a word definitely as either positive or negative ; words which

once were negative, e.g. " nonconformist," "unpleasant,"
" inconvenient "—often in course of time take on a positive
meaning; and other words, which have no negative prefix
—e.g. "starving" or "dead"—may sometimes be viewed as
negative[1]. Some use may perhaps be found for the distinction in guarding certain logical operations, such as
contraposition, against the elementary error of using the
contrary of a term instead of its contradictory. Each of
a pair of truly positive and negative terms should be the
contradictory of the other—e.g. "good" and " not-good," or
"equal" and "unequal"; and then the negative term is
said to be *infinite*, because it denotes innumerable different
things. Whenever two opposite names have a middle
ground between them — as " good" and "bad" have
" indifferent "—they are not contradictories, and therefore
not truly positive and negative.

Another way of explaining the difference between contrary and contradictory terms is by saying that with any
two opposed predicate terms, whether they are contraries or
contradictories, the assertion of the one implies the denial
of the other; but only when they are contradictories does
the denial of the one imply the assertion of the other. If
the reader will refer to the definition of contradictory *propositions* (p. 42), and the rules explaining the Square of
Opposition on p. 87, he will understand the reason of this.

The distinction between positive and negative terms has
suggested the question whether a term like " not-white "
should be taken to denote, as Mill supposed, everything in
the universe except white things. Most logicians now deny
this and consider that the reference is not to the whole
universe but to some particular part of it, which they call
the " *universe of discourse*[2]." Thus in contrasting " red "

---

[1] De Morgan held that " parallel" and " alien " were so.
[2] At p. 15 we met with a slightly different use of the notion of a universe
of discourse.

and "not-red" we have in view merely the universe of colour. Cases may no doubt occur where two parties disputing fail to make clear what their universe of discourse is, and so fall into confusion; but otherwise this puzzle has little reality in it. It seems to arise from the assumption that every term, whether positive or negative, *must* denote something—a necessity which is disputable. Where a negative term is used as predicate the question what it denotes is often irrelevant; and where it is used otherwise the assertion may always be viewed as a conditional one whose antecedent clause is a negative *proposition*[1]. Thus "Things which are not white keep comparatively clean" means "If (or when) things are not white, they keep, etc." The meaning of this assertion does not in any way depend on our recognising the precise extent of the class "not-white" things.

There is also a traditional distinction between negative and *privative* names, which must be briefly mentioned. The latter—e.g. such words as "blind" or "deaf"—are distinguished from the former as implying that the subject to which they are attached as predicates might normally be expected to have the quality—e.g. sight or hearing—which they declare to be absent. The difference between negative and privative names can in most cases—though by no means in all—be easily seen. But it is difficult to imagine what purpose can be served by the distinction, and it is seldom nowadays heard of outside the examination room.

Another useless survival is the distinction between *relative* and *absolute* terms. This was intended to mark the difference between on the one hand pairs of terms (e.g. "parent" and "child") each of which pre-supposes the other and is called its *correlative*, and on the other hand

[1] See p. 82.

those terms which have—at least on the surface—more
independence. It is an extremely loose distinction, besides
being seldom put to any use; and its defects are now
pretty widely recognised even by Logicians. Prof. Read[1],
for instance, expresses the view that since all knowledge
depends upon a perception of the resemblances and differences of things, all terms are really relative; but that
some words may on occasion be *used* without attending
to their relativity, and may then be considered as absolute.
Here we have one of the instances in which Logic is
reluctantly driven to take context into account.

Next, the distinction between general and *collective*
names is intended to mark an important difference. But
here again most Logicians[2] would admit that it cannot
be understood as a distinction between kinds of name apart
from context, but only between kinds of *use* which certain
names allow of. When a number of units—e.g. soldiers—
are spoken of collectively—e.g. as a "regiment" or an
"army"—the assertion that is made about them is made
not of the individuals as such, but of the group as a whole.
And in order to guard against mistakes of meaning it is
sometimes convenient to be able to say that we are using
the term X "collectively"; we may even say that *in a
given assertion* X is "a collective term." But when terms
are regarded in isolation from all context collective terms
cannot be contrasted with general terms, because many
terms have both characters. A better name for the non-
collective use of a term is the *distributive* (rather than
"general") use of it. We use a term distributively when
we speak of the individual units, collectively when we
speak of the group as such. It should also be noticed that
only the assertor himself can decide definitely whether in
a given assertion he intends to use the name X collectively

---

[1] *Logic, Deductive and Inductive*, p. 43.

[2] See for instance Keynes' *Formal Logic*, p. 13.

or not; from the form of the sentence alone his intention may often be presumed, but at a risk of error.

One more traditional distinction between kinds of term remains to be briefly noticed, namely that between *univocal* terms (terms that have only one meaning) and *equivocal* terms (those with more than one meaning). As far as its intention goes—that of discriminating between terms which are not and those which are *ambiguous*—this is the most important of all distinctions among kinds of term. We shall see, further on, why it fails to fulfil its intention. Some Logicians[1] admit that we ought in strictness to regard this distinction as not between terms but between uses of a term, since otherwise it is extremely risky to call any general name univocal. Nevertheless the distinction remains in most of the textbooks as naming two different "kinds of term" without reference to their special use or context.

§ 21. *The Predicables.*

The list of five "Predicables," as originally drawn up by Aristotle, was an attempt to classify exhaustively the ways in which a predicate term might be related to its subject, where the subject is the name of a "kind," or *species*, (e.g. "man") and not of an individual (e.g. "Socrates"). We may state (1) the *definition* of "man" (e.g. "rational animal"); or (2) the *genus* of "man" (e.g. "animal"); or

---

[1] E.g. Mr Joseph, *Introduction to Logic*, p. 34. And yet at p. 138 we find him saying "An equivocal term is not a term without a meaning; it is a term with more than one meaning." But this is true only of terms considered apart from their use in a given assertion. For if, owing to an ambiguity in the term "Y," the *statement* "X is Y" admits of being accepted in one sense and rejected in another, how can we regard *its* predicate term as having now *any* actual meaning? A term which has "more than one meaning" in a given statement is, for that very reason, "a term without a meaning," so far as that particular statement is concerned. It will hardly be maintained that a statement whose interpretation is doubtful *means more* than it would otherwise.

(3) his *differentia* from the genus (e.g. "rational"); or (4) a *property*—i.e. any quality common to the whole class but not expressly included in the definition; or (5) an *accident* —i.e. any quality not common to the whole class. For instance, where "a three-sided rectilineal figure" is given as the definition of a "triangle," the fact of its having its interior angles equal to two right angles would be a "property," and the fact of being drawn with chalk on a blackboard an "accident."

Later Logicians, however, following Porphyry[1], made an attempt to extend the scope of the predicables so as to take in the case where an individual is the Subject of the proposition. An individual, as such, has no "*essence*," and is therefore incapable of definition; yet we can mention his *species*. Accordingly the original list of predicables was altered into Genus, *Species*, Differentia, Property, Accident; and that is the form in which it is now usually repeated in the textbooks.

It must be confessed that both these lists have lost the importance formerly attached to them. Though most of the terms remain in modern use, both as technicalities of Logic and in looser everyday language, the notions which underlie them have changed considerably. We no longer think of genera and species as immutably fixed and only requiring to be known; and consequently, though we still use definitions and may still regard them as setting forth the genus and the differentia of the species defined, we do not suppose that the "essence" of any class can be— except in a rough way—distilled from all the varying aspects of that class which may suit our many different possible purposes[2]. For the same reason the notion of a "property" as distinct from the essence has lost its value in use. Under the old scheme a property was deducible from "the" definition without being actually a part of it,

---

[1] In the 3rd century A.D.　　　　　　[2] See p. 202 and § 36.

but with a variable definition this distinction becomes unmeaning; besides, why should we care to distinguish between an essential quality which a definition happens to mention expressly and one which is only tacitly implied?

It should be noted, too, that Porphyry's well-meant attempt to make the predicables applicable to the individual introduces confusion in regard to "property" and "accident." As Mr Joseph says[1], "A property is necessary to its subject, and an accident is not; but all the attributes which belong to Cetewayo are equally necessary to him as Cetewayo; on what ground then are some to be called properties, and others accidents?... If it is asked whether it is a property of Cetewayo to talk, or fight, or be remembered, we must demand of Cetewayo considered as what? Considered as a man, it is a property of him to talk; considered as an animal perhaps it is a property of him to fight; but considered as a man or as an animal, it is an accident that he should be remembered, though perhaps a property considered as a barbarian who destroyed a British force. So long as we consider him as Cetewayo, we can only say that all these attributes are predicable of him." It was probably the unsatisfactoriness of the distinction between property and accident as predicable of an individual which led to the distinction between *separable* and *inseparable* accidents. Since an individual has no essence, everything predicable of him is strictly an accident. Dr Schiller points out[2] that though an individual's qualities are all alike accidents, "Yet there are some qualities of an individual which he cannot alter, e.g. his race or the colour of his eyes. These then are *Inseparable Accidents*, as contrasted with *Separable Accidents*, like the state of his temper, or the fact that he is wearing a particular suit of clothes. The lines, however, both between separable Accidents and

---

[1] *Introduction to Logic*, p. 94.
[2] *Formal Logic*, p. 49.

Inseparable, and between the latter and Properties, become hard to draw. The Inseparable Accident is supposed to differ from the Property in that it could be conceived to be otherwise without destroying the identity of the subject. But is this really so? An Englishman may speculate as to whether he would have burnt his mother at his father's funeral if he had been born a Hindu, but there would hardly be enough identity between his two lives to give meaning to the question. The Inseparable Accident tends to take the position of a Property, of which the connexion with the Definition has not yet been made out, but is still a scientific hope."

It was from this old notion that every class had a single essence that the distinction between *essential* and *accidental* propositions arose ; which, in the form of a distinction between *verbal* and *real* propositions, was supposed by Mill and Bain, and is perhaps still supposed by some Logicians, to be applicable and useful. From a more modern point of view, if an assertor declares, or confesses, that a statement made by him is intended as merely verbal (or "essential") we know where we are ; he thereby confesses that he is not stating a fact, but merely defining a word[1] ; and we may also at times boldly bring this accusation against a statement in order to see whether the assertor will confess to it or not. But except on the supposition that a class has one and only one essence, and a word one and only one "correct meaning," we cannot decisively label a given proposition as essential or verbal. The difficulties into which Bain was drawn in dealing with this question are instructive. The statement that "a house is made to dwell in" he declares to be verbal ; also " Fire burns " ; and in one passage[2] he arrives at the startling doctrine that " All newly discovered properties are real predications on

---

[1] See p. 220.
[2] *Logic : Deduction*, p. 70.

their first announcement; although immediately on being communicated, they become verbal. When Faraday discovered that oxygen is magnetic, the intimation of the fact was for the moment a real proposition respecting 'oxygen.' After being once communicated, it was no more real than the affirmation of any other property of oxygen." When one thinks of the number of new scientific discoveries "announced," "communicated" and "intimated" in pamphlets and journals week by week, and of the uncertainty of their general acceptance and survival, one sees what a convenient weapon a doctrine like this might become in the hands of one who, having made what he thought was a discovery, desired to suppress all future criticism of it. " I have announced " he might say " that the ' canals' on Mars are potato-farms; henceforth, therefore, if you deny it you are making a contradiction in terms." Bain's doctrine is an example of the difficulties into which we are led unless we say that a proposition only becomes verbal by being *meant* to be so.

The good intentions which underlie the list of the Predicables are as evident as elsewhere in the old Logic. The contrast between what is essential and what is accidental is of perennial interest and importance, even though we now know that it cannot be so simply taken and so easily applied as the ancients supposed. And it is that contrast, interpreted on the assumption that every species has one "correct" definition, which the Predicables are chiefly concerned with. When Geometry was regarded as the ideal type of science, their defects in application were less easily noticed, and even the distinction between the essence and a property had some value. But the type of science to-day is remote from those early conceptions of it. Not petrified perfection, but gradually improving imperfection is our present ideal, involving a constant criticism and reorganisation of the genera and species which from time to time, for this or that purpose, are recognised as useful groupings of the facts.

§ 22. *Division, Definition, and Classification.*

The Logical account of the processes of (1) dividing a genus into species, and (2) defining a species, follows the same lines.   Certain rules were laid down, stating the ideals which Division and Definition should aim at, and difficulties in the way of reaching these ideals were insufficiently realised.

There was, for instance, the rule that we must use only a single *Principle of Division* (*fundamentum divisionis*) at a time.   The genus A must first be divided into those cases which are both A and B, and those which are A but not B; after which we may proceed to divide each of the species thus obtained into those which are C and those which are not C ; and so on as long as we can find further principles of division.   This has the effect—verbally at least —both of preventing the overlapping of the species through *cross-division,* and of ensuring that the species, taken together, account for the whole of the genus.   By the (verbally) simple process of always dividing into those members of a class which have, and those which have not, a given attribute—which process is called Division by *Dichotomy*—we obey the only rules that Formal Logic can give in this matter.   As to the difficulties of making our verbal distinctions useful when applied to the facts of a case, these must be reserved for § 37.

The process of Dichotomy may be illustrated by the celebrated *Tree of Porphyry,* which begins with the *summum genus*[1] " substance," which it gradually subdivides

---

[1] In any division the *summum genus* is the starting point, and the *infima species* the end, so far as division into species is concerned.   The division of a species into individuals is a different process.   The intermediate species are called *subaltern genera,* and the *proximum genus* of a species is the one that comes next above it.

till it reaches the *infima species* " man." Translated into English it runs as follows :

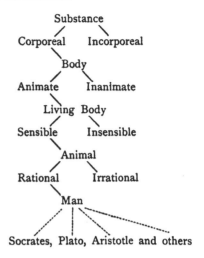

The chief Formal Rules of *Definition*, or the characteristics of an ideally perfect definition, are usually given as follows :

1. The definition must apply to everything included in the species to be defined.

2. It must state the essence of the species ; omitting both properties and accidents.

3. It must state the genus and the differentia of the species.

4. It must not be in negative terms.

5. It must not be expressed in obscure or figurative language.

6. It must not, directly or indirectly, include the name of the species which is to be defined.

The first three of these rules are different expressions for the same desideratum, namely that a definition must be such as to enable us to identify actual cases which come under it, and to exclude all others. Take for instance, " A chair is a piece of furniture with four legs and a back." This might be said to break the first rule because (*a*) it does not apply to three-legged chairs, and (*b*) it does apply to a sofa. It breaks the second rule because the essence of any species belongs to everything included in the species and to nothing else; if anything outside the essence is mentioned, it must be either a property or an accident. And it breaks the third rule because, though it gives the genus it fails to give a satisfactory differentia. It is worth noticing that the third rule implies that a *summum genus* is *indefinable*.

The other three rules are of the nature of literary advice with the same end in view; advice more or less important and trustworthy, but now seen to be open to some obvious difficulties of interpretation. It is true that to explain what a given species is *not* would (generally speaking) be a vague and therefore insufficient way of explaining what it *is*. Yet the objection may on occasion be pedantic and pointless; e.g. where a "busybody" is defined as " a person who is not content to mind his own business." The fifth rule evidently means well, though the line between figurative and plain language is not always easy to draw, and expressions which are well understood by one person may be obscure to another. Still, defining *per obscurum*, or by means of words whose meaning is open to question is a fault to avoid (if we can), and a fault which is often committed. Some of the attempts to define " Life" may serve as examples ; for instance, Herbert Spencer's phrase "the definite combination of heterogeneous changes, both simultaneous and successive, in correspondence with external co-existences and sequences." The sixth rule is directed against one special form of defining *per obscurum* —namely where the word whose definition is asked for (and whose meaning is therefore presumably obscure) is repeated, directly or indirectly in the supposed definition that is given. It is difficult to imagine this ever being done directly, or even where the adjectival form of the word is used in defining the substantive—as in the standard example "an archdeacon is a person who performs archidiaconal functions." But a less obvious form of the same fault is worth noticing; namely where, the problem being to draw a clear line between X and non-X, the supposed definition gives a differentia which is open to exactly the same line-drawing difficulty. If a "hero" be defined as "a man who behaves nobly," we may still want to know the precise difference between "noble" and other behaviour. Wherever there is a real difficulty in drawing a line, no mere substitution of one word for another can be trusted to do away with it.

What is called *circular definition* (or *circulus in definiendo*) is in effect the same fault. The typical form of it is when each of a pair of opposite notions is defined solely by reference to the other ; as in *Punch's* celebrated answer to the two questions, "What is mind?" (no matter), and "What is matter?" (never mind). Naturally, however, a circular definition usually hides its circularity as much as possible, and we do not commonly find the two definitions put side by side as *Punch* here put them. It is on this account difficult to find a concise example which would be likely to deceive anyone. But there is little real difference between readiness to accept a circular definition as satisfactory and readiness to be content with an "abstract" distinction—i.e. with the fact that the contrasted words are *intended* as contradictories — as an excuse for stopping enquiry into the precise application of the words. Some further remarks on this tendency will be found at p. 214.

Division involves the recognition of classes, and may therefore in a sense be called *classification*. But Logicians

usually mean by "classification" not the splitting up of a
summum genus into subordinate genera and species, but
the orderly arrangement of a number of different individuals or cases under wider and narrower heads, so as to
serve the general purposes of science as conveniently as
possible.   Thus "classification" is a larger and more
responsible operation than mere dichotomy where it does
not greatly matter what *fundamentum divisionis* we use so
long as we use only one at a time.   The attempt to serve
scientific purposes introduces the notion of *importance*, and
importance implies a reference to purpose[1], and is very
often confused by a conflict between purposes in general
and some particular purpose of the moment.   Again, there
must always be some conflict between different men's view
as to what kind of classification, in any department of
knowledge, suits even general purposes best.

Two main types of classification are usually distinguished, one of which is known by the name of "natural"
while the other is called artificial[2].   The former is explained
to be one in which, roughly speaking, the divisions are so
constituted that the objects included in any one of them
resemble each other, and differ from all others, in many
important respects; while the function of a diagnostic
classification is to serve as an index enabling us to find the
correct name of an object by means of marks which are,
even if superficial, easily recognised.   These two types of
classification are illustrated in Botany by the "Natural"
and the "Linnæan" systems respectively.

Though Logic can say nothing more definite than that
one classification is better than another in proportion as the
distinctions it recognises are "important," and must leave
the specialist free to judge—or to dispute with other

[1] See below, p. 203.
[2] Mr Boyce Gibson calls it *diagnostic*, since it may be used as an index for
the corresponding natural classification. (*Problem of Logic*, p. 63.)

specialists—which the generally important distinctions are, that does not prevent our noticing great changes in the notion of general importance after they have occurred. Among the most notable of these is the change that followed upon Darwin's convincing demonstration of the importance of a common ancestry in zoological classifications, and of the absence of fixity in species. Nearness of relationship often has little connexion with *obvious* resemblances. Again, as Prof. Read[1] notices, "ancient and important traits of structure may, in some species, have dwindled into inconspicuous survivals or be still found only in the embryo ; so that only great knowledge and sagacity can identify them ; yet upon ancient traits, though hidden, classification depends. The seal seems nearer allied to the porpoise than to the tiger, the shrew nearer to the mouse than to the hedgehog ; the Tasmanian hyæna, or the Tasmanian devil, looks more like a true hyæna, or a badger, than like a kangaroo ; yet the seal is nearer akin to the tiger, the shrew to the hedgehog, and the Tasmanian carnivores are marsupial, like the kangaroo."

The change in the notion of " important characters," though directly and specially due to Darwin's work, is also part of the general movement, already spoken of, away from the interest in classes that happen to be already recognised and accepted, towards an interest in the *causes* that have made and are still making things what they are. What we now want to know about things is not what they are usually *called*, but what they *do*, and how they may be produced or avoided ; and this enquiry leads us both to distinguish different kinds that were previously, for superficial reasons, classed together as one, and also to group together things which, though superficially different, have a deeper and more far-reaching resemblance.

---

[1] *Logic : Deductive and Inductive*, p. 313.

CHAPTER V

INDUCTIVE INFERENCE

§ 23. *The Problem of Induction.*

As said in the introductory chapter, we must not, in Part I, quarrel more than we can help with " Inductive Logic," though some cautions against exaggerating its value must be given. For our present purpose we may think of Inductive Logic merely as a body of doctrine— satisfactory or not—with which the reader wishes to make some acquaintance.

The development of it in comparatively modern times is due to J. S. Mill, whose *System of Logic, Ratiocinative and Inductive* had an immense influence for some forty years after it first appeared (1843), and set a fashion which most of the textbooks are still content to follow.   The opposition it met with from some contemporary writers, on the ground that it extended the "province" of Logic too far, is now of no interest.   The modern criticism is not that it brings material considerations into what is properly a purely formal science, but that it does not escape so entirely as it hoped to do from the excessive formalism which is the bane of Logic generally.

The problem of Induction arises naturally out of the admitted fact that syllogistic reasoning does not guarantee the *truth* of the conclusion (but only its "validity") unless the premisses are also known to be true.   How then is the truth of the premisses to be established?   And specially, how are we to establish the truth of " universal propositions" ?

It was held by Aristotle, and has indeed been held by many other philosophers ancient and modern, that a certain number of universal propositions are known to us by intuition.   Unfortunately, however, neither Aristotle nor anyone else has drawn up an authoritative list of these; and we may dismiss from our minds any expectation that such a list will ever now be attempted, or that if it were attempted it would be found generally acceptable.   Meanwhile, in its absence, how are we to know *which* principles, claiming to be self-evident, are really true and which are flawed with error?   It is always easy to *claim* that a so-called truth is self-evident, but to convince everyone else that the claim is justified is another matter.   A given assertion may at any time be undisputed by a particular person, or even by " all the world," but hitherto the only way to make it strictly *indisputable* has been to leave its application so vague that its truth cannot be tested.   An example of this kind of self-evident truth are the Laws of Thought, noticed in § 3.   It is indisputable, e.g., that every A is A, but this leaves it quite uncertain whether *any* actual case of " A " that we meet with is the genuine thing or not.   Such a "Law" therefore has no application except on the assumption that we no longer need the information it is supposed to give.   This kind of indisputability is common enough, and we can all manufacture as much of it as may content us.

But if we cannot know, apart from the weighing of evidence, whether a given assertion is true, it remains to ask how the evidence may be found and weighed; and this was the task to which Mill addressed himself.   Induction he defines[1] as "the operation of discovering and proving general propositions," and a concise account of the operation as he conceived it is that a general proposition is discovered and proved by the observation of particular facts under the guidance of rules deducible from the " Law of causation." We shall presently enquire what these rules, or "canons," were.

[1] *System of Logic*, Book III. chap. I. § 2.

But first we find him putting aside, as " Inductions improperly so called," some other processes which have at times been called by the name. Unless there is an *inference*—i.e. unless we " proceed from the known to the unknown "—there is, he says, no Induction. It is evident that what Aristotle regarded as the only " formally valid " Induction (now usually referred to as *Perfect Induction*) is here excluded. An induction is said to be " perfect " when *all* the instances coming under the supposed rule have been examined and found to be truly cases of it. If we examine every member of a definite group—say, the known planets, or the twelve apostles—and find that every member of such group has the attribute P, the summing up of such knowledge in the form of a universal proposition does not, says Mill, amount to what he would call Induction. Such a process is not an inference from facts known to facts unknown, but a mere shorthand registration of facts known.

Certain mathematical generalisations again he will not allow to be inductions, some because they are not (in his sense of the word) inferences, and others because in them " the characteristic quality of Induction is wanting, since the truth obtained, though really general, is not believed on the evidence of particular instances."

Again, the case where an island is gradually discovered to be an island by sailing all round it, is not to be called an induction, because it is not an inference from the particular facts but a summary of them. For this operation he borrows Dr Whewell's name, the " Colligation of Facts," but he thinks Whewell " mistaken in setting up this kind of operation which, according to the old and received meaning of the term, is not induction at all, as the type of Induction generally ; and laying down, throughout his work, as principles of Induction, the principles of mere colligation." Further on, he adds that " the scientific study of facts may be undertaken for three different purposes: the simple description of the facts; their explanation; or their prediction: meaning by prediction the determination of the conditions under which similar facts may be expected again to occur. To the first of these three operations the name of Induction does not properly belong: to the other two it does."

Mill spends some sixteen pages on this dispute with Whewell about the *correct* use of the word Induction, and supports his own view by saying that "nearly all the definitions of Induction, by writers of authority, make it consist in drawing inferences from known cases to unknown." These questions of usage are generally difficult to settle, and, whether settled or not, the direct interest in them is verbal and literary rather than philosophical. But the dispute is here noticed for its indirect interest—namely as helping us to see what the process was which Mill thought he could reduce to rule. Induction, as he regarded it, was the arrival at a generalisation, previously unknown, from a survey of particular facts; or, as he puts it more shortly, generalisation from experience. "It consists in inferring from some individual instances in which a phenomenon is observed to occur, that it occurs in all instances of a certain class; namely in all which *resemble* the former, in what are regarded as the material circumstances." And the general warrant we have for making such inferences, he explains, is our belief in the principle known as the "Uniformity of Nature." The universe, we believe, is so constituted that whatever is true in any one case is true in all cases of a certain description.

Mill speaks of this Principle as an "axiom," and it has generally been accepted as such by his disciples. But it is an axiom only in the sense in which the Laws of Thought are axioms. It is indisputable, but only because it carefully avoids making any assertion which can be tested in experience. What exactly is meant by "all cases of a certain description"? This is one of the numerous instances where the word "certain" might be changed into "uncertain" without making the smallest practical difference. Immediately after stating the axiom, Mill naïvely adds "the only difficulty is to find what description." The *only* difficulty! As if the axiom had settled a number of really important difficulties, and merely left this minor one on our hands.

Still, we can give the Principle of the Uniformity of Nature a meaning if, instead of—with Mill—supposing it to be an ultimate major premiss from which any inductive conclusion is deducible, we take it simply as stating the inductive *problem*—the problem how to find a correct general description for all cases to which a given particular inference should be extended. Anyhow, that always is the problem, and another name for it is the discovery of uniformities in Nature, both minor uniformities and those larger ones which we dignify by the name of Laws of Nature. If we interpret the "Principle" in this way we are set free from the task—which Mill found so difficult and which led him into some obviously weak positions—of explaining how the axiom was itself generalised from experience, and what our experience was like before we possessed this guide to it. To state a problem is to ask a question, not to make an assertion ; or, even if we grant that at any rate it implies that the problem is one which may in many cases be hopefully attacked, this statement claims to be nothing more than an expression of hope which is justified by reference to hundreds of past experiences of comparative success. Hope is reasonably satisfied with any improvement on our present knowledge of Nature, and need not die away when it finds that Absolute Truth is never attained but that further improvement is always possible.

Now there is a natural inclination on the part of mankind to generalise on flimsy evidence; either on too small a range of experience and especially by taking only the cases that happen to support a particular theory (*inductio per enumerationem simplicem*, as Bacon called it), or on too clumsy observation of a complex sequence of events (*post hoc, ergo propter hoc*). The nearer our inductive operations approach the type exemplified in the reasonings of children and savages, the more they suffer from one or both of these faults. At an early age, for example, we may assume that the trees cause the wind, or that blowing on a watch makes the case fly open. Later we may jump to the conclusion that all women are fickle, or that it was the salmon that caused the headache. The problem of induction, as Mill conceived it, was how to correct, systematically, these natural tendencies to error; how to reach generalisations (or "discover uniformities") which, being carefully drawn according to rule, shall escape both the charge of proceeding *per enumerationem simplicem* and that of arguing from *post hoc* to *propter hoc.*

Mill divides all uniformities under the heads of (1) co-existence and (2) succession. Under the former he classes, in effect, all generalisations asserting that the quality X and the quality Y are inseparably bound together and present at the same time, whether we can account for the conjunction or not. He gives as examples the laws of number and of geometry; but also any universal proposition must be regarded as belonging to this type if it does not assert succession in time. On the other hand the latter name is restricted to those generalisations which assert that X is universally followed by Y; and the special type of these are the assertions of causation. To say that X is "invariably and unconditionally" followed by Y is the same as to say that X *causes* Y; and the knowledge we can get of particular causal sequences is our best guide in all inductive enquiries, whether the resulting generalisations are of co-existence or of succession.

We need not follow in detail Mill's speculations about the Law of Causation, since they cannot be said now to have more than historical interest. The difficulties apparent to him have mostly changed their shape, and new difficulties have arisen. Besides, Mill allowed himself to be drawn into questions which are irrelevant to his theory of Induction. As far as that goes, it is enough to note that though he expressly disclaims meaning by a "cause" an *efficient* cause, and claims to mean invariable (and unconditional) sequence only, it may be doubted whether his theory could really do without the notion of efficiency. The truth appears to be that though Mill thought he was excluding the notion of efficiency in causes, he himself made exactly the same use of it that common sense and science make. Common sense and science do not profess to understand *how* the causal tie exists, but are content to assume that we can, more or less securely, become aware of its existence in particular cases. Thus, in striking a match, the friction on the prepared surface is said to *make* the flame. Mill is careful to admit that no induction ever takes place—at any rate if we leave out of account the first induction that ever was made—except by the help of generalisations previously accepted. When we set out on any inductive enquiry our minds are full of other generalisations of different degrees of strength and certainty, and "the stronger inductions are the touchstone to which we always endeavour to bring the weaker," the strongest of all our inductions being those which we dignify with the name of causal sequences. For example, it is by getting to understand the causes at work that we convert a "merely empirical" law of co-existence into a "fully proved induction."

§ 24. *Mill's Canons.*

The discovery and proof of causal sequences are thus the main operations that Mill tried to reduce to rule. What are usually called his "Inductive Methods" are the result. They are largely based upon nine "Rules of Philosophising" which were laid down by Herschel[1]. Mill reduced the number, but it is not quite clear whether as he conceived them they should be regarded as five, or four, or two, or one; for he lays down five separate Canons, calls them "The four Experimental Methods," and yet acknowledges that two of them, the *Method of Agreement* and the *Method of Difference*, are fundamental, the others being mere variations due to the special circumstances of the cases investigated. Finally, since he says that the Method of Difference is more particularly a method of artificial experiment, while the Method of Agreement is more especially the resource employed when experimentation is impossible, and that "it is by the Method of Difference alone that we can ever, in the way of direct experience, arrive with certainty at causes," it appears that Mill really recognised no more than one fundamental method, with four inferior substitutes, to one or other of which we may be restricted by the circumstances of a case.

However, there were at any rate five separate canons laid down.

FIRST CANON : *If two or more instances of the phenomenon under investigation have only one circumstance in common, the circumstance in which alone all the instances agree, is the cause (or effect) of the given phenomenon.*

The use of this Canon was called the Method of *Agreement.*

---

[1] *Discourse on the Study of Natural Philosophy*, §§ 145—158.

SECOND CANON: *If an instance in which the phenomenon under investigation occurs, and an instance in which it does not occur, have every circumstance in common save one, that one occurring only in the former; the circumstance in which alone the two instances differ, is the effect, or the cause, or an indispensable part of the cause, of the phenomenon.*

This is the regulating principle of the Method of *Difference*.

THIRD CANON: *If two or more instances in which the phenomenon occurs have only one circumstance in common, while two or more instances in which it does not occur have nothing in common save the absence of that circumstance; the circumstance in which alone the two sets of instances differ, is the effect, or the cause, or an indispensable part of the cause, of the phenomenon.*

The corresponding method is called either the *Indirect Method of Difference*, or the *Joint Method of Agreement and Difference*.

FOURTH CANON: *Subduct from any phenomenon such part as is known by previous inductions to be the effect of certain antecedents, and the residue of the phenomenon is the effect of the remaining antecedents.*

This is the Canon of the Method of *Residues*.

FIFTH CANON: *Whatever phenomenon varies in any manner whenever another phenomenon varies in some particular manner, is either a cause or an effect of that phenomenon, or is connected with it through some fact of causation.*

This is the Canon of the Method of *Concomitant Variations*.

The wording of these Canons needs some explanation. In the first place, what is called "the phenomenon under investigation" or "the phenomenon" is something whose *cause or effect* we are searching for. The problem of all the methods is to single out from among the circumstances which *precede or follow* " a phenomenon " those with which it is connected by an invariable law.

In the second place, all the Methods presuppose prepared material to work on. " The phenomenon " itself, and also the " circumstances," are supposed to be already definite enough to be named as separate things or events, and indeed to be capable of being represented by distinct letters of the alphabet—A followed by *a*, B by *b*, and so on. All this part of the work therefore must have been done—intelligently or otherwise—before the Method comes into operation ; and the success of the Method depends to a great extent on its having been done intelligently. For instance, in our conception of "the phenomenon" we must not leave out of sight any essential or relevant features, nor must we regard irrelevant features as part of it. Again, if we regard as " one circumstance " what would be more truly described as a group of several circumstances, some relevant, and some not so, we may seem to be using one of the Methods when we are in fact using only a parody of it.

What this involves is that the Methods are not capable of being applied at very early stages of any enquiry ; and also that even when, at a later stage, we think we are conforming to their requirements, we may be mistaken in thinking so. They do, no doubt, represent some of the ways in which, after a hypothesis has taken fairly definite shape, we set about *testing* it by observation and experiment ; but even in that operation our conclusion will suffer from any mistakes we have made in conceiving the nature and limits of " the phenomenon," and the singleness of the " circumstances." But where the mistakes are not serious, reasoning by means of the Methods will help us to pursue the investigation in an orderly manner.

§ 25. *The Method of Difference.*

We noticed above that the Method of Difference is the one that Mill regarded as the best, wherever the case admits of its being used. As we saw, he speaks of " arriving with certainty at causes" by means of it, and elsewhere[1] he speaks of its "rigorous certainty." We are supposed to get two "instances" of nearly but not quite the same sequence of events, one being expressible (in abstract symbols) as BC followed by *bc*, the other as ABC followed by *abc*. Then *if* the two instances are alike in all respects except the presence or absence of the sequence A followed by *a*, we may infer (with rigorous certainty) that A caused *a*. As Mill himself confesses, this " if " is a large one, and we have to interpret it with some discretion—which proviso ought to interfere more or less with the rigour of our certainty. For instance, we may leave out of account, in judging of the similarity of the two instances, any circumstances which are " known to be immaterial to the result," and in practice this means of course that we do leave out of account all circumstances which we *think* to be immaterial—some people's thoughts of this kind being more intelligent than others. The extent of our relevant knowledge obviously varies with the circumstances of the case. Thus if a man in full life (BC) is shot (A), and drops dead (*abc*) we all agree in assuming that BC without A would have become *bc* merely ; that all the other differences between the two cases are irrelevant. But suppose an aeroplane suddenly behaves in an unexpected manner, we can well imagine even experts differing on the question which of the circumstances that preceded the change were relevant and which were not. Again, Mill notes that even when the best use is made of such " knowledge " (or guess work) " it is seldom that Nature affords two instances of

---

[1] *System of Logic*, book III. chap. VIII. § 5.

which we can be assured that they stand in this precise relation to one another. In the spontaneous operations of Nature there is generally such complication and such obscurity, they are mostly either on so overwhelmingly large or on so inaccessibly minute a scale, we are so ignorant of a great part of the facts which really take place, and even those of which we are not ignorant are so multitudinous, and therefore so seldom exactly alike in any two cases, that a spontaneous experiment, of the kind required by the Method of Difference, is commonly not to be found." On this account the chief use of the Method of Difference, according to Mill, is in careful experiments where we can know pretty well what we are doing. " A certain state of surrounding circumstances existed before we commenced the experiment; this is BC. We then introduce A ; say, for instance, by merely bringing an object from another part of the room, before there has been time for any change in the other elements....We choose a previous state of things with which we are well acquainted, so that no unforeseen alteration in that state is likely to pass unobserved; and into this we introduce, as rapidly as possible, the phenomenon which we wish to study; so that in general we are entitled to feel complete assurance that the pre-existing state, and the state which we have produced, differ in nothing except the presence or absence of that phenomenon."

What this comes to is that, in investigating causes, we naturally *try* to follow the Method of Difference, and very often are afterwards satisfied (rightly or wrongly) that we have done so. The Method itself, regarded as an ideal, is in the happy position of being safe against all attack; if our satisfaction with the inference is justified, that goes to the credit of the Method of Difference, while if it is not justified that only proves that when we thought we were using the Method we were mistaken in thinking so.

The following are among the examples of the Method of Difference given by Prof. Read : Galileo's experiment to show that air has weight, by first weighing a vessel filled with ordinary air, and then filling it with condensed air and weighing it again ; when the increased weight can only be due to the greater quantity of air contained.   Again, "the melting-point of solids is determined by heating them until they do melt...for the only difference between bodies at the time of melting and just before is the addition of so much heat.   Similarly with the boiling-point of liquids. That the transmission of sound depends upon the continuity of an elastic ponderable medium, is proved by letting a clock strike in a vacuum...and standing upon a non-elastic pedestal : when the clock may be seen to strike, but makes only such a faint sound as may be due to the imperfections of the vacuum and the pedestal."

§ 26.   *The Inferior Methods.*

Carefully arranged experiments are not always possible, and that is why we often have to put up with Methods that are either obviously inferior to the Method of Difference, or at any rate different from it.   As regards the Method of *Agreement*, the inferiority is clear.   The abstract formula for this Method is :

First Instance.   Second Instance.

Antecedents   —   ABC   —   ADE.

Consequents   —   *abc*   —   *ade*.

Then, as far as our instances go, A is shown by them to be the invariable antecedent of *a*, and the two instances agree in no other circumstance.   We have therefore some evidence for the conclusions (1) that B and C are not the causes of *a*, since they were absent in the second instance; (2) nor are D and E, since they were absent in the first. These are called (following Bacon) "negative instances."

The force of the Method consists not only in showing what events are in invariable sequence, but also in eliminating those which are not so.   Merely to collect instances of the sequence A*a* would be *inductio per enumerationem simplicem*. There must be as far as possible exclusion of the accidental circumstances, and by means of such exclusion the essential ones are *selected*.   This is one reason why, in practice, a couple of instances are seldom thought sufficient.   The larger the number, the further the process of elimination is carried, and the more probable therefore the conclusion becomes.   Still, there is no means of knowing exactly when we have carried the eliminative process far enough. Mill says that this uncertainty does not "vitiate the conclusion," and what he seems to mean is that such a conclusion is at any rate of *some* value ; that we have taken a considerable step towards finding the really invariable sequence, and can then very often proceed to get nearer to the desired result by planning further experiments, and if possible using the Method of Difference in them.   In this way, he seems to think, the Method of Agreement may be a useful preliminary way of preparing the material for the Method of Difference.

What Mill himself regarded as the characteristic imperfection of the Method of Agreement is the fact that "the same" effect may often be produced by different causes. This fact is generally known by the name of the *Plurality of Causes*.   Expressed in symbols, the effect *a* may sometimes arise from A, sometimes from B.   Thus many different causes may produce "death" on different occasions.   Now if we have two sequences, ABC followed by *abc*, and ADE followed by *ade*, and if we admit that *a* can be produced by different causes, why should it not in the second of the instances have been produced by D, and the *d* in that instance have been produced by A?   This possibility evidently interferes considerably with the value of the eliminative process on which the Method of Agreement relies, though something can be done to guard against it by increasing the number of the instances observed.

It is worth noticing here that what renders the Plurality of Causes possible is merely some vagueness in the *description* of the effect we call *a*. If two instances of *a* have different causes, it is because, in spite of their both deserving the general name *a*, there is some difference between them. One case of "death," for instance, is never in all respects exactly like another case of it. We shall see in Part II that such vagueness is a necessary incident of all description ; and therefore the Plurality of Causes is a real objection to the Method of Agreement. Mill rightly claims that the Method of Difference is free from it ; but it is not free from other uncertainties which are due to the same defect of language on which the Plurality of Causes depends. If it be true that all description is indefinite, the abstract symbols of the Method of Difference assume more knowledge of the fact than is ever *strictly* possible.

The *Joint Method* of Agreement and Difference has for its formula two different sets of instances, one showing the presence of the sequence A followed by *a*, and the other its absence, e.g. :

Presence.	Absence.
⎰ ABC	⎰ CHF
⎱ *abc*	⎱ *chf*
⎰ ADE	⎰ BDK
⎱ *ade*	⎱ *bdk*
⎰ AFG	⎰ EGM
⎱ *afg*	⎱ *egm*

Here the inference that A and *a* are cause and effect, which is suggested by the series of instances in which they are both present, is further confirmed by finding them both absent in the second series of instances. Evidently the two sets together amount to something nearly resembling the Method of Difference. In order to make the resemblance complete we ought, as Mill says, to be able in some of the instances, say ABC, to leave out A and see whether *a* disappears; but supposing we are not able to do this, we may at least get some light on the question what to expect if we could do it. And this suggestion we get by means of the second set of instances, which establish (by the Method of Agreement) the same connexion between the absence of A and that of *a* which was already established by their presence. "As, then, it had been shown that whenever A is present *a* is present, so it being now shown that when A is taken away *a* is removed along with it, we have by the one proposition ABC, *abc*, by the other *BC*, bc, the positive and negative instances which the Method of Difference requires." This method, he adds, can only be regarded as a great extension and improvement of the Method of Agreement, but not quite as fulfilling the requirements of the Method of Difference. Mill claims for it the merit of not being affected by the Plurality of Causes; but, as Dr Schiller points out[1], such a claim involves the assumption that the "effect" is not further analysable; which is never strictly true.

An example taken from A. R. Wallace is condensed by Prof. Read as follows: "In the Arctic regions some animals are wholly white all the year round, such as the polar bear, the American polar hare, the snowy owl and the Greenland falcon: these live amidst almost perpetual snow. Others, who live where the snow melts in summer, only turn white in winter, such as the Arctic hare, the Arctic fox, the ermine and the ptarmigan. In all these cases the white colouring is useful, concealing the herbivores from their enemies, and also the carnivores in approaching their prey; this usefulness, therefore, is the

[1] *Formal Logic*, p. 306.

cause of the white colouring. Two other explanations have, however, been suggested; first that the prevalent white of the Arctic regions directly colours the animals, either by some photographic or chemical action on the skin, or by a reflex action through vision (as in the chameleon); secondly, that a white skin checks radiation and keeps the animals warm. But there are some exceptions to the rule of white colouring in Arctic animals which refute these hypotheses, and confirm the author's. The sable remains brown throughout the winter; but it frequents trees, with whose bark its colour assimilates. The musk-sheep is brown and conspicuous; but it is gregarious, and its safety depends upon being able to recognise its kind and keep with the herd. The raven is always black; but it fears no enemy and feeds on carrion, and therefore does not need concealment for either defence or attack. The colour of the sable, then, though not white, serves for concealment; the colour of the musk-sheep serves a purpose more important than concealment; the raven needs no concealment. There are thus two sets of instances: in one set the animals are white; (a) all the year, (b) in winter; in the other set, the animals are *not* white, and to them either whiteness would *not* give concealment or concealment would *not* be advantageous. And this second list refutes the rival hypotheses: for the musk-sheep and the raven are as much exposed to the glare of the snow, and to the cold, as the other animals are." Taking the two lists together, therefore, we draw the conclusion that the presence of whiteness is due to its biological utility.

The Method of *Residues* is "a peculiar modification of the Method of Difference." Here the phenomenon may be symbolised by *abc*, and its antecedents by ABC. Now if we already know that B and C together account for *b* and *c*, we may regard the sequence BC *bc* as the negative instance required by the Method of Difference, and thus infer that A is the cause of *a*. The use of this Method is for those cases in which we cannot find or make a direct experiment with BC, and yet have grounds for imagining what the result of such an experiment would be if we could make it; and it is specially employed for discovering " residual phenomena" which deserve to be enquired into. Prof. Read quotes Lord Rayleigh's observation that nitrogen from the atmosphere was slightly heavier than nitrogen got from chemical sources. It was the search for the cause of this difference which led to the discovery of argon. Mill quotes from Herschel as follows: " Almost all the greatest discoveries in Astronomy have resulted from the consideration of residual phenomena of a quantitative or numerical kind.... It was thus that the grand discovery of the precession of the Equinoxes resulted as a residual phenomenon, from the imperfect explanation of the return of the seasons by the return of the sun to the same apparent place among the fixed stars. Thus, also, aberration and nutation resulted as residual phenomena from that portion of the changes of the apparent places of the fixed stars which was left unaccounted for by precession. And thus again the apparent proper motions of the stars are the observed residues of their apparent movements outstanding and unaccounted for by strict calculation of the effects of precession, nutation, and aberration. The nearest approach which human theories can make to perfection is to diminish this residue, this *caput mortuum* of observation, as it may be considered, as much as practicable, and, if possible, to reduce it to nothing, either by showing that something has been neglected in our estimation of known causes, or by reasoning upon it as a new fact, and on the principle of the inductive philosophy ascending from the effect to its cause or causes."

Finally, the Method of *Concomitant Variations* is a quantitative application of the Method of Difference, and

its chief use is in the investigation of natural forces—
such as gravitation or heat—that cannot be eliminated
altogether, where accordingly a perfect negative instance
for the Method of Difference cannot be found. We then
put up with a *comparatively* negative instance. Instead of
having ABC, *abc*; BC, *bc*, we have BC with more A
followed by *bc* with more *a*; and BC with less A followed
by *bc* with less *a*. This Method is very largely used in
scientific enquiries, partly because it is generally easier of
application, and partly because it gives a quantitative precision which makes the result more definite than when we
can merely infer that A causes *a*. Prof. Read quotes from
Deschanel some experiments of this kind. It was found
that "whenever work is performed by the agency of heat"
[as in driving an engine] "an amount of heat disappears
equivalent to the work performed; and whenever mechanical work is spent in generating heat" [as in rubbing two
sticks together] "the heat generated is equivalent to the
work thus spent." Again, there was an experiment of
Joule's "which consisted in fixing a rod with paddles in
a vessel of water, and making it revolve and agitate the
water by means of a string wound round the rod, passed
over a pulley and attached to a weight that was allowed
to fall. The descent of the weight was measured by a
graduated rule, and the rise of the water's temperature by
a thermometer. It was found that the heat communicated
to the water by the agitation amounted to one pound-
degree Fahrenheit for every 772 foot-pounds of work
expended by the falling weight. As no other material
change seems to take place during such an experiment,
it shows that the progressive expenditure of mechanical
energy is the cause of the progressive heating of the
water."

This Method is often very convincing. Yet, as Mill
confesses, it has two characteristic infirmities. First, it is

possible, until we have reason to know the contrary, that A and *a*, instead of being cause and effect, are different effects of the same cause. The only way to decide between these alternative suppositions is to try whether we can produce the one set of variations by means of the other. Thus we find that by increasing the temperature of a body we increase its bulk, but not that an increase of bulk will increase the temperature. Secondly there is always some risk in assuming that the law of variation which the quantities follow within our limits of observation will hold beyond those limits. Different laws of variation may produce numerical results which differ but slightly from one another within narrow limits, and it is often only when the absolute amounts of variation are large that the difference between the results given by one law and those given by another becomes appreciable.

§ 27. *The Deductive Method.*

Though Mill at times[1] claims for his Experimental Methods more than they are able to perform, he has also at other times a glimpse of their defects as practical guides. In the account of the Methods themselves there are scattered phrases which suggest this, but it is chiefly where[2] he comes to consider the *Intermixture of Effects* that we find him confessing plainly that there are situations with which the Methods are "for the most part quite unable to cope."

By the "intermixture of effects" Mill meant specially the disguising of one piece of "invariable sequence" by another, or others, that are entangled with it. Sometimes, as in Mechanics, the separate effects continue to be produced but are compounded with one another and disappear in one total. This he calls the *Composition of Causes.* At

[1] E.g. in his controversy with Whewell, referred to at pp. 188—190.
[2] *System of Logic*, book III. chap. X.

other times, as in chemical action, the separate effects
cease entirely and are succeeded by phenomena altogether
different.   It is specially the former kind of cases which
in Mill's opinion show the kind of complexity that renders
the experimental methods by themselves comparatively
useless.   The *abc* required by the Methods are no longer
separately discernible as such, but some cancel each other,
while others merge in one sum "forming altogether a result,
between which and the causes whereby it was produced
there is often an insurmountable difficulty in tracing by
observation any fixed relation whatever."   Thus a body
may be kept in equilibrium by two equal and opposite
forces.   Laws or uniformities which are liable to combination are properly called *tendencies*; by means of this phrase
we can express the fact that the law itself holds good in
all cases, but that its effect may be disguised.   How, then,
are we to investigate such cases ?

What Mill called the *Deductive Method*, and what is also
sometimes referred to as the Combined Method of Induction
and Deduction, he conceived as consisting of three stages :
first, direct induction ; second, deduction ; third, verification.   The "direct induction" of the first stage is, however,
something much looser than what the Experimental
Methods demand.   It corresponds rather to the previous
knowledge by which the material for the use of those
Methods is prepared.   In order to enter upon the second
stage—deduction—we must have something to deduce
from ; we must have as trustworthy rules as we can get.
But, as Mill confesses, there is often much difficulty in
laying down with due certainty the inductive foundation
necessary to support the deductive method.   We get what
knowledge we can, and then proceed to use it deductively ;
that is to say, if we know what are the separate causes concerned we can calculate what their joint effect will be.   By
this means "we may, to a certain extent, succeed in

answering either of the following questions : Given a
certain combination of causes, what effect will follow ? and,
what combination of causes, if it existed, would produce a
given effect ?   In the one case, we determine the effect to
be expected in any complex circumstances of which the
different elements are known : in the other case we learn,
according to what law—under what antecedent conditions
—a given complex effect will occur."

But our results still being, as Mill acknowledges, liable
to error, we need a third stage of the enquiry, namely
Verification—" without which all the results the Deductive
Method can give have little other value than that of conjec-
ture."   We must test our conclusions by comparing them
with the results of direct observation wherever it can be had.
" If our deductions have led to the conclusion that from
a particular combination of causes a given effect would
result, then in all known cases where that combination can
be shown to have existed, and where the effect has not
followed, we must be able to show (or at least to make
a probable surmise) what frustrated it : if we cannot, the
theory is imperfect, and not yet to be relied upon."

In a much later chapter of Mill's Logic[1] we are introduced to what he calls the *Inverse Deductive Method,* which
is sometimes called the *Historical* Method.   Here, instead
of verifying our deductive result by comparing it with
observed facts, we call in deduction to verify a previous
induction.   We begin with a rough generalisation from
a number of cases, and then we show its likelihood deductively from what we know of the nature of the cases
regarded as made up of known causes.   The proper field
for the application of this Method is in large and vague
enquiries like those of Social Science, when the complexity
of the phenomena is more than usually evident.

In the Deductive Method, both direct and inverse, Mill

[1] Book VI. chap. IX.

comes nearest to recognition of the actual procedure of Natural Science, its vision of complexity in what may at first look simple, and the consequent gradualness of its approach to a satisfactory result ; a result which is nevertheless only to be taken as satisfactory in the absence of future results still better guarded against error. If we substitute in the first step " hypothesis " for " induction," the Deductive Method corresponds very closely to that of causal research, not only in those sciences which—like Sociology—are obviously complex, but in many cases where Mill thought his five Methods applicable and sufficient. Complexity and vagueness of outline are not exceptional qualities in the facts of Nature ; we can find them anywhere if we look for them carefully ; and wherever Science finds them it will deal with them as best it can. As Prof. Read says[1] " Only a ridiculous pedantry would allot to each subject its own method and forbid the use of any other ; as if it were not our capital object to establish truth by any means."

A much fuller account of inductive procedure in its actual working is that given by Jevons in his *Principles of Science*. Scientific enquiry, generally considered, consists, he says[2], in forming hypotheses as to the laws (uniformities or causes) which are probably concerned in the case investigated, and then observing whether the combinations of phenomena are such as would follow from the laws supposed. The investigator begins with facts, and ends with them. He uses such facts as are in the first place known to him in suggesting probable hypotheses ; deducing other facts which would happen if a particular hypothesis is true, he proceeds to test the truth of his notion by fresh observations or experiments. If any result prove different from what he expects, it leads him either

[1] *Logic, Deductive and Inductive*, p. 236.
[2] Vol. II. p. 137.

to abandon or to modify his hypothesis ; but every new fact may give some new suggestion as to the laws in action. Even if the result in any case agrees with his anticipations, he does not regard it as finally confirmatory of his theory, but proceeds to test the truth of the theory by new deductions and new trials.

The investigator in such a process is assisted by the whole body of Science previously accumulated. He may employ analogy to guide him in the choice of hypotheses. The manifold connexions between one science and another may give him strong clues to the kind of laws to be expected, and he thus always selects out of the infinite number of possible hypotheses those which are, as far as can be foreseen at the moment, most probable. Each experiment, therefore, which he performs is that which seems to him most likely to throw light upon his subject, and even if it frustrate his first views, it probably tends to put him in possession of a better clue. It should always be remembered that what is called a *crucial experiment*— an experiment which, like a finger-post at cross-roads, points the way—is only *taken for crucial*, and may be wrongly so taken. It is always possible that some future investigator, going over the same ground, will be able to show that the information given by the experiment was ambiguous. But this possibility we shall have to consider in Part II.

CHAPTER VI

THE NAMES OF THE FALLACIES

The attempt to classify fallacies under heads has led to some hopeless confusions, even as to the main division with which the classifications start. There was first Aristotle's division of them as *in dictione* and *extra dictionem* where the former class comprises only certain mistakes of meaning to which words and statements are liable, while the latter is a receptacle for certain other kinds of error which happened to be noted by him as effective in his time. This division was gradually altered by later writers who, as Mr Joseph says[1], "have given new meanings to the Aristotelian names in certain cases; or have invented names for special forms of some of the Aristotelian fallacies; or have included in their list what are not forms of erroneous argument, but sources of error of a different kind." In Whately's time the principle of division had so far changed that the two main kinds were called respectively *Logical* (or Formal) and *Non-Logical* (or Material), the former including an intermediate class called *semi-logical*, which consisted entirely of certain ways in which the middle term of a syllogism may be ambiguous. By the purely Logical fallacies Whately meant all cases in which a supposed conclusion does not follow from its premisses; and by the Material (or non-Logical) those in which, owing to falsity in the premisses themselves, a "valid" conclusion is untrue. The classifications of fallacies given in our leading textbooks are far away from any general agreement, though they all make use of several of the traditional special names. In these circumstances our best plan here seems to be to take the chief traditional names which have survived, whether important nowadays or not, to arrange them in alphabetical order and to give a short explanation of the meanings that are usually attached to them.

Accent (Fallacy of). This is from Aristotle's list of fallacies "in dictione." Mr Joseph says[2] it "meant to Aristotle one arising through the ambiguity of a word

---

[1] *Introduction to Logic*, p. 533.
[2] *Ibid.* p. 542.

that has different meanings when differently accented. It was perhaps distinguished from Equivocation, because words differently accented are not strictly the same words. The Latin writers illustrate it in words which have different meanings when their quantity is different, e.g. "omne malum est fugiendum, pomum est malum: ergo fugiendum".... In English, which does not distinguish words by tonic accent, the name is generally given to arguments that turn on a wrong *emphasis* of some particular word in a sentence; in which, if the emphasis were placed differently, the meaning might be very different. The words of the Catechism in the "Duty towards thy neighbour"—"to hurt no body by word nor deed"—have by laying the stress on *body* been wrested to include the injunction to be kind to animals. In modern reasonings quips and blunders of this kind have very little importance.

Accident (Fallacy of). This heads Aristotle's list of fallacies "extra dictionem." As understood by him the fallacy consisted in assuming universally that what is predicable of a thing is predicable of its "accidents" (the "equation of subject and accident"). The examples he gives would be recognised by a modern child as obvious verbal trickery, e.g. "You do not know the person approaching with a muffled face; he is Coriscus: therefore you do not know Coriscus. The statue is a workmanship; the statue is yours: therefore the statue is your workmanship. The dog is yours; the dog is a father: therefore the dog is your father[1]."

But later Logicians have extended the notion of this fallacy so as to make it another name for the fallacy called *Secundum Quid*, which is explained below.

Affirmation of the Consequent. See p. 75.

Ambiguity. This word can be translated "Vagueness

---

[1] *Sophistici Elenchi* (Poste's Translation), p. 73.

of Meaning," but such an account of it leaves room for much difference of opinion as to its actual nature, its causes and results. The difference between the older and newer notions of it is too complicated to be given shortly, and is explained at length in Part II[1]. The general tendency of Logicians, even now, is to identify it with " Equivocation" in the sense explained below. But Whately, and some other writers, had glimpses of a more important view of its nature. In view of the fact that thoughts have to be expressed in words before their truth can be examined, and that small differences in expression may be overlooked and may yet make all the difference between truth and error, ambiguity represents the main type of all error that is most likely to be taken for truth.

Amphibology. Defined as ambiguity of phrase rather than of word. But this is a distinction that vanishes as soon as we recognise—as the ancients did not—that the actual meaning of words is dependent on their use in phrases. The standard examples of " amphibology " are oracular statements—such as " Crœsus, by crossing the river Halys, will destroy a great empire"—where the oracle neglects to mention which of the two great empires is referred to.

Argumentum ad so and so ; e.g. ad *baculum*, ad *hominem*, ad *ignorantiam*, ad *misericordiam*, ad *populum*, ad *verecundiam*. " Argumentum " may here be translated " an appeal " ; e.g. an appeal to force, to a man's own professions or admissions, to ignorance, to pity, to popular views, to respect for authority. The second, third, and sixth in the above list were contrasted by Locke with the *argumentum ad judicium*, which he described as " the using of proofs drawn from any of the foundations of knowledge or probability.... This alone brings true instruction with it and advances us in our way to knowledge."

[1] See especially § 32.

Begging the Question. An English translation of *Petitio Principii.* The accusation is often made in disputes, and it is often difficult to see whether it is justly made or not. As now used its meaning is wider than as conceived by Aristotle, who was thinking only of formal debates. Mr Joseph says[1] "the word *petitio* belongs to the terminology of disputation, where the questioner *sought* his premises in the admissions of the respondent. He had no right to ask the respondent to admit the direct contradictory of his thesis...the term *principium* is a mistranslation. The fallacy lies in *begging* for the admission not of a principle to be applied to the determination of the matter, but of the very matter, in *question.*"

In more recent times we find some who would restrict the name to cases where one of the reasons given for a conclusion depends on the truth of the conclusion itself, or even those only where one of the premises of a syllogism does so. On the other hand, we find others who would extend its application to *concealed assumption* generally. And by failing to distinguish between concealed and open assumption, a few have gone further and accused the syllogism itself—which *openly* assumes its premises—of begging the question. A question can only be begged by a syllogism when doubts as to the truth of the premises are denied a hearing. There is no covert assumption in asking whether the person who disputes a conclusion disputes also one of a pair of premises which together contain it; else to ask a question would be the same as to answer it. A Logician who does not understand the difference between begging and *raising* a question may find question-begging in any unanswerable piece of reasoning the conclusion of which he disputes.

Circular Argument. In view of the difficulty of knowing exactly how an assertion made in support of a

[1] *Introduction to Logic,* p. 550 *n.*

conclusion would itself be supported, until this question has actually been answered, it is only where an argument is "circular" that we get anything like a clear case of begging the question. An argument is called circular when it admits of being analysed into two assertions each of which is used to prove the other. But since this analysis usually involves some re-statement of the argument in a shorter form, there is always the possibility of misinterpretation. Very few actual arguments show their circular character clearly on their face; as a rule the critic has to dig it out from the surrounding verbiage, with opportunities of discovering meanings that were never intended.

Composition and Division. These are two of the heads in Aristotle's list of fallacies "in dictione," and may be taken together because they are the counterparts of each other. The examples given by him are so remote from modern ways of faulty reasoning that a different usage of the words has now grown up, and these fallacies are now identified with the opposite confusions that are possible between the "collective" and the "distributive" use of words[1]. Even so, however, it is difficult to imagine examples which are likely to occur. Dr Schiller suggests as a case of *composition* the argument "all the angles of a triangle are less than two right angles ; ABC, ACB, BAC, are all the angles ; therefore they are (together) less than two right angles." And of *division* the argument "all the angles of a triangle are equal to two right angles ; therefore the angle ABC is equal to two right angles." Apart from the question whether such reasonings, or anything resembling them, are likely to be met with in real life, they may serve to illustrate what has now become the traditional meaning of these technicalities.

Consequent (Fallacy of the). This again is one of the

[1] See p. 107.

heads in Aristotle's list "extra dictionem." By De Morgan[1] it is identified with *Non Sequitur* as "the affirmation of a conclusion which does not follow from the premisses"; or, in other words, with Formal fallacy in general. Mr Joseph[2], however, takes a different view, and identifies it with "Affirmation of the consequent" (see above).

Denial of the Antecedent, see p. 75.

Equivocation. This heads the list of the fallacies "in dictione." Here Aristotle seems to have had in view the simplest and most obvious kind of ambiguity—when a word has two or more senses distinguishable in a dictionary. The defects of such a conception of ambiguity are discussed at some length in Part II.

False Cause (or *non causa pro causâ*). This is one of the fallacies "extra dictionem." Aristotle seems to have meant by it an attempt to deduce absurd consequences from a theory by misrepresenting it. Later writers have identified it with "*post hoc, ergo propter hoc*," or the supposition that because an event B follows an event A, therefore A was the cause of B.

Figure of Speech. The last of the list "in dictione." Of this Dr Schiller says, "It is the most trivial of the ambiguities and consists in mistaking one part of speech for another; and though this might conceivably occur to persons who have an imperfect knowledge of a language, Formal Logic here does not seem to afford much assistance even to Grammar." Whately explains it as the unjustified assumption that "paronymous" words (i.e. those belonging to each other, as the substantive, adjective, and verb of the same root) have a precisely correspondent meaning; an example he gives is "Projectors are unfit to be trusted; this man has formed a project; therefore he is unfit to be trusted."

---

[1] *Formal Logic*, p. 267.　　　　[2] *Introduction to Logic*, p. 555.

Ignoratio Elenchi. This comes in the list "extra dictionem." Originally it meant proving something other than the contradictory of an opponent's assertion, but it has now come to be identified with irrelevant argument in general. Both the fallacy itself, and the accusation of it, are as common as possible; and the more we understand that all thought is purposive[1] the more we shall be able to discover the less obvious kinds of irrelevance in argument. The irrelevance of a fact and a rule to each other is, as we shall see in Part II, the explanation of all error that is well disguised.

Illicit Process, see p. 20.

Inductio per enumerationem simplicem, see p. 124.

Many Questions. This is, strangely enough, one of the fallacies "extra dictionem," and its presence there adds to the general effect of casual collection which that list makes upon us. It is still an important kind of trick, and consists in putting a question so that it appears simple—appears to admit of the simple answer, Yes or No—when in reality it is complex, and accordingly either answer may be misleading. A classical example is, "Have you left off beating your father?" where either answer admits the fact of the previous beating. In modern every-day discussion, a man of ordinary intelligence would refuse to answer such questions, and if through carelessness he should for a moment be caught there is nothing to prevent his correcting the mistake afterwards. But in the ancient disputations, admissions were held to be binding; and in our Law Courts to-day, where rules have to be made with the object of keeping the proceedings short, a witness may find it difficult to point out the real complexity of a question without giving a jury the impression that he is trying to hide something. Strictly speaking, every *ambiguous* question is a case of "Many Questions," so that wherever the

[1] See p. 153.

predicate term is ambiguous in the question whether S is P, the only accurate answer is Yes *and* No.

Non causa pro causâ, see *False Cause*.

Non Sequitur, see *Consequent*.

Petitio Principii, see *Begging the Question*.

Post hoc, ergo propter hoc, see p. 124.

Quaternio Terminorum. Though this literally applies only to the case of pseudo-syllogisms with four terms, it is generally taken to cover any breach of Rule 2. Its most important actual form is " Ambiguous Middle " (see § 32).

Secundum Quid. This comes in the list " extra dictionem." Two opposite forms of it are usually recognised : the argument *a dicto simpliciter ad dictum secundum quid* (from a general rule to a case whose " circumstances " make it an exception); and *a dicto secundum quid ad dictum simpliciter* (from a particular case to a rule which is too wide). Both of these are important forms of error, covering a wide range of application. The former may be identified with the most effective kind of ambiguity of the middle term, and the latter with faulty induction of every kind.

As regards the former, Dr Schiller (who identifies[1] it with the " Fallacy of accident ") notices that in applying a rule to a case there are *always* particular circumstances to reckon with, so that the problem involved is precisely that of *all* deductive reasoning—" We are always reasoning from a universal rule to what we take to be an example of it ; we are always liable to find that we were mistaken, and that the rule does not apply in this case. If, so soon as we apply a rule, we become liable to a ' fallacy of accident,' a new and startling light is thrown on the use of rules. For if they may betray us so soon as we try to use them, they are indisputable and *safe* only while they are *not* applied. Here, then, is the reason why Formal Logic, which has

[1] *Formal Logic*, p. 355.

instinctively scented the danger, fights so shy of application in its pursuit of *a priori* safety. Yet what is the use of *inapplicable* rules?" The need for taking individual differences into account, in applying rules, is the chief point insisted upon in Part II.

Sorites. This "fallacy" is also important, though it has no place in Aristotle's lists, and is usually classed along with a few miscellaneous tricky arguments, on special points, that have been preserved from ancient times. It should be described rather as a source of difficulty than as a fallacy; and we shall meet with it in connexion with Distinction, in § 37[1]. It gets its name from σωρός, a heap, because the original form of it was the difficulty of saying how many grains of sand constitute a "heap" when you begin with a number so small as not to deserve the name, and then add a grain at a time till the difficulty arises. In its modern forms we generally call it the difficulty of "drawing the line."

Undistributed Middle, see p. 21.

[1] See especially pp. 210—212.

PART II

THE RISKS OF REASONING

CHAPTER VII

THE CHANGED POINT OF VIEW

§ 28. *The Type of Modern Difficulties.*

As noticed in the Introduction, some detailed knowledge of the old Logic is worth acquiring not only for the purpose of passing examinations but also in order to understand better the reasons for the new departures. Briefly it may be said that the necessity for these has arisen out of the discovery that the old system is of very little use in distinguishing between better and worse reasoning in actual life. Bits of reasoning of a certain kind can indeed be dealt with by it, namely those concerned with the extensive relation of classes to each other when the constitution of the classes is assumed to be clearly understood and the premises are assumed to be true. But in the first place such reasonings, though still occasionally met with, are far from being representative of reasoning in general, still less of contentious or disputed reasoning; it would be truer to say that from any modern point of view they represent only the least interesting part of our mental operations, and that the errors they contemplate are trivial. In the second place, the assumption that a given pair of premises are true is more easily attacked nowadays than it used to be when authority rather than experiment was regarded as the chief source of knowledge. Most of our knowledge is now recognised as progressive

and therefore always unfinished and requiring to be held
with reservations. And in addition to the general need
for caution which the progressive character of science is
continually bringing to our notice there has lately been
discovered a previously unsuspected source of weakness in
the Syllogism itself, due to the fact that a premiss may be
in some vague general sense " true," and yet untrue *for the
purpose of drawing a particular conclusion.* The notion
that a " truth " is only trustworthy when it is " true for the
purpose in hand " is due to the school of thought called
Pragmatism, whatever errors may (justly or otherwise) be
credited to that school. By modern logic I shall here
mean the logic which is modern enough to recognise that
" thought is purposive throughout."[1] The new logic, in any
of its possible developments—of which, no doubt, there will
be many in years to come—is mainly an attempt to dis-
pense with the cramping assumptions of the old Logic
where they have been found to interfere with the fulfilment
of its excellent aim. It was necessary, even in Part I, to
make some occasional references to these assumptions and
their misleading influence, but now we are free to pursue
that subject further, and more constructively.

The old Logic has long been decaying, and as an active
force it hardly exists now except in some of the backwaters
of philosophy, where men who are often both learned and
ingenious make efforts to soar above the truth that is
" merely practical," and are rewarded by reaching results
that are very much the reverse. With them we are here
not concerned. What we have to consider are the risks
of error in reasoning, as science and the better kind of
common sense conceive them — mistakes which are important just so far as they do affect our practical dealings
with Nature and our fellow men ; and chiefly mistakes

---

[1] See Schiller's *Formal Logic*, chap. x, § 9 ; *Studies in Humanism*, p. 10 ;
and my *Application of Logic*, p. 300. Also § 36 below and pp. 223, 233, 239.

about the precise *causal* relation between various occurrences.

Slow as the change has been in our way of conceiving the reasoning process, it is already large enough to be easily seen. Anything like disputation in the old forms is dead. If we look at modern writings or speeches we may search a long time before we find a syllogism formally expressed or even before we find propositions of the AEIO types. The greater part of our thinking does not run into these forms at all, because we are pre-occupied with causes rather than with classes—with causes assumed to be subtle and complicated to an unknown extent, rather than with classes assumed to be fixed and definite; we are concerned with the way things act or behave under changing conditions, and so we lay less weight than formerly on the class-names that custom has attached to the things considered apart from their circumstances. Changes in the circumstances or conditions are, we know, always producing exceptions to even the best of our settled rules, and science has taught us that the study of exceptions is the chief source of progress in knowledge. Besides, the line between "the thing itself" and the thing's surroundings or conditions no longer seems so clear as it used to seem. We are accustomed to recognise that every actual case of A is A *secundum quid*, and so differs more or less from A *simpliciter*.

For these and other reasons we seldom find in modern talk or writing statements that can be naturally translated into the old forms. Certainly, classes are spoken of, and freely enough, but it is unusual to find them spoken of or thought of in the way Logic requires. Instead of "All X," "No X," and "Some X," what we find is "Most X" or "Few X" or "X as a rule" or "for the most part," or "broadly speaking," or "the typical X," or still more cautious and insinuative phrases—recognitions of "tendency" by means of our knowledge of the causes in operation. In contentious matter, at any rate, the "universal" form is seldom used, and when we do meet with it we generally know that it is not quite strictly intended. Often it is a mere literary device for attracting attention by means of a consciously exaggerated form of speech; as where a modern writer tells us that "No nobleman dares now shock his greengrocer." What he apparently means is no more than that respect for the prejudices of our social inferiors is on the whole stronger now than it used to be.

Again the "Some" of the particular proposition is too vague to satisfy a mind which is interested in causes. No doubt the form is still occasionally used. For example, we may use it in denying a rash generalisation ; against an assertion that "All men have their price" we may still bring forward the assertion that "Some[1] have not." But even then, and still more when our "Some X is Y" repre- sents an early stage of acquaintance with the behaviour of X—e.g. "Sometimes Radium fails to cure"—we are uneasy under the vagueness of the knowledge, and regard it rather as a starting point for further enquiry than as any- thing more substantial. Its use is chiefly negative and cautionary till the fuller knowledge of the *conditions* comes.

In these obvious ways a great change has come over the form of our contentious reasoning and of our perplexi- ties. Deeper insight into causes is what we are nowadays always trying to get and to use, and in order to get it we have to consider concrete cases in their details and their setting ; we have to take their individual differences into account as well as their general aspects. That is one reason why we are no longer so content as formerly to stop at the class-name which at first sight seems to belong to the

---

[1] If this is not quite the logical "Some," that fact does not and cannot appear in the mere form of the sentence.

case in question.   Instead of tamely assuming that " A " is
A, and supposing the matter settled, we try to discover
under what conditions a case of apparent A loses its right
to the name *for such and such a purpose*, and so makes the
case an exception to some otherwise useful rule about
A in general.   When the Government is unexpectedly
defeated, it does not deny that a defeat is a defeat, but
calls it a "snap division."

In consequence of this changed point of view the most
general form of modern difficulties in thought is that of
knowing how to interpret some valuable general rule so as
to use it as far as it will bear using, but no further.   In
pure Mathematics possibly this difficulty is not felt[1].   But
wherever we have to deal with causation in concrete cases
it is liable to arise, owing to the fact that concrete cases are
always more full of detail than our best description (or
conception) of them can take into account, and that some
of the details that are necessarily left obscure may be
causally important.   Hence a given case may always on
closer inspection turn out to be an exception to a rule that
it seems to come under.

The full extent of this all-pervasive difficulty is not yet
generally recognised, and there are several ways in which
we are tempted to overlook it.   Regard for accepted truth
still has plenty of influence, both rightly and wrongly,
so that we sometimes hesitate to criticise established rules
even when they deserve it.   Again, what is often loosely
called the "practical" spirit, anxious to overcome obstacles
to action, dislikes and distrusts the critical spirit which
discovers the obstacles.   The common-sense contempt for
casuistry is, at its best, based upon a fear of tampering with
useful general rules by dwelling upon their exceptions;

---

[1] If, as Dr Schiller seems to suggest (*Formal Logic*, p. 58), there is room
for it even in pure Mathematics, still we may here be content to waive the
point. See also *Mind*, No. 89, pp. 10—13.

while at its worst it is due to a simple and natural dislike of taking trouble. It is always easier, and often more virtuous, to follow a plain rule than to complicate the matter by troubling about its possible exceptions. And in general neither of these two different motives holds undivided sway over us, but our sturdy virtue and our idle impatience support each other in disguising the real nature of the problem.

A secondary obscuring cause is the survival of some of the old excessive respect for the Laws of Thought; which itself is an instance of uncritical acceptance of rules which are superficially useful. The recognition that a statement can be true in one sense and false in another—true for one *purpose* and false for another—renders the Laws of Thought available only for the setting of problems, not for solving them. A is *primâ facie* A, and not non-A, and clearly distinct from B. But if A can be A for one purpose and non-A for another the supposed authority of these rules *in application* crumbles away to nothing. If we grant that they are, in a sense, valuable rules, still their value is of a different kind from what Logic supposed. If they have any use, it is neither as giving us true information nor as an official statement of truths that are never neglected, but merely as calling attention to the need of justifying our actual neglect of them; the very fact that they seem at first sight undeniable leads us definitely to ask why in a given case they have been disregarded; and so they help to bring to light the particular ambiguity which justifies our doing so.

Take the " Law of Identity," which exhibits the defect even more simply than the others. The statement is that " A is A," or that "a thing, to be at all, must be something, and can only be what it is." How then shall we interpret and apply this ? The descriptive term "Things which are A" is ambiguous until we are told whether it means "Things which are *taken for* A," or "Things which *really are* A"; and in the former sense the rule is false unless no mistakes of fact are ever possible, while in the latter sense it is undeniable, but only because it gives no information, since as soon as we get a case which is known to come under the rule we know already about that case everything that the rule pretends to tell us. And the special harm of this rule, and of any other axiom which has one meaning in which it is applicable but false, and another in which it is undeniable but uninstructive, is that the latter interpretation is never thought of except as a refuge from criticism. People do not naturally interpret rules so as to make them inapplicable. And the only "Things which are A" which are not already known to be *really* A—and therefore the only "Things which are A" about which the rule conveys information—are "Things which are *taken for* A"; and then the effect of accepting the rule as perfectly true would be to make criticism of *any* alleged fact impossible. Even if we accept it with some tacit reservations, its operation must be to hinder our criticism of alleged facts except where we are already inclined to doubt them. At its best therefore it tends to support those errors of fact which are not easily seen to be errors.

Speaking generally of the "Laws of Thought," their actual effect, when accepted uncritically, is to hinder the discovery of ambiguities. No one indeed ever accepts these Laws quite consistently, for this would involve total inability to recognise ambiguity anywhere, and even Formal Logic does theoretically admit that a syllogism, though perfect *in form*, may be vitiated by ambiguity in its terms, while even the most wordy reasoner has occasional insight into the fact that a thing may be A for one purpose and non-A for another. Still, belief in the value of a rule may be excessive without being entirely uncritical and consistent; and that is the character of the belief in the Laws of Thought which is inevitably held by those who fail to understand that truth is relative to purpose.

The new way of treating the eternal problem of using general rules with discretion instead of either trusting them with stupid blindness or discarding them altogether is based on the philosophical belief that if we have any ideally perfect truths we cannot by any conceivable means distinguish between them and truths less perfect—truths that are merely the best attainable at the present time but which will later be superseded. So far as we are influenced by this belief we cease from what we then see to be the vain attempt to discover ideally perfect truths. Instead of crying for this moon or sinking into a dead and hopeless scepticism because we cannot get it, we try to make the best of the situation by taking care that our "truths" are at any rate sufficiently true to serve our purposes. That is made the criterion of the only kind of truth we ever experience or expect. The falsity of any judgment is thus identified with the failure of that judgment to serve some particular purpose. *For that purpose* we find it false, however many other purposes it may satisfy.

A few common examples will help us to get some general representative notion of modern difficulties of thought and reasoning. Wherever men take opposite sides on a subject they care about, each side is apt to suspect the other of holding views that are too *simple*— of trusting rules too blindly and without enough discrimination. It may be the fact, as cynics tell us, that in some of the great battlefields of thought—such as politics or religion—the men who are most prominent do not greatly care for the truth, or care for it only when it happens to seem useful in persuading other people to support them in power. Still, even if we allow this, at any rate they use the semblance of truth; they pretend to argue a question on its merits; and the great public innocently takes the pretence in all good faith. It reads, and listens, and sincerely thinks one set of arguments right and the other wrong.

In politics, for example, every contention is easily viewed as an attempt to apply some principle. There is the general principle of caution, called "conservatism," opposed by the general principle of social experiment, called "reform." There are special pairs of opposite principles, such as Individualism and Socialism, Aristocracy and Democracy, Imperialism and its opposite. And the commonest assumption made by the adherents of such principles is not that their own principle can be applied without limit, but that their opponents are pressing the opposite principle too far. Here and there we may find a man who assumes that his own favourite principle may be trusted absolutely, and in the case of some particular principles—e.g. Free Trade—most of the adherents take this simple view. But generally speaking we recognise nowadays that principles need applying with discretion; that, for example, complete conservatism and complete revolutionary change (if the latter conception has any meaning) are absurd and impossible ideals, the real problem being that of giving each opposite principle its due weight. And translated into practice this means that we must discriminate between different cases which are liable to be thought the same. The only reasonable method, we recognise, is that of treating each case on its own merits; which lets us in for the difficult task of taking its individual differences into account as well as its *general* aspects.

There are probably few people at the present day who would confess to holding that the general rules by which our thoughts and our lives are mostly guided deserve to be applied through thick and thin. We may trust the multiplication table, and perhaps the axioms of Geometry, and there are always a certain number of general truths which never lead us astray. But just in these favoured—and exceptional—regions dispute does not arise; there are no opponents to trouble us, and no inner doubts. Where dispute or doubt does arise, and where consequently a knowledge of the risks of reasoning may be useful, there it will generally be found that the crux of the difficulty lies in deciding whether a certain case—in all its concrete detail—does or does not come under a rule which, though broadly sound and useful, needs, like most other rules, to be applied with moderation.

There is hardly a decision we make of any kind in the course of a day, into which this perplexity cannot enter if we allow it to do so. Our codes of morals, of manners, of art-criticism, our business maxims, our Acts of Parliament, our rules of nearly every kind, present to us continually the problem " Is this case, as it appears to be, within the rule or just outside?" We may, and often do, stifle these doubts; but there they lie in waiting for us if it should seem worth while—and not too disastrous—to raise them. So that even in order to disregard them justifiably we are confronted with the question whether the *principle* of facing them, or that of avoiding them, is *in the particular case* the wiser course. All that logic can do in the matter is to help us to get a clear view of the problem itself. Any successful solution of the problem depends, in the end, on the accuracy and the comparative extent of our knowledge of the relevant facts, and their meaning, or consequences.

§ 29. *The Change in Logical Method.*

Before describing more fully the nature of the reasoning process as it now exists in use, we may stop for a moment and make a brief survey of the ways in which the change already noticed must affect our logic. In general, we have seen, the difference is that the chief assumptions underlying the old system are no longer considered either binding or even methodically expedient. The "Laws of Thought" are one such group of assumptions, and we have already noticed (p. 157) how the recognition that a statement true for one purpose may be untrue for another, cuts away the ground from under them and, while leaving them "undeniable," renders them—in any case where a doubt has arisen—irrelevant and therefore not worth attempting to deny. A radical change in our notion of the nature of ambiguity is, as we shall see, a result of this recognition. We must keep ourselves ever prepared to find these Laws *when applied* misleading; to find not only that what is called A is often wrongly so called, but also that what (from some points of view, or for some purposes) is rightly called A is, for other purposes, rightly called non-A. As we shall find, instead of there being even a presumption that a given predicate term, A, is free from ambiguity, the presumption—especially in contentious assertion and reasoning—is to the contrary. In the absence of clear reasons for thinking any disputed statement "S is A" unambiguous, we must expect to find it true in one sense and false in another. And we must re-organise our logic so as to include and allow for this expectation; which implies that we must cease to regard proof as strictly coercive.

Why, then, should we seek to bind ourselves by any (applicable) Laws of Thought? The reason why "necessary truths" have been sought for has always been the hope of getting an absolutely firm foundation on which to build. It was early understood that the enquiry into the material truth of any premiss necessitated a new syllogism in which that premiss becomes the conclusion, with two more premisses the material truth of which has also to be enquired into. And it is clear that if we are to avoid an infinite regress with an ever increasing number of statements requiring proof, we must imagine a stopping point somewhere. This point, now that we no longer expect "proof" to yield absolutely final truth, we must be content to conceive as relative, in dependence upon the progress of our knowledge. When any two people disputing arrive at a foundation they can agree to accept as true, that is enough *for them* until later doubts arise. But in so far as the old ideal of making proof strictly coercive remains with us, this reliance on mere agreement seems unsatisfactory. Those who hanker after complete and final proof of an assertion are compelled to assume that somewhere in the regress we can reach the downright impossibility of raising further doubt. What they fail to see is that a statement can only be made undeniable by depriving it of all application, and that this makes it empty of all meaning.

　　Closely connected with its uncritical acceptance of the "Laws of Thought," is the other main assumption of the old Logic—that it is possible, and advantageous, to separate the Form of reasoning from the Matter. This was briefly referred to at p. 66. The chief apparent justification of the method was that you thereby separated the process of judging evidence into two distinct steps, in the first of which absolute certainty might be claimed. First you judged whether the "reasoning" was sound, and then (if you wished to) you were free to pass beyond Logic and to enquire into the material truth of the premisses. Logic only claimed infallibility as regards this first step, and disclaimed all direct responsibility for the second.

　　But we now see what is the cost of thus artificially creating a region in which Logic cannot commit an error. In the separate "reasoning process" thus conceived, the terms and propositions of which it consists *have to be assumed* free from ambiguity. Every syllogism, Logic admits, must have an unambiguous middle term. Very well ; *and how*

11—2

are we to know whether a given apparent syllogism has one or not? Here Logic is content to give us an answer which ignores the real difficulty—namely how to detect the kind of ambiguity which only comes to light through asking in what sense each of the premisses is *true.* So that until we take the "material truth" of the premisses into account there is no way of deciding whether we have before us a syllogism or only a syllogistic form vitiated by an ambiguous middle. If we try to decide this question without reference to material truth we can only take account of the kinds of ambiguity which are obvious enough to be recognised in the dictionaries; and we have to exclude from logical jurisdiction all the most dangerous and seductive errors to which our reasoning is liable. Is Logic's infallibility worth preserving at the price?

We saw, too, how this assumption draws support from the belief that the A E I O forms are (owing to the fixity of "classes") fairly representative of thought. Just so far as they do represent thought, the separation of Form from Matter is feasible and harmless. We do occasionally reason about the extensive relation of two accepted classes to each other by means of the relation of each of them to a third class, and for that purpose we may put letters like X, Y and Z in place of the terms and so test the validity of a syllogism apart from the truth of its premisses and conclusion. If the kind of mistakes that can be made in this "reasoning process" were important, or likely to occur when ordinary care is taken, the tests of validity would have some justification[1], when strictly limited to this exceptional operation of thought. What logic quarrels with is the use of the assumption on a much wider scale. It is when the attempt is made to restrict logic as a whole to this petty function that the harm begins: mainly through

[1] But even then they need not be so elaborate and cumbrous as in the old syllogistic doctrine. See pp. 77—84.

the consequent neglect of the risk of ambiguity, but also partly because the difficulty of translating from ordinary language into Logical Form involves our accepting some other assumptions, equally baseless on the whole, and these other assumptions in their turn lend support to the original one.

For instance, if forms of proposition are to represent meanings we are under strong temptation to assume that a form of sentence we happen to meet with shows its only possible meaning unmistakably on its face; which is only true by accident. Here and there this rough assumption may work very well; for instance, everyone would naturally agree that "All that glitters is not gold" should be translated into the O form, and that "Great is Diana" should be expressed "Diana is great." Yet no satisfactory rule in the matter is possible, because in countless instances the same sentence may, without violating either common custom or a sensitive literary taste, be intended differently by different people, or by the same person on different occasions. Some examples were met with at pp. 61—64, and it is difficult to set or to answer examination questions of the kind there quoted without encountering this insoluble doubt. The more life-like the examples are, the more uncertainty as a rule attaches to their translation into the required forms. A natural result is that the examples used in Logic tend to be the reverse of life-like.

This is one of the many cases in which the attempt to separate Form and Matter almost compels Logicians to avoid facing a difficulty. Instead of recognising its full extent they keep to the fringe of the subject, and half-heartedly make little rules about the interpretation of words like "or," "most," "few," "only"; rules of which the best that can be said is that they generally try to reach a sort of safety by seeking for the minimum of assertive meaning that the sentence can grammatically bear.

Preoccupied as Logic has chosen to be with *forms* of statement, it cannot wholly desert the idea that the meaning of a statement is something that belongs to its form, instead of the form being a more or less successful attempt on the part of a speaker to express a meaning. Logicians cannot allow themselves to see that the question what a given sentence, used by a speaker, *means* (i.e. is meant to mean) is different from the question what, in the opinion of most people who use language carefully, it *ought* to mean, or may with fair probability be supposed to mean, in the absence of further information.

Closely related to this idea that a given meaning belongs of right to a given form is the whole attitude of Logic towards the question how distinctions are to be drawn between different kinds of term, and of proposition. Here the effort to keep Form and Matter separate leads in general to a merely grammatical treatment, in which the average customary use of a word, or a sentence, is what decides its " Logical character." But in certain cases common sense has forced Logic into deserting its principle; into taking account of the Matter, and admitting that the Logical character can only be decided by the actual use on a given occasion. Thus Logic allows that we cannot tell by the form of a disjunctive proposition whether it is "exclusive" or not, but that when an argument in the *modus tollendo ponens* is founded on it, our judgment of the argument's validity depends on our knowledge of the facts[1]. Again, the " universe of discourse "[2] is arrived at by taking actual meanings into account ; so far as the form of a negative term is concerned, there is nothing to show any limit to its reference. Again, most Logicians now admit that the distinction between a collective name and a general name depends upon actual use in a given case[3]. These

---

[1] P. 76.   [2] P. 105.
[3] P. 107.

definite and free admissions, however, affect only a few of
the distinctions. In other cases, like that of the distinction
between equivocal and univocal terms[1] and that between
hypothetical and categorical propositions[2], the admission is
made—on the rare occasions when it is made at all—with
some reluctance, and is not welcomed into the Logical
system. But in regard to the majority of the distinctions
the method adopted is that of skating lightly over the thin
ice and hoping that the reader will do the same. We have
had occasion to notice this tendency not only in regard to
the general difficulty of translating from ordinary language
into Logical Form[3], but also in regard to various special
points; such as the distinction between abstract and concrete names[4], positive and negative names[5], simple and
compound propositions[6], the distinction between one proposition and "another,"[7] and the value of the inference by
added determinant[8].

Blemishes of this kind, it may be pleaded, regrettable
though they are, do not deprive Logic of the power of
supplying some roughly useful knowledge about language
as an instrument of thought; and they have the merit (if
" merit" is the right word) of creating a number of little
puzzles upon which the student may exercise his wits and
the examiner may frame his questions. Perhaps this faint
praise is justified. But it is more difficult to find even so
slight a justification for two other tendencies which are
directly fostered by Logical method, and which draw
support partly from the Laws of Thought and partly from
the belief that the attempt to separate Form from Matter
is on the whole worth making. There is, first, the tendency
to view reasoning as a mechanical process, and secondly the
habit of confusing good intentions with good results, well-
meant rules with effective guides, and of taking the obvious

[1] P. 108.　　[2] § 15.　　[3] §§ 5 and 13.　　[4] P. 101.
[5] P. 104.　　[6] P. 69.　　[7] P. 85.　　[8] P. 89.

importance of a distinction as a guarantee of its value in application.

What is here meant by the mechanical view of reasoning is not merely the restricting of the name " reasoning " to that part of the whole process which—as Jevons showed—can be worked by a machine. So long as it is made perfectly clear that that is the limited sense in which Logic chooses *always* to use the word "reasoning," no harm need be done, and anyhow the objection would be merely verbal. The real objection lies rather against some corollaries of this attempted limitation of the scope of Logic, and specially against the conception of propositions as constructed by taking two unattached terms and joining them together ; and of syllogisms as similarly built up out of ready-made propositions with an independent value and meaning. The way in which this conception helps to support a false view of the nature of ambiguity will be seen further on, and is summarised at pp. 230—232.

The second habit or tendency just referred to is encouraged by Logical method rather than created by it. To accept an apparently axiomatic statement as true, and a distinction as valuable, without troubling about their precise application, comes naturally enough to those who are not of an enquiring turn of mind. All that Logic does is to take advantage of this inertness, and so to gain a reputation for wisdom at small expense in trouble. To lay down the rule, for instance, that a term used in a piece of reasoning " must not be ambiguous" is thought sufficient, especially when supported by an abstract distinction between equivocal and univocal terms. A distinction is drawn between verbal and real (or essential and accidental) propositions, which everyone can see is an important distinction, but we are encouraged to apply it as dogmatically as we please[1]. Rules are given for Definition,

[1] See p. 111.

Division, and Classification, and Canons for the interpretation of experiments; but always the question how to apply such rules in cases of difficulty is kept out of focus. Yet the difference between correct and incorrect *application* of any rule, or any distinction, is precisely that in which its value consists[1].

Such being, in outline, the defects that are found in the old Logic, the next question is how to build up a logic which shall as far as possible avoid them. Since the defects are due to shallowness and excessive simplicity (or "abstractness") of view, it would seem at first that any doctrine which shall escape them must involve a greater expense in labour of thought. This is true in regard to each of the points that the new logic has to consider, but there are great compensations both in the number of doctrines and technicalities that we are able to discard as lacking logical purpose, and in the avoidance of many insoluble puzzles and awkward inconsistencies that the old method involved. In the first place the intricacies of Mood and Figure are swept away; also (as we saw at pp. 77—84) the distinction between the categorical and the hypothetical syllogism, and all the trivial minor distinctions belonging to the former; also (as we shall see in § 33), the distinction between inductive and deductive Logic. And of the numerous old distinctions between kinds of term, and between kinds of proposition, the few that are retained require to be seen from a different point of view, with a radically changed interpretation. An ordinary acquaintance with Grammar is presupposed—the kind of acquaintance which every sixth-form boy finds sufficient for writing his essays or his letters, and which is not much concerned about the precise grammatical names of the various parts of speech, or with the pedantry of the subject

---

[1] See also pp. 185, 211—214, 223, 236.

generally[1]. What the student of logic has to remember is that Grammar, at its best, represents average custom ; errors in Grammar are mere solecisms and have nothing directly to do with errors in reasoning. It cannot even be assumed that ungrammatical expressions are generally more ambiguous than grammatical ones ; and, in any case where they happen to be so, it is to logical method that we must appeal for their correction.

The central subject of logic is the risks of reasoning, so far as they admit of being recognised and understood[2]. In our next chapter an account of the reasoning process will be given, from which it will be seen that the structure of reasoning consists throughout of the *application of rules to cases*. If any material fault can be found in a piece of reasoning it must be traceable either to an error of fact in some rule accepted as true, or to an error of fact as to the nature of some case supposed to come under the rule, or—where the error is often most difficult to discover—to a lack of connexion between the rule and the case, due to an ambiguity.

As regards technicalities in general, the attitude required by the student of logic is the reverse of what it used to be. Our chief business now is not to "learn how to name our tools," but how to use them. Formerly the meaning of the traditional technical terms was a subject of study for its own sake—or rather for the sake of being able to show acquaintance with them on paper. But when we make a knowledge of the risks of reasoning our chief object,

[1] A sufficient treatment of Grammar, for those who need more knowledge of it than they can pick up unconsciously, is given in that excellent book *The King's English*.

[2] There is no need to make any pretence of securing infallibility of judgment, even in a single instance. If Absolute Truth means Truth as it would appear to a superhuman mind, how can we presume to have reached it ? Or, if by any chance we did reach it, what means should we have of distinguishing between it and the truth that merely suffices for human purposes ?

technicalities become purely subordinate to that purpose. So far as they are needed at all, they are needed only as instruments of expression; they help us to say concisely what would otherwise have to be said at inconvenient length and subject to doubts of interpretation. And in order to keep them in this subordinate place we must set ourselves free from the notion that the ideal of a philosophical language is that every word should have one and only one meaning in all its possible uses. Convenient as such simplicity might be if it were possible, the effort to reach it is certain to be wasted, and the time and trouble will be much better spent in other directions. Anyhow, that is the belief which underlies the following discussions. After we have been through them, there will be no harm in reconsidering the few technicalities employed, and doing what we can to regulate their meaning.

CHAPTER VIII

THE PROCESS OF REASONING

§ 30.   *Verbal and Real Reasoning.*

Though all reasoning is verbal in so far as it involves the use of words, there is a kind of reasoning which is sometimes called specially "verbal" as contrasted with "real" because it stops short of an enquiry into the truth of things, and contents itself—if only as a preliminary step —with developing the consequences of some admission, in the interests of *consistency*. If you admit so and so, it says, you are thereby committed to such and such a consequence of that admission. If you have called a thing white, you must not also call it black; if you have admitted the truth of the axioms of Geometry, you are bound to stick to these admissions until you openly desert them. This kind of reasoning serves two purposes mainly. First, where we are admittedly in possession of an undisputed truth which is also completely intelligible—let us call the multiplication table an example—we can follow out its consequences to the utmost. And secondly, where we have before us a statement which seems to us open to criticism, we can sometimes "reduce it to absurdity" (or at least get it corrected in expression) by pointing out its strict literal consequences.

One of the great differences between ancient and modern logic is shown in our attitude towards "verbal" reasoning. Instead of regarding it as final and conclusive, we now regard it only as preliminary—as an attempt to clear away initial misconceptions due rather to the expression than to the thought expressed. The notion that any statement, even an axiom, may be defectively expressed and may conceal a truer (or a less true) view than it literally states; and the corresponding notion that an apparently undeniable statement may be misleading; are gradually superseding the earlier notion that all statements need to be interpreted strictly, and either to be trusted as "true" or condemned as "false" on the strength of such literal interpretation. The more modern we are, the more we recognise the necessary defects of language and the frequent difficulty of expressing a meaning in words so unmistakable as to need no alteration for any possible purpose. It has become our normal logical experience that statements are often true in one sense and false in another, or true for some purposes but not for others. Hence instead of assuming that because a statement is "true" it may be blindly trusted, we look out for a possible limit to its value. And instead of being content with condemning a statement out of hand because it cannot be strictly interpreted without leading us into absurdity, we seek rather to get it amended in order to make out how much truth there may be in it, or on what sort of occasions (for what purposes) it may be trusted. And we have begun to see that the range of "undisputed truth which is also completely intelligible" dwindles away in the light of our knowledge of the conditions under which language performs its functions. Language we find to be at best an affair of compromises, of rough and ready purposes. We can only justify it as an instrument of purely human invention, liable to criticism and liable to misuse. In consequence, "verbal reasoning" is a less important matter than it used to seem ; and in the following chapters we will turn our attention away from it and think of "real reasoning" only.

§ 31.   *Facts and their "meaning."*

Except when we are merely concerned with verbal consistency, the reasons we give for any belief consist entirely in *alleged facts* ; and in order that such "facts" may serve their purpose as evidence for the belief in question, they must be (1) true, and (2) sufficient for proof. When evidence fails to be satisfactory it is always in one of two ways : either (1) the alleged facts are false, or (2) their supposed *meaning* is disputable.

It is rather unfortunate that the same word "meaning" is used for a quality possessed by facts, and also for another quality possessed by words. Confusion sometimes arises from this source, and we must be careful to avoid it. When we say that a red sunset "means" fine weather to-morrow what we are speaking of is *indication*. When we say that "Hund" means "dog," or that an "abacist" means a particular kind of calculator, or that a "sardine" means "any kind of small fish tinned in oil," what we are speaking of is the *translation* of words. Facts, so far as they are understood, always indicate further facts, past, present or future; words, however well they are understood, tell us no more than the intention of some person who uses them. There is no reason why these two sorts of "meaning" need be confused. The difference between them is plain the moment we think of it. If we like, we can call the one kind of meaning "indicational" and the other "translational," but it is seldom necessary to be so explicit since the context will generally make clear which kind of meaning is spoken of.

However far back we go in memory we cannot recall a time at which *no* facts had meaning for us. The assumption that facts have a meaning, which we may more or less successfully learn to read, lies at the root of the whole of our thinking, from childhood onwards, and we pass our lives in becoming better acquainted with the facts we encounter. Even the lower animals, so far as we can observe, often seem to recognise that facts have a meaning; for instance the fact of my taking a stick from the hat-stand may be read by my dog as a sign that he will presently be taken for a walk. Facts are *signs* of other facts; and their value to us, their interest for us, consists entirely in that quality. Facts are better or worse guides to action according as we know more or less about their meaning.

To a great extent our reading of the meaning of facts is so vague and subtle that we can only lamely express it in words. When we take a liking or a dislike to a face at first sight, it is often beyond our power to give any satisfactory account of the facts on which it is based; and when we are experts in any subject a great portion of the judgments we form in regard to questions that belong to it have this quasi-instinctive character. If we try to reduce to words the precise weight which this or that fact has had in a judgment of ours, we often find it a very difficult

matter to do so with clearness and completeness.   Expert
judgments, as such, rest on complicated grounds, the whole
of which cannot be produced, or even definitely remembered.

Still, the problem of stating the meaning of a given fact
is one that we all very often have to deal with as best
we can.   Not only in discussion but also for the purpose
of clearing our own ideas, it is necessary to reduce to
words our notion of what is meant by—what is to be
inferred from—this or that fact, or this or that detail in
a fact.   And our usual and simplest means of doing this
is in the form of *general rules*.   If we believe that a fact or
detail, X, is a trustworthy sign of a fact or a quality Y, we
commonly express this belief in some form like "All X is Y"
(e.g. All with that trade mark are good); or "If (or when or
where) X, then Y" (e.g. If the ice bears you, it will bear me;
when that signal drops, the train is coming; where there is
smoke, there is fire); or "X indicates Y" (e.g. Confusion
shows guilt).   The forms in which such rules are commonly
stated are various, and the rules are of all possible degrees
of supposed certainty; from axiomatic or quasi-axiomatic
rules like "the whole is greater than its part" or "all matter
gravitates" down to consciously uncertain ones like "a red
sky at night means fine weather next day."   Thus facts
and rules are what evidence as a whole consists of—the
facts being such that they *come under* the rules, and the
rules being such that they *apply to* the facts alleged.   It
must always be remembered that any detail in a fact is
also a fact on its own account.   And we all conceive of
facts as made up of a number of details.

We noticed just now that there are many cases in which
it is impossible to give a complete account of our reasons
for a belief, and difficult to give even a sufficient account to
convey to another person the real strength of such reasons.
This occurs, we saw, where our judgments are complex and

subtle or "expert" in character. But of course complexity in judgments is a matter of degree; complex judgments are not sharply marked off from simple ones, nor expert judgments from inexperienced. Nearly always—perhaps in strictness always—our judgments lack complete simplicity, and rest on more facts than can be conveniently stated in any concise form. Instead of being able to prove a conclusion by producing one fact (minor premiss) and one rule under which it comes (major premiss), and so putting the proof into a single compact syllogism, we generally find it necessary to produce fact after fact, each contributing its share to the proof, and all together frequently falling short of conveying to another mind the same certainty that they give to ourselves. The process of proof, instead of being simple and short and conclusive, thus tends to be complex and extended and questionable. A change of conviction is a growth from seed, in favouring conditions, rather than a sudden inevitable result of a threat from Logic's pistol.

In two ways chiefly these considerations differentiate the modern from the medieval conception of proof. On the one hand proof is no longer regarded as strictly coercive; there may always conceivably be more details that ought to be taken into account; and so any statement of reasons always leaves room for a possible later supplement or correction. But on the other hand it is now recognised that a slacker kind of general rule may be enough to give a fact all the "meaning" that is claimed for it, or needed for it, in regard to this or that conclusion. A fact X may be relevant to the proof of a conclusion Y not only where it is claimed that X *universally* indicates Y (e.g. smoke and fire) but also where it is claimed that this particular concrete fact X points to Y, not by virtue *only* of its quality of Xness, but also because of its individual peculiarities ABC... which make it the particular kind of X it is. For example there are endless possible kinds of "red sky"—different shades of colour, different shapes of clouds, slightly different atmospheric appearances of all sorts; and so, though it cannot safely be maintained in strict generality that a red sky at night indicates fine weather, a sufficiently expert eye may be able to see in *this* red sky a combination of details which makes the prediction highly probable.

For logical purposes the chief consequence of this great change in the conception of the nature of proof is that now we look more to *facts* than to *names* as evidence; we are more ready than the Logicians were to criticise the application of the name X to a given case by appealing to the facts—the circumstances of the given case—in the light of all we know or surmise about *causes*. X is X, of course; we never dream of denying that, and no one has any interest in doing so; but in this particular case here and now before us we see that "X" is X with a difference. We see that it departs in certain particular ways from the pure or abstract type of the X's; and to us its departure from the type is an important factor in the problem of reading its meaning. From the pure type of X, perhaps,—if such a thing could ever be found in the actual world—we may believe that Y is inferrible with certainty; for instance we may believe that perfect goodness leads to perfect happiness; but when we have to deal with a concrete case which we find to be ABC...X, any knowledge we may possess of the causal relations of A and B and C to Y will rightly affect our reading of *this* X's meaning. Perhaps all these details are antagonistic to Y; or some of them antagonistic and some favourable; and in different degrees.

Before going further, it will help us if we stop for a moment to compare this modern view of the process of proof with the old doctrine that all proof is syllogistic. That may still be regarded as true in a sense, but in a very different sense from what the reader of the traditional text-books is led to imagine. "Facts" and "the meaning of facts" do respectively correspond to minor and major pre-misses[1]; and since evidence in general is entirely made up of these two elements the complexities we see in a fact only bring new syllogisms into operation. Thus the whole structure of reasoning is syllogistic, even when we break it into fragments. But on the other hand the effect of this admission is to destroy the *coercive* force of any one syl-logism, however verbally perfect it may be. Theoretically always, and practically very often, the premisses "S is M," and "M indicates P" may fail to yield a conclusion because S is aM, and a may be antagonistic to P. In any given case, therefore, of syllogistic reasoning, however small or large, we have to face this possibility. Wherever we dis-regard it we take a risk of error. We thus get the requisite practical certainty—when we get it at all—not from the syllogistic form as such, but from our knowledge (external to it) of the details belonging to *this* S and of their causal relation to P. So that although every part of every piece of reasoning is syllogistic, no part of it is perfectly safe against the charge of "ambiguous middle term." To guard against this ubiquitous source of error as well as we can, and to recognise that when we have done our best to guard against it we may still have failed, is the chief business of modern logic. Our next aim therefore must be to get a clear view of the nature of ambiguity in a middle term.

§ 32. *Ambiguous Middle.*

Any reader who has been thoroughly infected with the old Logic will find a difficulty in recognising as a case of ambiguous middle the form "S is aM; M indicates P; there-fore S is P." To him it will seem that either both these premisses are true or one of them is not true; and that if they are both true the conclusion follows of necessity. If

---

[1] I.e. in the first figure ; to which, as we saw, the others are reducible.

S is aM, he will say, it is none the less M; and the major premiss speaks of M in general, and allows no exceptions for sorts of M.

Such a reader may however be asked to notice that he would be bound to bring the same objection against any attempt to expose an ambiguous middle (as distinct from undistributed middle) in a formula at all. He would have to maintain that there could not be such a thing as an ambiguous middle where the formal conditions are satisfied; that a syllogism in *Barbara*, for instance, could never suffer from this defect. Now even the traditional Logic does nominally recognise the possibility of a formally correct syllogism with an ambiguous middle, though in practice it makes light of the risk, and obscures its importance; the student is led to suppose that the only ambiguous terms are those which have two or more meanings distinguished in the dictionary. And though it is true that undistributed middle is at bottom a form of ambiguous middle[1], it is after all only one special form of it, and comparatively unimportant. One of the differences between it and the more dangerous kind here spoken of consists in the fact that while an undistributed middle can easily be expressed in a formula, the very conditions of formal expression prevent our finding any formula in which ambiguous middle (in a formally correct syllogism) can be expressed.

But there is really no need to seek for a formula here. The defect of a syllogism with an ambiguous middle is that the fact " S is M " and the rule " M indicates P " have the *verbal appearance* but not the reality of belonging to each other; and the problem of understanding how this happens, and what can be done to correct it, is forbidden ground to Formal Logic. Every piece of reasoning, we shall see, is *liable* to this defect, owing to the necessary

---

[1] See above, p. 21.

vagueness[1] of all descriptive language; and the only possible remedy lies in recognising this necessary vagueness and allowing for it.   Before entering on the subject of language, however, we may usefully look at some of the commoner forms of ambiguous middle, so as to get a general idea of its operation in actual reasoning.

For this purpose the first thing to do is to put aside as of scarcely any importance the only kind of "ambiguity" which the old Logic is able to recognise—namely when a word has two or more meanings which can be registered in a dictionary[2] or allowed for as a grammatical idiom[3].   Such ambiguities may perhaps trip up a careless reasoner now and then, but both the prevention and the cure of their ill effects is easy[4].   What we here want to investigate, rather, is the kind of ambiguity which constitutes a real danger even when the utmost care is taken.   *It is precisely the words which are supposed to be "univocal" that exemplify ambiguity in its most effective form.*   And ambiguity, instead of being—as formerly supposed—a comparatively rare defect, avoidable by taking ordinary care, is now seen to correspond to the kind of error which is most difficult to detect; instead of being a purely verbal affair it arises out of ignorance of fact.

A syllogism with a middle term ambiguous in this manner differs only on the surface from a syllogism with

---

[1] Dr Schiller and Captain Knox would here prefer to speak of the *indeterminateness* of descriptive words, rather than of their *vagueness* or *indefiniteness*. As explained, however, at p. 197, I use the latter expressions as equivalent to the former.   The important distinction is that between vagueness (or indefiniteness or indeterminateness) and *ambiguity*.

[2] E.g. "Light is a mode of motion; a feather is light; therefore a feather is a mode of motion."

[3] E.g. "Nothing is better than wisdom; dry bread is better than nothing; therefore dry bread is better than wisdom."

[4] Dr Schiller (*Formal Logic*, p. 27), uses the phrase "Plurality of senses" to express what Logic calls "ambiguity"; and points out that, so long as the word serves to convey the meaning actually intended, the more meanings it can convey *the better it is, as a word*,—the more useful and economical.

one of its premises false ; the difference being that one
of its premises, instead of being *simply* false, is true in
one sense and false in another, or true in a sort of way but
not in the way required for the conclusion drawn—not true
for the purpose for which it is used in the given argument.
It is "true" (in a sort of way) that S is M, and also (in a
sort of way) that M indicates P ; and yet, because of a lack
of correspondence between the two "sorts of way," the conclusion that S is P fails to be supported by these premises.
We will look at some examples presently.   The fault may
sometimes be traced to the fact that a concise and slightly
inaccurate expression is sufficient for most purposes but
not for the purpose in hand ; and sometimes to the fact
that we do not yet know the importance of some detail in
which *this* S, though for most purposes it may be described
as M, differs from the pure type of M, or that we do not
yet know this particular exception to the broad serviceable
rule that M indicates P.   Thus in both cases ambiguity of
the middle term is due to ignorance of *fact*, which hides
from us the need of greater accuracy of language for the
purpose of the particular inference.

A further reason why the nature of ambiguity is still so
little understood is the difficulty of giving an example of
ambiguous middle plain for everyone to understand and
yet capable of deceiving a reasonable man.   It is easy to
give examples of this or of any fallacy if we are content
with coarse and obvious ones, effective perhaps with the
ancient Greek populace and with some modern children ;
but if we try to illustrate well-concealed fallacy of any
kind—fallacy which can deceive our judges, statesmen, or
scientific men of to-day—we are brought up at once against
the fact that to most people such examples will seem to
illustrate sound reasoning rather than fallacy.   There is
only a razor edge on which to balance our examples between
the transparent and the obscure.

To meet this difficulty, let us notice first a class of comparatively simple examples and then another class where the ambiguity is more difficult to see. As illustrating the first of these classes we may take almost any instance where a proverb is used as a major premiss by someone who interprets it too literally. A proverb is a rough general rule, and to take a rough general rule too literally is to ignore its unspecified exceptions. In the case of well-known proverbs the extent to which we do this is largely a result of our temperament or our habits. If, for instance, I am timid or miserly I shall interpret the proverb "A penny saved is a penny gained" more strictly and literally than it is interpreted by a venturesome man of business. Some occasions that to me appear to come under the general designation of "a penny saved" will to him appear to come under some such name as "an opportunity missed" or "a short-sighted policy." On the face of it the occasions on which I save my pence *are* savings; and yet, to a more acute business eye, they are not so. The middle term of the syllogism is "a penny saved," and the truth of the minor premiss (where my niggardly action really is uneconomical) depends upon this term being taken in a different sense from that which belongs to it in the major premiss (where the major premiss is interpreted in a sense which allows it to be true).

On the other hand I may be a reckless and improvident person, and then I shall interpret to suit my own nature that other well-known proverb "Don't spoil the ship for the sake of a ha'p'orth of tar." That is the way with proverbs generally; their interpretation is (more or less) known to be elastic. The more we know this and remember it the less likely will a proverb be to mislead us. But, other things equal, it is just as easy for some people to form the habit of viewing almost any extravagance as a ha'p'orth of tar, as for others to take excessive care of the pence.

Generally less transparent, and often extremely obscure, are the cases where the ambiguity is due to our ignorance of the facts of a situation which seems more simple than it is. For instance, we may be ignorant of the effect of some detail *a* which we know to be present in S; so that, though S is undeniably M, it is M with a difference, the importance of which remains unseen; or on the other hand, the detail *a* (even when its effects are known) may be difficult to recognise—may escape our closest powers of observation. Almost any "small" but important error in interpreting a scientific experiment will illustrate one of these kinds of ambiguous middle. So far from being a rare occurrence in experimenting, this risk is the normal condition under which all such work is done. To engage in scientific research is to look for—and for someone sooner or later to find—important details which have been overlooked by all previous experimenters, using what seemed to them to be the greatest available care that the case required. For instance, experiments are made with a certain substance, and the results are found on the best authority to be of such and such a character. Some years later it is discovered that these results were not due to the substance itself, but to a change that had happened to it through the lapse of one day between obtaining the substance and experimenting with it. S (the substance in question) *is* M, and M, *when unspoilt, is* P; but S that is twenty-four hours old is S with a difference—liable to pass unnoticed—which prevents its being P[1].

From the most obscure cases of ambiguous middle down to the most transparent ones which can deceive only the thoughtless or the ignorant, there is an unbroken

---

[1] This case occurred in some French experiments with splenic fever infection. A parallel instance—now fortunately too transparent to deceive most people—may be found in the premisses "Boiled fish is safe invalid food"; and "here is some [stale] boiled fish."

series of more or less respectable errors essentially the same in character; cases where S is undoubtedly M, and yet where the really valuable rule that M indicates P does not apply to it. It is open to anyone to say that in such cases the rule may be "valuable" but is not *strictly* true. That is, in fact, all that the old Logic can say in the matter; and the result of saying it is that we thereby cut ourselves off from any hope of dealing with hidden ambiguities at all. Such a method cripples our power of correcting the errors to which reasoning is most liable. In actual reasoning we seldom have to do with rules which are strictly universal and true. We have *valuable* rules in plenty, but their value depends on their application not being taken too literally and stretched too far. The problem of right reasoning is that of taking our valuable rules with the requisite pinch of salt. Rules applying to pure abstractions, like a straight line or a triangle, can be taken as strictly universal, because there we openly postulate that individual differences shall not be considered. But in the case of a rule applicable to *facts* such a postulate would be fatuous. A fact's individual difference is always important for *some* purpose, and the question whether it is important for a given purpose in hand—the purpose of inferring P—cannot be ignored where our object is to get at the truth. In all our rules which are applicable to facts there is some vagueness and therefore some risk of misinterpretation. Risk of misinterpretation of a rule is in practice the same as risk of error.

Not only is ambiguous middle a risk that every smallest piece of reasoning runs, but it is also the typical form of all respectable error, or error for which there is a good excuse. Where there is error in real reasoning there must be *misdescription* either of facts or of rules; and any misdescription whether slight or gross can take effect only when it occurs in a middle term[1]. That follows from our recognition that

---

[1] On this account we will generally take the form " S is M " as typical of

thought is syllogistic throughout. If I wrongly describe S as "M," no harm is done till I couple this with the rule "M indicates P" and so give point or meaning to the description. In the absence of any such rule of inference the statement that S is M would mean nothing. Similarly, if I am mistaken in saying that M indicates P, no harm can be done till I couple this with the minor premiss "S is M." It is doubtful whether in real life it ever happens that a statement either of a fact or of a rule of inference is accepted as true without *any* view of its applications; the nearest approach to this is when we repeat, as a parrot might, some accepted formula which we take from authority. But in its extreme form that would not be thinking at all, and in anything less than its extreme form we do make some sort of vague application of the statement. All meaning, in short, whether vague or definite, consists in recognising applications of a statement and so getting information out of it. A predicate term is meaningless to us unless it gives us information about the Subject through one or more rules of inference, and a rule of inference is meaningless to us except so far as we can recognise cases about which it gives us information. We may thus apply a statement of fact to a rule of inference, or we may apply a rule of inference to a statement of fact; without such application neither the one nor the other would have any meaning. And where a rule and a fact have, through ambiguity of expression, a false appearance of applying to each other, there we get a false appearance of a justified conclusion.

§ 33.   *Induction and Deduction.*

It may occur to the reader to ask what room is left in the above account of reasoning for "Induction." I would

predication, rather than " S is P "; for wherever a conclusion "S is P" has a meaning, it gets its meaning through an agreement that the fact of being P " means " something particular; and " P " thus becomes the middle term of a further syllogism.

reply by another question—Why should Induction be treated separately? The separation of Logic into two departments, deductive and inductive, is responsible for much needless difficulty due to the belief that a different process is required for proving a general rule by means of particular facts, from that required for proving any conclusion by means of a minor and a major premiss. The distinction between deduction and induction does not warrant this belief, and is in fact chiefly of value from the point of view of the idler kind of teaching and examining. It separates Logic as a whole, artificially and misleadingly, into two distinct branches in which instruction, of a sort, can be conveniently given.

Since we are always at liberty to make distinctions, and to use what names we please for them, there is not necessarily any harm in calling the process of generalising from facts "induction," and that of following out the consequences of a generalisation "deduction." But such a distinction does not help us to understand the process of judging evidence in general, any more than the distinction between "stalactite" and "stalagmite" helps us to understand the chemical and other processes concerned in the formation of both. In fact the distinction between induction and deduction is not so harmless, because of its liability to make us imagine that the process used in judging the evidence for a general rule is somehow different from that which is used in the case of particular facts. And whether Aristotle did or did not fall into this error, it is certain that at some point in the history of Logic it has become established.

As soon as we recognise that all thought is syllogistic however small be the fragments into which we analyse it, and also that every syllogism is liable to have an ambiguous middle term, we are safe against the supposition that general rules are proved by a different method from that which is

used in proving particular facts.   In arriving at both kinds
of conclusion whatever success we may reach depends upon
the grip we have of the evidentiary facts and their "meaning"
—depends, that is to say, on our having a proper and sufficient selection of minor and major premises relevant to
our conclusion.   The recognition that any given syllogism
may suffer from ambiguous middle breaks down the supposed simplicity of "deductive" proof, since in order to
guard against the fallacy we have to make sure in what
sense each of the premises is *true*.   And since every fact
we use in proving a general rule is either a fact with a
"meaning" or else a fact of no use in proving anything, all
proof of a general rule involves a considerable amount of
deduction.   The more complete we make our proof, therefore, whether of a particular fact or a general rule, the more
of *both* processes—if we care to regard them as two—is
involved in it.   It is only by forgetting that middle terms,
as such, are liable to ambiguity, or that facts cannot prove
anything except through their "meaning" that we can think
of induction and deduction as separate methods of proof.

Since Mill's time there has been a fashion, in the textbooks, of treating Inductive Logic as mainly concerned
with the proof of *what caused what* in particular cases
observed, or arranged for experiment.   The importance of
guarding against error in this process is obvious, whether
our conclusion claims to be a true particular fact or a trustworthy general rule.   For just as we cannot recognise the
exceptions to a general rule, and therefore cannot know
when to trust it, till we know what details in the facts concerned operate for and against the rule's trustworthiness, so
on the other hand our knowledge of the real as contrasted
with the merely apparent nature of any fact is bound up
with our knowledge of its causes and consequences.   Just
as, for instance, we estimate the value and the weakness of
the major premiss "Familiarity breeds contempt" through

our knowledge of different kinds of familiarity and their modes of operation, so it is through our causal knowledge of the details of any case of "familiarity" that we judge whether it does or does not deserve that name for the purposes of the inference.

What logic has to say, however, about the interpretation of experiments is mostly by way of caution against the excessive simplicity, and the useless or delusive formalism, of the inductive Logicians' results. If Mill and his long line of imitators were not so unmistakably serious, we might think they were mocking the enquirer when they tell him that all we want for the Method of Difference is two cases alike "in every circumstance save one." When do we in fact know every circumstance? And besides, what exactly are we to mean by "one" circumstance? A circumstance *not* composed of smaller details? If so, where are we to find it? Considered in themselves, and apart from the previous knowledge which gives us the material for them, and from the discretion which leads us to regard their results as tentative and unfinished, the rules for correctly interpreting a piece of observed causation are about as valuable as the rule that in business "all you have to do" is to buy cheap and sell dear. The important question always is How are we, with the best intentions in the world, to recognise *before the event* the wrong steps we may take in trying to follow these excellent principles?

This fundamental defect in the Inductive Methods is no new discovery. It was already brought to light in the controversy between Mill and Whewell about their value. Dr Whewell[1] found fault with them on the ground that they only come into operation after the chief part of discovery has been accomplished—namely the reduction of the crude phenomena, as actually encountered, to the neat

[1] *Philosophy of Discovery*, pp. 263, 4. Mill's account of the matter is in his *System of Logic*, Book III. chap. IX. § 6.

formulæ which the methods demand. In answer Mill points out that a similar objection has been brought against the Syllogism itself, and argues that though as a matter of fact both objections are true, they are unimportant. For, he says, we cannot successfully reduce the phenomena to the formulæ unless we know what kind of formulæ to reduce them to; we need rules and models to which if the arguments conform (and only if they do so) they are conclusive. And moreover, if it be true, as Whewell seems to suggest, that no discoveries were ever made by the methods, then none can ever have been made by observation and experiment; "for assuredly if any were, it was by processes reducible to one or other of those methods."

As regards the latter part of this answer, Mill shows in the next paragraph that what he means is that in the beginnings of discovery men made use *not* of the methods in all their strictness, but of some much looser form of them in which there is no attempt at the precision which the canons expressly require. He here gives as an example of the Method of Agreement the arrival at the generalisation "Dogs bark" from the mere experience of a number of barking dogs—an induction "by simple enumeration" if ever there was one; and as an instance of the Method of Difference the arrival at the law that "Fire burns": "Before I touch the fire I am not burnt; this is BC; I touch it and am burnt; this is ABC, aBC." Mr Bradley's[1] comment on this is worth quoting : " The Canons we think are not hard to content if this will satisfy them. But surely their author had forgotten them for the moment. By seeing three barking dogs I perceive that they *'have only one circumstance in common.'* By standing in front of a burning fireplace, and then touching the fire and being burnt, I am to know that the two facts *'have every circumstance in common but one.'* Is not this preposterous? Surely it is clear in

[1] *Principles of Logic*, p. 336.

the first case that Mill's way of arguing might prove just as well that all dogs have the mange, and in the second that every fireplace blisters."

Now Whewell's point was not to deny that science may have originated in some such clumsy observations and experiments as these, but to notice that the *strict* methods, as conceived by Mill himself, require a great deal of work done upon the given material before they can be used. Everyone admits that savages use Agreement in the form of simple enumeration, and Difference in the form of *post hoc, ergo propter hoc*; but these, instead of being respectively the methods of Agreement and of Difference, are the very mistakes against which these methods are supposed to guard us. And what was meant by Whewell, and is now meant by logicians, is that all the safeguards which the canons elaborate depend for their value on work that must be done before the strict method can be applied. Therefore, we say, it is the quality of this previous work to which the credit is due. If this has been badly done we may think we are using (e.g.) the method of Difference when we are in fact only using a poor imitation of it.

But the first part of Mill's answer is more instructive as indicating the deep difference between Mill's whole view of experimental work and the view which has grown up within the last half century. We no longer look for perfect rules and perfect models, to which our arguments shall conform ; we no longer expect to get *conclusive* results, but only results guarded against such errors as our best existing knowledge and our utmost care may enable us to foresee and prevent. Though we still use our observation of Agreement and of Difference—there is obviously nothing else to use—we recognise that there is no advantage in formulating a Canon or a Method whose strict provisions we can never be sure we have reached. Indeed, what information can such a Canon be supposed to give us ? It is each particular problem itself which sets before us the desired ideal. The attempt to discover which of the antecedents was the cause of *a*, or which of the consequents was the effect of A, presuppose just as much knowledge of the ideal sought for as the strictest statement of the Method of Difference. For in asking *which* out of all the antecedents or consequents is the one we want to discover we already recognise the need of getting an answer that shall single out as far as possible the *one* relevant circumstance; we set before ourselves the task of excluding *all* the irrelevant circumstances; we thus confess our recognition of the same need that the Canon of Difference superfluously expresses. But we recognise it only as a problem to attack, instead of as a rule that can be supposed to guide us[1].

On the view here taken, then, of the process of judging evidence, there are no Canons which can tell us how to avoid error. Instead of them we have a review of the difficulties in the way of guarding our conclusions, whether main or subsidiary, against ambiguity of the middle term. We have to learn how to look out for this defect under its most specious disguises, and we have to accept the fact that with all our care and trouble we may in a given case be deceived by them. No logic can seriously pretend to reveal those secrets of Nature which science is only gradually and laboriously discovering. Nor can it cure a dull mind of all its dulness, or make a careless temperament consistently careful, or remove by word of command those deep-seated habits and prejudices which are the results of our training and character. Any pretensions therefore which we may be inclined to make for logic, of providing security against error, must be of a humbler kind. The most it can do is to give us the same sort of insight that common sense and daily experience give us, but to give it

[1] The reader who wishes to see the case against Inductive Logic more fully stated may refer to Chap. XIX in Dr Schiller's *Formal Logic*.

in a more generalised shape. And it is specially in generalisations about the use of words in reasoning that logic finds
its opportunity of reducing to comparative definiteness and
coherence certain truths the force of which is *on occasion* felt
by common sense. Thus logic makes use of the fact that
the man of common sense already acts—in certain cases
and irregularly—as if he knew these general truths about
the relation between language and reasoning ; it suggests
his taking a firmer hold of them and extending their scope.
The assumption that will here be made is that such
generalisations are neither wholly strange to the reader nor
sufficiently known.   Many of them may seem familiar, and
yet the full extent of their application is in general little
understood.

CHAPTER IX

THE GENERAL CONDITIONS OF LANGUAGE

§ 34. *Description and Indefiniteness.*

The fundamental defect of language is its necessary indefiniteness, and the consequent risk of its being ambiguous
in a given case ; that is to say, the risk that any given
statement runs of being true in one sense and false in
another, i.e. that a statement which is "true" may be
used in such a way as to lead us to a false conclusion by
means of an ambiguous middle term.   As we saw above,
the "true" statement that a penny saved is a penny gained
may—through the different possible conceptions of what
constitutes "a penny saved "—be used to justify a short-
sighted economical policy.   Thus the Manchester Corpora-
tion, when they laid on the water from Thirlmere, "saved"
money by providing only a single conduit pipe.   But they

found, a few years later, that they had to spend a much larger sum on laying a second pipe alongside the first.   So that what was in one sense a saving might equally well be described as a loss.

It must always be remembered that both " facts " and " rules," when recognised as such, are *statements*.   However possible it may be to think without words—and that depends entirely on what we choose to mean by " thinking " —it is only in the form of statements that we can deliberately examine our thoughts and either accept them as true or reject them as false.   This is fairly obvious in the case of rules, and we need not here spend time in showing either that rules are always open to criticism or that to criticise a rule is to criticise its expression in language.   But it seems to be less universally recognised that facts are only statements.   It is tempting to suppose that the undeniable truism that " facts are *facts* " (or that facts, as such, cannot be false) tells us something; whereas it tells us nothing about " so-called facts " and " apparent facts "—which are the only facts that ever can come before us for acceptance or rejection, and then they come before us in the shape of statements.

A further point must also be kept in mind ; that all statement of fact is *descriptive* statement, or that we can never state a fact except by describing it.   Some people seem to think that the " bare " statement of a fact is one thing and the descriptive statement of it another ; and what probably leads them to think so is the obvious truth that of two statements of the same fact one may be comparatively bare and the other comparatively full of detail.   Probably they would say that " It is raining " is a bare statement of fact, while " It is pouring " or " It is raining cats and dogs " is a descriptive statement.

There certainly is a difference in the relative descriptiveness of these statements.   But it is not the difference between describing and not describing ; it is only the difference between a more and a less incomplete description. We may say, if we like, that the first statement is less obviously descriptive than the other two, or again we may even say that it is less descriptive, since the description it gives is scantier. It is, however, only in a loose and careless way of speaking, inadmissible for logical purposes, that we can call it a *bare* statement of fact, a statement wholly devoid of description.

These may be very elementary truths, but they enable us to find in language, and specially in the descriptive function of language, the source of that quality in facts and rules which renders them liable to ambiguity. When we speak of the necessary indefiniteness of language we do not mean that every " part of speech " that Grammar recognises is an indefinite word, but that indefiniteness belongs to all *description*—to every word when and while its function is to describe. Since in all assertions there are one or more words intended to perform a descriptive function, the defect attaches to the *use* of language generally.

The simplest and the typical case of a word used descriptively is any predicate term—the term M in the statement that S is M. Its special function is to describe the Subject. It does not necessarily profess to give a full enough description to enable us to identify a Subject as yet unknown to us,—say, a criminal wanted by the police, or a locality we are seeking—but every predicate term claims to give *some* information about the qualities of the Subject, and so is to that extent a description. If I am told that Jones is a Theosophist, this would hardly be descriptive enough to enable me to pick him out from a crowd ; and yet, so far as it goes, it does (truly, or falsely or ambiguously) describe the man. And if we can understand how it performs this function, and what are the risks of giving a false or an ambiguous description, we shall see why it is that predicate terms, as such, are always indefinite.

A convenient short account of the act of predicating is that it consists in putting the subject into a *class*. Predicate terms are in effect general names[1]. Jones, for instance, is said to belong to the class called Theosophists. But the word " class " must here not be taken only in its narrower senses ; must not, for instance, be restricted to the natural history classes and social classes, nor even to classes of objects generally. There are also classes of qualities, of actions, of words, of assertions, of reasonings, and so on. The word " class " as here used is equivalent to " kind " or " sort." We shall presently[2] see that there is a further extension required, but let us at first think only of the classes that correspond to what Logic calls " general names " or class-names, which may be either substantives, adjectives, or verbs. Such statements as that S is a rhododendron, or a barrister, or a photographic camera, or a snowflake ; or that S is tyrannical, or is growing, or plays cricket ; or that S is a verb, a major premiss, or a case of ambiguous middle ; all such statements are predications about a Subject, and they all consist in putting the Subject into a class.

Now the fundamental logical fact about a class, or kind, or sort, is that it consists of *different* individual members which, in spite of all their differences, are supposed to have some points of resemblance on which the class is founded. That fact holds true of everything which has at any time been regarded as a class, or which can be so regarded, whatever other conceptions we may also have of the nature of classes generally. It holds true equally of " natural "

---

[1] Thoroughgoing Formalists may be unable to admit this, on account of statements like "Londres is London," where two proper names are so connected that one of them looks like the predicate. But when we cease to take the mere form of the *sentence* as decisive, there is no reason why we should not analyse such statements differently ; e.g. "Londres and London " (S) are (copula) "names for the same place " (P).

[2] See p. 201.

classes and of the most artificial ones, of classes that are universally recognised and that never change, as well as of classes that are only recognised locally or for a passing purpose.   Whether a class consists of innumerable members or of only two, still those members are alike in some respects and different in others.

That fact is the reason of the necessary indefiniteness of predicate terms.   To put S into a class is never to say all that can be said about S.   The general name or names by means of which the description of S is given in the act of predication *must* (because of their generality) omit to specify the points in which S differs from the rest of the class.   For however far we may carry the process of adding closer and closer descriptions of S, the same is true at every step.   At every step we are only putting S into a smaller and smaller sub-*class*.   Each descriptive name in the list is also general, and therefore neglects the individual differences which nevertheless are there.   So that the fullest description that can be given of S—with anything short of infinite time at our disposal—inevitably leaves out some of S's individual peculiarities.   However true therefore it may be that S is M, and however lengthy the description " M " may be, it is also always true that S is M *with a difference.* And in the absence of further knowledge it is an open question whether such difference is or is not important. The risk of its being unexpectedly important is the risk to which we succumb when our middle term becomes ambiguous.   S is not only M, but *a*M, and *a* is a quality which may spoil the otherwise justified inference that S is P.

This risk, then, is always present when we make a predicative statement, however carefully worded the statement may be.   There is no way of escaping it, short of ceasing to make any predications at all.   It is the price we pay for the power either of generalising or of describing a

Subject; it is a defect that belongs to a quality.   Consider
what language would be if we had no class-names.   We
should be unable to mention any of S's qualities, and also
unable to state (or to conceive) any general rules—the
" meaning" of any fact.   It is commonly supposed—but
without much evidence—that the lower animals are under
this disability, and at any rate their concepts and their
command of general rules seem to be (in some directions at
least) less developed than ours.   But wherever language is
used, even among savages, there we find this instrument of
thought—the class-name—and it is doubtful whether we can
even imagine the blankness of mind which the absence of
it would involve.   As the quality of living involves the defect
of being liable to die, so the quality of descriptiveness
involves a constant risk of reasoning through an ambiguous
middle term.   The pervasive character of the risk follows
from the fact that *all* description of S is indefinite.

Some readers may think that the word " indefinite "
is here misused ; that a descriptive name is only indefinite
till it has been " defined," and that this operation can
always be performed, and often with complete success
so far as the avoidance of ambiguity is concerned.   Why
then, in these cases—which are common enough—continue to call the word indefinite ?   Is it not enough, and
less confusing, to say that all description is necessarily
incomplete ?

If the latter phrase is really less confusing, by all means
let us use it.   The indefiniteness we are here speaking of
is the indefiniteness due to incomplete description, and
the latter name for it therefore need not mislead us.   So
long as we understand that a descriptive word, even after it
has been " defined," is still *liable* to need further defining,
that is sufficient.   It is obvious that a given definition may
be complete enough to remove this or that particular
ambiguity, and thus to render the word definite enough for

a particular purpose. But for this possibility, there would be no justification for taking the trouble to define any word. Still, we cannot proceed far in the study of logic without discovering two things about definition : one is that definitions are not always successful even for a strictly limited purpose, and that therefore the question always remains to be asked about a given definition whether it is sufficient or not—whether it removes the doubt about the word's meaning or only translates that doubt into other language ; and the second point is that, even when a given definition satisfies all the purposes for which it is required to-day, a new purpose may arise to-morrow for which it is insufficient. Not only does it often happen that the giving of a "definition" fails to make the word definite enough for a given purpose, but also the value of even the best definitions is limited. To recognise that we have no guarantee of *any* definition's sufficiency for to-morrow's purposes is to recognise that perfect definition is an unattainable ideal. In the case of the most nearly definite words we have, that is all that their indefiniteness amounts to ; their definiteness is never complete. The point of interest for logic is that however nearly definite a descriptive word may be there is always enough shortcoming to make it liable to become ambiguous when used as a middle term. A descriptive word is "definite" only in the same way that the *Titanic* was an " unsinkable " ship.

§ 35. *Predication and Analogy.*

In speaking just now of the nature of classes we had occasion to notice that a class is always " founded " on points of resemblance between the members. Classes, that is, are based on men's *recognition* of the facts, and so are made by man ; all that is made by Nature are the resemblances and differences which men have thought it worth while to notice in the things they want to classify.

If the reader finds any difficulty in accepting this truth, the reason probably is that in the impressionable years of childhood our business is to accept names as belonging to things *of right*. To a less extent this is also true of grown-up men in the comparatively childish ages when Logic was developed. Each of us when he begins to learn his native language finds the world already furnished with innumerable classes. For each of us, at first, the problem is neither to *make* nor even to criticise and improve classes, but to recognise them as facts that are independent of our choice. It is only later, as we gradually discover that along with the convenience of classes goes much inconvenience and confusion, that we are led to see the human and fallible element in them—their dependence on the thoughts men happen to have had about the things classified ; and we may easily live all our lives without getting any clear general view of the extent of the defect, and its consequences.

In this connexion it is worth while to look at the way in which classes are actually formed. It is true that most of the classes now recognised were formed so long ago that to discover the detailed history of their formation is impossible. Still, the same is true of the history of the stratified rocks, which is nevertheless capable of some intelligent reconstruction. It is difficult to imagine for instance that classes were ever made except to suit (what seemed to be) human convenience. Primarily it was because certain things were found to act or behave in the same sort of way that men cared to " sort " things into classes at all. Things are "the same" if they serve us in the same way. One kind of animal was found to be good to eat, another dangerous, another useful in hunting, and so on. And with the growth of men's knowledge of the properties of things there would arise the need of sub-dividing the broad classes that were first made. We find it useful, for instance, to break up the wide class "dogs" into a number of sub-classes with different characteristics. Classes would be too broadly conceived at first, things *importantly* different being included in the same wide class, and so needing to be distinguished. In this way the progress of knowledge always involves further discrimination.

Can we imagine any other origin for classes than men's desire for general rules based on the recognition of (supposed) *important* similarities in the things classified— resemblances which are thought to be important enough to justify our leaving the individual differences out of account? No other suggestion has, I believe, ever been made, and moreover the probability of this explanation is increased by everything we know about the recognition of new classes now. When a new invention or development is made in everyday life, or a new discovery in science, the need is at once felt of finding a class-name for it, even if the name be so little descriptive as " X-rays " or "argon." The maker of a new soap, or a new pill, or a new variety of rose, may prefer to give his own name to it ; in other cases, like the "taxi" or the "tube," the general public finds a convenient descriptive name. But, however the name is chosen, some *general* name there must be. The names are given in order that we may speak of the newly discovered things. And the only two ways in which we ever want to speak of a thing "M" are either to use the name as a predicate (S is M) or to speak of the class generally (M indicates P) without noticing the individual differences. But each of these ways of using the name is only valuable for the sake of the other. If nothing at all were known *generally* about the things called M, the name would be exactly in the position of a nonsense name like "Jabberwock." And except for the purpose of writing intentional nonsense such names are never in fact invented.

Some knowledge—often scanty at first, but growing—of the qualities of the things named always precedes the adoption of a class-name.

It was said above (p. 195) that the notion of a "class" is further extensible. Let us turn for a moment to another familiar mental operation—the recognition of an *analogy* between two things or cases, S and ♄. Now and then we may hear it said that the things compared are "exactly" alike, but no one supposes that this expression is strictly accurate, and often the difference is on the surface more apparent than the resemblance. Here again we have resemblances and differences combined, and the resemblances judged more *important* than the differences. The phrase "*essentially* alike" is generally used as stating strictly—where "exactly alike" states with exaggeration —the relation between S and ♄ where an analogy is claimed.

The reader may now be asked to consider whether predication (putting S in a class) is not essentially like the recognition of an analogy. The operations are certainly different ; for instance, in the former we have the use of a class-name while in the latter we have not. Other differences may also be found ; such as that predication usually has a matter-of-fact air, while the recognition of an analogy requires some use of imagination or fancy, and is nearly allied to the use of metaphorical language. But along with all these differences there is the fact that both operations involve comparison between S and something else, and both involve a judgment as to the relative *importance* of the resemblances and differences. Finally— and this has a special interest for logic—the fact that both involve this judgment implies that both are liable to the same kind of error.

A further light on the closeness of the connexion between predication and the recognition of an analogy is thrown by the phrase itself—"*essential* resemblance." The modern conception of " essence " differs from the ancient one in recognising the relation of the essence to passing purposes, and therefore its variability ; but in both the old and the new logic the essence is something that belongs to the class of which the individual is a member, and not to the individual as such.   Whether, like the ancients, we think the essence is something invariable and discoverable, or whether we think it something to be settled by agreement and therefore open to settlement in various ways, our knowledge of the essence (or " essential attributes ") of a class M is the test to which we bring the question whether S does or does not deserve a place in that class.   The members of every class therefore " essentially resemble " each other, just as S and 𝔖 do when they are analogous cases.   Both in predication and in claiming an analogy real differences are neglected because they are judged unimportant (i.e. " accidental " or not essential) ; and this judgment, like every other, is fallible.

Nor can we say that the risk of error is different in *amount*.   In the first place the whole conception of risk as a calculable amount is, when applied to a particular case, misleading.   It belongs to the rough method of calculation which is suitable only when large numbers are taken into account and when the average is what we want to get.   As regards any particular judgment what we want to know is whether it actually is erroneous or not.   A knowledge of the amount of *risk* does not answer this question—the question whether the risk (great or small) has or has not been avoided.   And even were this not so, a further reason for doubting whether predication is on the whole safer than the vision of an analogy is that everyone is awake to the risk in the latter kind of judgment, while it takes some acquaintance with modern logic to make us aware of the weak point in predication.   To many people predication seems matter-of-fact assertion as contrasted with the fanciful character of the analogical judgment; and so it is apt to lull our critical powers and give us a false security.   The chief point of logical importance is that a predicative statement, however plain and matter-of-fact it claims to be, may be false in exactly the same way as the most poetical glimpse of an analogy. There is no other error possible in a predicative statement than that of taking an unimportant resemblance for " essential " ; and the risk of this error is not only in theory present in every predication we make, but is in practice the source of all the most excusable errors of fact into which we fall.

§ 36.   *Variations of Purpose.*

We have seen that the right of S to a place in the class M—and therefore the truth of the statement that S is M— depends on the relative importance of the resemblances and differences between S and the other members of that class.   If we think the resemblances more important than the differences when the reverse is in fact the case, then S's position is outside the class M, and our statement that S is M is false.

But what is here meant by " importance " ?   In a general way, and apart from the application of the word to resemblances and differences, importance is a quality that we are accustomed to estimate roughly.   As a rule we judge that a thing is more or less important without going minutely into the question *what* it is important for.   Certain things, certain people, books, theories, discoveries, events, or whatever it may be, strike us as important *on the whole.* Though we know very well that the same thing is often not of the same importance to everybody, or even for all of our own purposes, still the notion of general importance has a value, and we use it continually.   It is also a trouble-

saving notion ; it saves us the trouble of discrimination—
whether discrimination happens to be needed or not.

As we saw in Part I[1], Logicians have from of old applied
this simple method to the question whether S is "essentially"
M. The importance of the resemblance on which the
class M is founded has been supposed to be importance
in general, and they never allowed themselves to view it as
varying with the purpose of the moment. They assumed
that any class M has some *one* essence, which may be
told us by authority or discovered by enquiry into the
facts. In their view every descriptive word M (except the
few that have obvious double meanings) has some one
definition which is "correct," all departures from it being
more or less erroneous. "The" definition of a class-name
M was, for them, simply the statement of "the" essence of
that class, and was performed by mentioning M's *genus* and
differentia. When you had defined "man" as "rational
animal," or "Logic" as "the science which regulates our
thought," you had done all in the way of defining these
notions that anyone could rightly expect.

There could hardly be a more deadening doctrine as
to the meaning of descriptive words, or one which gives
more encouragement to error in reasoning. It allows
only for the ambiguities that a dictionary can notice,
and neglects just the one kind of ambiguity that is most
delusive. We have seen[2] that the risk of reasoning with an
ambiguous middle term is mainly the risk that S's individual
difference from the rest of the class M is unexpectedly
important ; and what the old doctrine of essence does is
to ignore this possibility. It makes S's right to the
predicate M depend on the *general* unimportance of S's
individual difference ; and this is exactly what we must
always be on guard against assuming where "S is M"
is put forward as proving a conclusion. There is always

the possibility that, though *for most purposes* S is truly M, yet it is not truly so for the purpose in question.

Before going further it may be worth while to disclaim at once certain obvious follies which this modern view of the "variable essence" does *not* involve; misconceptions of it are easy, and appear to be the only source of anyone's hesitation in accepting it. For instance, in saying that no word has a "correct" meaning we do not overlook the fact that dictionaries supply true information about the correct meaning of words to those who are ignorant enough to need it ; nor the fact that an incorrect use of technical terms is always possible, is often met with, and admits of correction by expert authority. Again, in saying that the meaning of a class-name cannot be discovered by intelligent enquiry into facts, we do not deny that in the case of many natural classes or kinds there is room for the discovery of hitherto unknown "essential" qualities. And lastly we do not deny that the meaning of many words remains the same for centuries, and may remain so for ever. Let us admit freely that (e.g.) the word "euphuistic" may be *incorrectly* used for "euphemistic" ; that there is a *correct* meaning for words like "voltage" or "maintopgallant mast" or "monocotyledon" ; that there is room for further enquiry into the essential differences between black and white men ; that the word "crocodile" means now exactly what it meant in Greek, and that its use never varies or is likely to vary. Indeed the great majority of names of common objects in the animal, vegetable, and mineral worlds have stable meanings, and meanings which seldom or never present any important difficulty.

All these obvious truths being admitted, what remains of the doctrine of the variable essence? In the first place none of them conflict with the fact that *meaning depends on agreement*. The dictionaries tell us what meanings are customary—i.e. agreed upon either by the public at large, by average educated people, or by experts; "incorrectness" therefore means no more than solecism or disregard of authority.   And since this is so, the discovery of new characteristic facts about a class M can at most produce an agreement to change the existing custom, while as a rule for a long time it merely tends to divide custom against itself, and so weakens authority.

In the second place the fact that many names keep their meaning steadily does not conflict with the fact that *meaning varies with our varying purposes*.   The most it can prove is that in these cases, however numerous, our purposes have not actually varied importantly.   What was said is that the essence of M is *variable*, not that it *must* vary.   The doctrine is therefore merely permissive; it says that there is nothing in custom or authority to bind us to a given meaning *if and when* a new purpose drives us to make a change.

We have already referred[1] to the purposiveness of all thought as such.   But the use of the word " purpose " in the present connexion requires perhaps some explanation. The assumption underlying its use is that no statement is ever made except for a purpose, such purpose being that of *inferring* something further.   It is not necessary—and indeed it would be ridiculous—to suppose that everyone who makes an assertion has a clear idea of all that can be inferred from it.   We may regard that as an ideal extreme which is never reached.   But we do assume that every assertor, in so far as his statement has a meaning at all, has *some* idea of its consequences, even if only a regrettably vague and incomplete one; and that his idea of the statement's consequences is the precise index and measure of the meaning that he intends by it. Purpose, then, as affecting the meaning of a word M, is in effect the same as *context*.   Each occasion of the use

[1] P. 153.

of the word M has its own context, its own purpose for
which the class-resemblances are rightly or wrongly supposed
to be important; and this purpose may or may not be in
harmony with the general purposes of the use of the word.

Suppose I describe S as a "pragmatist." So long as
I have only a vague general idea of what follows from this
minor premiss, a vague general idea of what constitutes
"pragmatism" will suffice. There is as yet no reason why
any difficulty about the precise definition of the word should
arise. But as soon as I have a particular inference in view
—for instance, that S, since he is a pragmatist, must hold
that the "working" of a doctrine is a perfect criterion
of its truth—then it becomes important to ask what are
S's actual opinions on this point, even if they differ from
those of the class as generally conceived. No doubt it
would save trouble not to go into these questions, and
to assume that there is one "correct definition" of the word
pragmatist, no individual differences being important. But
if in making a statement we are more interested in saving
ourselves the trouble of thought than in getting as near
the truth as we can, why concern ourselves with logic at
all? The traditional Logic will then fulfil our object
sufficiently.

It may be said that the example just quoted illustrates
an obviously "wordy" kind of question, since difficulties
about the precise meaning of any *ism* are notorious. Still,
the notoriety of one group of difficulties may help us in
recognising other groups of them which are the same in
nature, though better disguised. Since what we accept (or
dispute) as "facts" are always statements, there can be
no question of fact which is not also a wordy question—
a question whether some descriptive word that is used
is, for the particular purpose in view, a misleading description or not. What is commonly meant by a "wordy"
question is only a question where, owing to the *recognised*

vagueness of a word, this aspect is obtrusive, and where in consequence there is less actual danger of being misled. Indeed, in the case of a predicate term like " pragmatist " (or " atheist " or " socialist," and so on) the doubts of application are so well known that some inclination to draw particular inferences without caring much whether they are true or not seems almost required to explain the error.

Often, indeed, wordiness is more apparent to some people than to others, and there are certain kinds of enquiry in which the " others " are always the great majority. The terms used in the sciences which—like Logic and Economics —run a special risk of abstractness, lend themselves easily to arguments of this kind. We arrive, say, by some extended process of reasoning at the rule that " Labour is the source of all value," and then, forgetting the varieties that are included under this extremely wide notion of Labour, we think of the wage-earning class as essentially the " labouring class " and conclude that *its* labour is the one source of value ; or we lay down the Canon of the Method of Difference, and then take some highly complex fact for the " one circumstance " which that Method requires.

Perhaps the least wordy questions that we ever encounter are those that arise in experimental science. But every respectable error that is made in interpreting an experiment is a case where a fact is " truly " and yet misleadingly conceived or described. The difference between M *simpliciter* and the M *secundum quid* which is taken for it and therefore wrongly used to draw a particular inference is here seldom as easily seen as in the case of notoriously vague words like " pragmatist " or " socialist." In scientific problems it is not the conflict between a rough usage of a word and a careful usage, but rather between a careful usage and the still more careful one that the case happens unexpectedly to require. The experimenter presumably does what he can to get a sufficient knowledge of the facts he is dealing with, but (as we have seen) the individual facts always have more in them than can be comprised in even the fullest description or conception. Beyond the completest possible account of them in descriptive terms there lies *some* individual difference ; and this may be enough—it is often afterwards found to have been enough—to spoil the inference.

In each man's special line of work, or play, whether it be scientific research, or business, or sport, or any other pursuit which leads him to be careful in dealing with facts, the risk of drawing false inferences is mainly of this latter kind. In his own line he is perhaps above the risk of falling a victim to what is commonly called wordiness, but only because the wordiness that does lie in wait for him is better disguised and is therefore not commonly called by that name. Outside his special subject, however, —and we all make excursions into an outside region of less responsible thinking—even what is commonly called wordiness often trips him up. Words always imply distinctions ; and distinctions, as we shall presently see, are generally valid for some purpose or purposes, but their value is always limited, and we are liable to use them for purposes to which they do not apply.

§ 37. *Distinction and Definition.*

What are commonly known as " distinctions " are pairs of contrasted predicate terms—e.g. good and bad, tall and short, luxuries and necessaries. As a rule, distinctions exist to meet a felt want, namely to mark a difference which is taken to be for some purpose important, and also which is in some danger of being overlooked. Though distinctions are occasionally made without much deliberate thought about the importance of the difference noticed, they are never made except on the ground of a noticed difference of some sort, and it is probably safe to assume that every difference has importance for *some* purpose[1]; and we do not speak of a " distinction " between such disparate things as, for instance, a fortnight and a soup tureen, or between vaccination and a sonata. These things are certainly different, but can hardly be regarded as *pairs* of different things; they are so obviously different that they do not need distinguishing. Distinctions are always either between two kinds of " the same thing "—whether two sub-classes within a wider class, such as flowering and non-flowering plants; or between two points separable from each other on what is confessedly a continuous scale, such as heat and cold, or age and youth. Any scale, by virtue of its continuity from end to end, may easily itself be regarded as " the same thing "—for instance, the scale of temperature or of age—and thus as a class including all the different degrees we mark along it; and where, as often happens, two sub-classes shade off into each other—e.g. Semitic and non-Semitic races of mankind—they may also be regarded as points on a scale, or names of cases possessing different *degrees* of a special quality or set of qualities.

It is well known that many of our troubles of thought turn upon doubts as to the right way of making and using certain distinctions. The mere importance of a distinction between M and N—e.g. between truth and error, or good and evil—may lead us to suppose these things more definitely and certainly distinguishable from each other than they are; we are then unexpectedly brought up against difficulties in " drawing the line " between them. This is the basis of the *sorites*

---

[1] For example, even the trivial distinctions between the AEIO forms of proposition had a purpose of a kind. A "distinction without a difference" means no more than a distinction based on a difference which we think to be unimportant.

puzzle noticed at pp. 92, 151. On the other hand we may be so convinced of the fact that M and N, when closely looked at, shade off into each other, that our sense of the difference between them is weakened, and the distinction loses much of its value for us and fails to serve its purpose sufficiently. If the danger were always that of exaggerating the clearness of a distinction, or if it were always that of whittling away the difference, the task of guarding against it would be far simpler than it is. As so often happens in life, the real feat required is that of picking our way along a narrow ledge between the too much and the too little. We have to use the distinction, but to use it with discretion; we cannot always make light of the line-drawing difficulty, and yet we cannot afford to let it destroy all the snap and point of our beliefs.

The reader will remember what was said at p. 156 about the chief problem of modern thought—that of using general rules moderately and wisely, instead of either accepting them as perfect guides or discarding them as worthless because they fall short of being strictly universal. The use of distinctions is a particular case coming under that general conception. Every distinction between M and N is itself a rule—a rule not strictly universal—and needs applying with discretion. To trust the distinction entirely is to hold that every case of " M " is outside the class " N "—that we may disregard the possibility of a case being on the fence between them and belonging as much to the one as to the other. And even if we avoid this extreme rigidity, it is easy to take a distinction for a little more than it is worth, and so to trust it excessively. Some people, for instance, make this mistake in regard to the distinction between " gentlefolks " and those who are outside that pale ; others, again, forget that there are degrees of " orthodoxy," and imagine a line of division between the orthodox and the un-orthodox as clear and sharp as that between sheep and goats.

14—2

The difficulty is that when and while we *use* a distinction which we know to be loose, we do believe in its value ; we treat it *as if* it were perfectly sharp. It may be asked, How can we believe in the sharpness of a distinction which at the same time we know to be only a distinction of degree ? The answer seems to be that that depends on the quality of the belief in question. Belief may be either stolidly rigid, held without wavering, through thick and thin, or it may be held with discretion and related to a purpose. In some instances, no doubt, self-contradiction is a possible explanation of the process, but it is not the only explanation nor even in general the likeliest. I incline rather to the view that this is one of the many cases where common sense instinctively acts in a manner which logic can afterwards justify, and that the reason why it does not always act so—the reason why common sense now and then gets into confusion—is that it fails to see the principle involved as clearly as logic sees it. That principle is that we can *on occasion* trust in the sharpness of a distinction without supposing it to be above criticism *in all its possible contexts ;* we may see that it is sharp enough for a particular purpose, and that so long as that purpose is in view, the looseness of the distinction is irrelevant.

As to the line-drawing difficulty itself, the mere fact of continuity between M and N is enough to account for this. But it is further complicated by difference of standard. Not only do different people use different standards—for instance, of good and evil—but also each of us uses different standards on different occasions. Broadly speaking, this latter case resolves itself into a difference between two types of usage; one that is sufficiently exact for what may be called ordinary purposes, and one which is as exact as we can make it. It sometimes happens, for instance, that what we loosely call M and N are, strictly considered, two contrasted degrees of M. The whole scale is, in strictness, M ; but we reserve that name, in common usage, for the end of the scale which is most typically (or most obviously) M, and we give the name N, *contrasted* with M, to the cases in which the quality of M-ness is less apparent. For example, everything we experience suffers change, more or less ; to the best of our knowledge change is everywhere on the earth. Yet it suits our convenience to restrict the term " change" to the more evident cases of change, and to contrast with these, as permanent or unchanging, things that are *comparatively* durable, like the " permanent " officials in a Government office, or the customs of the " unchanging " East.

A somewhat similar case is that of the distinction between the "white" and the coloured races. Strictly speaking, " white " is an incorrect description of any human being except perhaps a leper. Yet this is a kind of incorrectness which for all our ordinary purposes does not matter. On the other hand, however correct it may be to describe the colour of a carpet as green, such a description may be insufficient—and therefore possibly misleading— for the purpose of choosing curtains to match the colour. Thus there are some occasions on which a mere hint of a description suffices, and other occasions on which a much fuller description may be insufficient. All depends on what the occasion, what the purpose, is.

Several illustrations of this double usage may be taken from the technicalities of logic itself, especially those which are also terms in everyday use. For example, there is the distinction between definite and indefinite as applied to terms. Although, as we have seen, all descriptive terms are, strictly speaking, indefinite, yet for rough everyday purposes it is convenient to use the distinction, classing as definite those that suffer least obtrusively from this uni-versal defect. Again, for rough purposes, we use the distinction between a bare statement and a descriptive statement of fact, though strictly all statements of fact are descriptive. A similar instance is the distinction between a simple and a complex assertion — a distinction which Logic accepts but which logic is compelled to criticise. If we are speaking of *sentences* only, this distinction can be interpreted. But what can possibly be meant by an *assertion*, a judgment, entirely devoid of complexity? Judgments differ widely in the amount they discard from the complex facts they refer to, but they never can get rid of the complexity altogether.

Some of us are at times tempted to think that as long as a distinction is clear in its aim, or idea, that is sufficient. But sufficient for what purpose? Not for distinguishing between the *things* so named when there happens to be a difficulty in doing so. It is only when the words are unfamiliar—e.g. " categorematic " and " syncategorematic " that we learn anything by recognising the abstract (or verbal) distinction. In all other cases we might just as well repeat the Law of Contradiction itself and think we are giving or getting real information. At most an abstract distinction gives us information—if we need it—as to the customary meanings of words. A distinction taken in this abstract way is the setting of a problem, not the answer to it. If we know that " M " and " N " are contrasted with each other, that does not even begin to tell us *what* either of them is; it does not begin to tell us how to apply the distinction. The whole value of a distinction, the whole fulfilment of its purpose, depends upon its application in actual cases. Every distinction between M and N professes to separate, in thought, things which are *essentially* M from those which are *essentially* N ; and thus every mistake of fact, every misapplication of the predicate M, involves a mistake in applying the distinction.

It is clear, then, that the looseness of a distinction and

the indefiniteness of a descriptive name are two aspects of
the same truth, and present to us the same difficulty of
judging of their importance on different occasions. The
looseness of a distinction, like the indefiniteness of a name,
is the price we have to pay for an advantage. The difficulty of knowing when to view it as important is one of a
group of difficulties which are not due to the defect itself
but rather to the varying conditions under which words
and distinctions must be used. In using language several
accidental circumstances have to be taken into account
in order to get the best results. I am not here speaking of
beauty of expression or of any literary quality except the
conveyance of an intended meaning. It is notorious that
the same statement will often convey a different meaning to
two different people; that one person is able to fill in the gaps
or read between the lines better than another ; and also
that in general the most strictly accurate statement is not
always the best for rousing attention or for helping us to
understand a difficult point. Things that strictly will not
go "in a nutshell" are sometimes advantageously put
there. Artificial simplifications of what is really complex,
the judicious omission of disturbing details, even undue
emphasis on this or that feature or aspect of a matter, are
often necessary—in different degrees for different people—
if we wish to get our statements understood. Thus a loose
expression may convey a clear and pointed meaning where
a more accurate expression would be flat or clumsy or
difficult to follow, or would even be almost certainly misunderstood. And so we are under strong inducements, of
the most practical kind, to run a small risk of misleading
an audience for the sake of avoiding a greater likelihood of
the same misfortune. This difficulty takes various forms ;
one is where a slight exaggeration may be expected to
produce a truer effect than the literal "truth." If the fish
we want to sell are *fairly* fresh, we tell the truth about them

better by leaving out the qualifying adverb ; and it is often difficult to make it clear that we really believe a thing unless we exaggerate our certainty and say that there is not the smallest shadow of a doubt. A good many of these difficulties are so dependent on local and passing fashions of speech, or on the personal characteristics of our audience, that logic can do no more than note their existence and draw the conclusion that the value of a distinction must be looked for not in the distinction itself, but in the use we propose to make of it on a given occasion.

From the connexion between indefiniteness in a word and looseness in a distinction it follows that to "define" any predicate M is to explain how the distinction between M and another predicate contrasted with M should be applied. Thus the real difficulties of distinction and those of definition are the same. The continuity that joins contrasted terms, and the habitual employment of different standards, are what unavoidably render exact definition difficult. But in addition to these real sources of confusion there are some which are avoidable because they are due to slack ways of thought about definition generally ; partly to the old assumption that every class has one essence, instead of having a number of different essences dependent on our changing purposes ; and partly to the fact that the term " definition " is commonly used for several different operations which need to be distinguished.

There is (1) the kind of definition that we get in a dictionary. Of this there are two varieties : (a) where a more or less technical word is carefully explained, or distinguished from other words likely to be confused with it— e.g. " Collectivism " explained as the theory that all the instruments of production ought to belong to the State— a peculiarity which distinguishes this form of Socialism from others ; and (b) where the object is to give a rough general idea of a word to anyone who may need it,—e.g.

"Alkekengi" explained as "a kind of medicinal resin." In either case the sole business of a dictionary is to register past and present custom in the use of words. On this account dictionary definitions would be more suitably called translations[1].

Then there is (2) the effort that is sometimes made to find the *best* meaning of a word—not necessarily the most authoritative meaning, nor the etymological meaning, but the meaning which is supposed (by the person defining) to be on the whole the most convenient or the least likely to cause confusion. Here some criticism of existing customs is often required. In this respect it differs from dictionary definitions, though popular thought often overlooks the difference. Many people, that is, assume as a matter of course that the existing authoritative custom *is* the best ; an assumption which has about as much to be said for it as the kindred assumption that safety in investments can be strictly measured by the low rate of interest they yield.

Then there is (3) a process which hardly makes a pretence of being definition at all, though it is commonly called by the name. It does not aim at giving a complete account of the word " defined," but only at bringing out prominently some one feature—generally a feature thought likely to be overlooked—in the thing named. Words with very complex and uncertain meanings — like "humour," "gentleman," "poetry"—are familiar exercise grounds for this kind of mental activity. Statements like " Gratitude is a lively sense of favours to come" or "Genius is an infinite capacity for taking pains" are the result of it. They seem to have been called "aphorisms " (and so "definitions"[2]) chiefly because they resemble in their brevity, and also usually in their form, the kind of definition that Formal Logic regards as typical.

[1] See my book *The Application of Logic*, pp. 249, 252, 261, 269—71.
[2] The word *definitio* is a translation of ἀφορισμός.

This formally typical kind (4) of definition is only a little more precise and careful than the (*a*) kind of dictionary definition. Here, in order to define the word M, "all you have to do" is to state M's *genus* and *differentia*, which together make up M's *essence*. It is plain that if M has only one essence, knowable precisely, and capable of statement in language which cannot be misunderstood, then definition must be an easy matter. With such a weapon ready to hand for preventing ambiguity, why fear it? And, as we have seen, Logic did not fear it. On the same principle why fear to conduct an orchestra, since "all you have to do" is to wave a stick about in the right manner? The traditional six rules[1] for correct definition suffer from this kind of fatuous inutility. They give us a purely abstract account of the ideal definition, and ignore the difficulties of attaining it.

There remains (5) one other conception of the nature of definition, namely that its function is neither that of giving the customary meaning, nor of finding the best meaning, nor of emphasising a special part of the meaning, nor of putting "M" into its proper place in a ready-made system of *genera* and *species ;* but something different from all of these. It recognises that effective ambiguity can by no amount of forethought be securely prevented, and it concentrates attention on the problem of removing an ambiguity *after* it has occurred.

Leaving out of account the minor differences between this kind of definition and the others, there are two that deserve special notice. First, it is true that all the others, except perhaps (3), did probably originate in the desire to combat ambiguity ; but at best their success in doing so is limited to the kind of ambiguity which, as we have noticed so often, is of the smallest importance. And secondly not one of them does anything to dispute the old fatal

[1] These were given at p. 114.

assumption that every class has only one essence, which is unchanging and discoverable. That assumption has, as we have seen, been entirely discredited by the progress of science in recent times. It may linger in popular thought, but it will never revive in logic. Classes, we saw, are *made* to suit our purposes, and our purposes change and vary, with corresponding effect upon the essence of the class. Only in one way can a sort of spurious singleness and rigidity be given to the essence ; and that is by taking the average of the variations and choosing to regard that as something real. This involves isolating the class-name from its context in an assertion ; and by doing so we leave the definition free to be irrelevant to any particular ambiguity that has arisen. The aim of these kinds of definition is to give the meaning of " the word "—i.e. the word in most of its usual contexts—instead of its meaning as used in a particular assertion.

Now the ambiguity which spoils a piece of reasoning is, as we have seen[1], always ambiguity in a middle term ; and this implies that it exists only in a context, and in relation to that context. The word is not ambiguous *in itself*, but only when its particular context happens to make it so. For a simple example, too transparent to deceive most people, let us take a predicate term like " wise." We all know that there are different kinds of wisdom, and that the wisdom which is important for one purpose may be useless for another—e.g. that a wise Head of a college may be " a child in matters of finance "—so that the fact that S is wise, and the rule that the wise are trustworthy advisers, need not persuade us to consult S about our investments. But though this particular " M " does not deceive us, others may. And wherever they do so, it is through our overlooking the precise importance of a distinction between *different kinds* of M. That is why, as a remedy for an

[1] See p. 184.

actual ambiguity, the *general* definition of M is of no use whatever. The doubt as to meaning only begins after the broad meaning of the word is understood, because the deception itself is dependent upon that understanding. In these cases we all know what " M " means in a general way, but have to find out what it means in a particular context. The dictionary can tell us nothing further ; the " best" definition, even if we knew it beyond a doubt, might be equally irrelevant ; epigrams about "M " (e.g. "wisdom") would be too vague for application; and a formal definition, showing "M" as a species under a higher genus, would ignore the question about the differences *within* the species itself—which is the question raised. And in addition to these shortcomings, all these four kinds of definition profess to tell us *facts* which, as such, are disputable ; whereas the fifth kind of definition is not an assertion of fact, but a voluntary limitation of meaning. It is more in the nature of a postulate, even though the person making it—the arguer who under pressure gives the definition — would often prefer to leave his meaning vague. All the other kinds of definition are expressions of opinion which may be erroneous, but definition in view of an actually seen or suspected ambiguity is merely a declaration of the speaker's own *intention* in using the word ; an intention which he is free to change, and about which he (and no one else) can always give the latest intelligence. The speaker is, in effect, taking his choice between two suggested meanings, whether he likes being placed in the dilemma or not. Instead of his asserting something as against an opponent, his opponent is dragging from him what may amount to a confession of weakness in the argument, and which anyhow is not disputable. If a man explains that when he asserts that S is M he does *not* intend M to be taken in such and such a suggested meaning, we may perhaps be able to claim that he has not kept to this limited meaning consistently, but we cannot claim to decide for him which of the meanings he *now* chooses to abide by. That is entirely for him to declare. Otherwise what point, or reality, would there be in our offering him the choice? If I ask " Heads or tails?" and my friend answers " Tails," how could I maintain that "Heads" is what he really meant?

Definition of this kind, then, namely in order to remove an ambiguity from a particular argument, differs fundamentally from the four other kinds. It has nothing to do with the statement of facts either about the things commonly denoted by the word " M," or about custom or general convenience in the use of the word. It is a purely personal postulate or declaration, made with a definite purpose in view and restricted to that purpose. The real difficulties that may be felt in discovering either the most usual, or the most convenient, or the most illuminative explanation of a word do not exist for the speaker who answers the question what exactly he intends by the predicate when he tells us that S is M. Moreover, when the request for a definition arises out of a discovered ambiguity, the question always indicates the choice that is offered. The questioner thinks he has discovered an important difference between two kinds of M—a difference which is important in regard to the soundness of the conclusion. There is one sense of the word M in which the questioner would agree that S is M, but would perhaps dispute the truth of the major premiss; and another sense in which he would dispute the truth of the predication. The question which of two alternative meanings the speaker himself intends can always be answered, even if he had not previously seen that there were two; and neither ignorance of fact nor ignorance of custom can be pleaded in excuse. Reluctance to answer the question tells its own tale about the value of the argument.

The importance of these considerations comes into view when we remember that descriptive words, from their very nature, are not susceptible of complete or perfect definition, but only of definition sufficient to suit this or that limited purpose. Impossible though it is to draw a finally satisfactory line between M and not-M for use in every conceivable argument, future ones included, yet the line can always be drawn for the purpose of removing an ambiguity that has been found in a particular piece of reasoning. The necessary trouble of making the alternatives clear falls entirely on the finder of the ambiguity. It is he, and not the arguer, who discovers the importance of a distinction within the too vaguely conceived class M. It is he who discovers that things which are rightly called M for one purpose are wrongly called so for another, and who on the strength of this (true or false) discovery thinks the particular argument unsound. But until he knows which of two alternative meanings of "M" the arguer is willing to declare, he does not know which of the two premisses the clearing up of the ambiguity will falsify. If for instance the predicate "wise" is intended to include financial wisdom, he may dispute the assertion that S is "wise"; if it is only intended to mean "wise in a general way," then he may dispute the assertion that so vaguely conceived a quality allows us to infer the trustworthiness of S's advice on a special subject.

Apart from this view of the nature and purpose of definition there seems to be no way out of the difficulty that every predicate term *claims* to be perfectly definite, while no predicate term *is* so. The claim to perfect definiteness rests on the fact that every predication makes a choice between the answers "yes" and "no" to a question. To say that S is sober is to answer "no" to the question whether he is drunk; and the same with every predicate term that may be used in asserting. The predicates M and not-M are supposed to cover the whole range of possibility, so that to assert the one is to deny the other.

This claim is, as we have seen, generalised in the " Laws of Thought," which refuse to admit the theoretical possibility of S possessing both predicates at once, or neither. If there were no way open to us of ignoring the assumed authority of the Laws of Thought—if we were compelled to accept them as *applicable* to actual predications—then, wherever we use a predicate term which is indefinite, or a distinction which falls short of being perfectly clear and sharp, we should be convicted of making an unsubstantiated claim.

Fortunately, however, the Laws of Thought have no longer any power to put us in this position. The recognition that S may be M for one purpose and not-M for another deprives these oracular maxims of all their authority over our actual statements or reasonings. So long as they are not applied they certainly mislead nobody ; and, as we saw above[1], even when they are applied they have a sort of *primâ facie* value. The harm begins with the supposition that there need be anything illogical in refusing to admit their inapplicability in a given case, and so refusing to pay attention to their irrelevant cautions.

It is again the notion of "truth for a purpose" that saves us from the traditional slavery to words. Misplaced trust in a distinction, and so in the definiteness of a predicate term is, we saw[2], merely a special form of misplaced trust in a general rule. The question whether the distinction between M and not-M is clear enough *for its purpose* is nothing else than the question whether S really or only apparently comes under the rule " All M are P." Useful or relevant doubts about the precise defining line of a predicate term are limited to the doubt whether S is or is not (through its individual difference) one of the exceptions to some particular rule that the predicate M appears to bring it under. Since " M " is always indefinite—i.e. since S's individual difference is never completely known—there

[1] P. 157. [2] P. 211.

is always room for a question whether S comes under the rule or not. But to attempt to clear up a doubt which is limited by reference to a particular rule is a very different thing from what Formalism attempts, namely to reach *perfect definiteness* in the word M. Imperfect definiteness will often serve a particular purpose sufficiently. There is, for instance, a vague yet valuable rule that a small dose of arsenic (or of alcohol) is not a poison but a tonic. The line between "small" and "not small" is quite vague. But if a given dose (S) is nowhere near the border line it becomes an irrelevant piece of pedantry or quibbling to press for closer definition. For the particular purpose of the moment we recognise that S's individual difference is *not* a disturbing factor.

On the other hand, take the apparently definite rule that promises should always be kept. S is a promise (M) but its individual difference is that it was made without a clear understanding of what might be involved in it. Does a "promise" mean "a promise as intended by its giver," or "as understood by its receiver?" In a case of this sort one can easily imagine a genuine disagreement arising between the parties concerned.

The habit of using the name "definition" for the four processes first mentioned is so securely established that it will probably continue. But that does not matter much so long as we keep clearly in view the difference between the whole group of them on the one hand, and the fifth process just described. The dictionary definition offers us a verbal translation professing to explain the customary usage; the "best" definition offers us an opinion of a highly complex (and disputable) kind; the "aphorism" offers us a partial view, also disputable, which we may have overlooked; and the formal definition offers us not the removal of a discovered ambiguity, but a statement of the meaning as it was before the discovery was made. These kinds of definition may have some value in preventing possible ambiguities before they occur, and it is conceivable that certain elementary ambiguities may even be removed by them ; but they are entirely worthless against that more effective kind of ambiguity which depends on S's individual difference from the type of the class M. For the purpose of correcting that, definition is a choice between presented alternatives, and does no more than state which of the two meanings the arguer is *now willing* to acknowledge and abide by. Instead of asserting anything it merely makes a confession ; and that is probably why the request for this kind of definition is so often resented. There are many people who hate being dragged out from the convenient shelter of an ambiguous middle term.

CHAPTER X

DOCTRINES AND TECHNICALITIES

THE weak point of the new logic as contrasted with the old is the greater difficulty it presents to the examiner and perhaps, as yet, to the teacher. Apart from this, it is probable that most of the established teachers and examiners would prefer to keep to the accustomed lines. But, even if we look forward to a time when a younger generation will be in office, the new system will require from all parties concerned in its working more flexibility of mind and a larger distrust of the pretence of definiteness and certainty. It will not lend itself easily to the arts of the examiner ; there will be no new mnemonic verses to take the place of the old ones, and no unquestionable Rules or Canons to be committed to memory. Not only are the new doctrines

s.   15

and technicalities less numerous, but our whole method admits of less verbal finality.

Still, the time must come when the rising tide of impatience with Logic will make itself felt in our universities. Outside them, it is common knowledge among the educated public that Logic has lost its authority; and since there is no one among its professional exponents who attempts to stand up for it against the definite attacks, judgment goes by default. Thus the present position is unstable, and before many years the subject will have to be either banished from the schools or else reformed. Those who hope that reform is possible will do well to consider what can be done to avoid the old defects and yet make the new system teachable.

One thing we can do, even now, is to express some of its leading doctrines and to discuss the technicalities needed for their expression. And if we can at the same time show how one doctrine leads to another and helps to explain another, we shall be moving in the right direction and clearing a way for further progress on the part of those who come after. With that hope in view the attempt is at least worth making. We shall find that the doctrines which seem at first to be merely negative—e.g. that the Laws of Thought cannot be taken as binding when applied, and that the separation of Form from Matter is delusive— imply certain positive doctrines as their ground, and lead on to others equally positive; and all these require technicalities for their expression.

We may begin with some technicalities the use of which is not confined to expressing a few special doctrines, but which are of wider application and may therefore be called elementary. First come the names for various aspects of what used to be called a "proposition." These are *judgment, thought, assertion, statement*. Between a "judgment" and a "thought" there is no logically important difference. A judgment (or a thought) is expressed, if at all, in a "statement"; and an "assertion" is a statement's meaning, whether the meaning intended by the assertor or the meaning put upon it by the audience.   In fact, the first three of these words are often harmlessly used as synonymous, though "assertion" may also on occasion be contrasted with "judgment" or "thought" as being expressed instead of tacit. All three are contrasted with "statement" as referring to *meanings* rather than to the words in which a meaning is expressed. "Proposition" is a word to avoid, on account of the confused way in which it has always been traditionally used.   It ignores the distinction between "assertion" and "statement," probably owing to the Logical habit of assuming that statements seldom present any serious difficulties of interpretation.

Next let us take the word *Syllogism*.   A syllogism may be shortly described as "the application of a general rule to a particular case."   Any general rule, as such, speaks of a number of particular cases, and when we can identify any case as being one of them we can apply the rule, and so infer something about the case.   For example, we use a syllogism when we infer that a certain picture, because it is by Van Dyck, is valuable.   We have the rule that Van Dyck's pictures are valuable, and we apply it to any picture that we can identify as a case coming under the rule.

A syllogism may thus be regarded as consisting of three parts : the rule ("major premiss"); the identification of a case as coming under it ("minor premiss"); and the conclusion inferred as a result of applying the rule to the case.

Next, the word *Reasoning* :—

(*a*) *Reasoning and Thought*.   If we could find any unmistakable instance of unreasoned thought, we should have a basis for a distinction between reasoning and thought in general, or between reflective and unreflective thought.

But no one can say (except dogmatically and unconvincingly) how much reflection has entered into a given thought. Probably any thought which has got so far as to be expressed in language represents *some* reflection and reasoning, whether much or little, slow or rapid, sound or unsound. It is natural to draw a verbal (or abstract) distinction between reasoning and thought, but the difficulty is to apply it. If we assume that it is easy to apply, we are tempted to interpret it as turning on whether one sentence only is used or more than one. This method, however, does not solve the difficulty except on the delusive assumption (hidden by the old word " proposition ") that a sentence and the thought it tries to express are the same thing. In effect it commits us to all the formalism and verbalism of the traditional Logic. At that price it has the advantage—from a labour-saving point of view—of restricting the field of Logical enquiry.

On the other hand no harm is done by confessing that the line between reasoned and unreasoned thought cannot be drawn. The effect of that confession is merely permissive ; it allows us to look for reasons, good or bad, even where they have not been previously expressed.

(*b*). *Reasoning and Syllogism.* Is it possible to reason otherwise than by means of syllogisms ? Since no line can be drawn between reasoning and thought, it follows that we may " reason " without expressly setting out the process in the form of syllogisms. And even where the reasons for a belief are expressly given it is very common to find that what is called a " piece of reasoning " cannot be analysed into one major premiss, one minor premiss, and a conclusion[1]. But this is because of the vagueness of the phrase " a piece of reasoning," which says nothing about length, or shape, or complexity, and which is therefore as vague a phrase as " a piece of chalk." A whole book, such as the

[1] See p. 176.

Origin of Species, may be called a piece of reasoning, but it would obviously be too complex to be expressible in a single syllogism. And even much smaller pieces of reasoning may often be found too complex for such expression ; for instance the argument that a certain witness is not to be believed, because his manner of giving his evidence was unsatisfactory.

It remains true, however, that if we break up any piece of reasoning, however long and complicated, into smaller pieces, we sooner or later discover that it is throughout composed of the application of rules to cases, and so of syllogisms. In this sense there is no kind of reasoning (or thought) the *structure* of which is other than syllogistic. For instance, an unsatisfactory manner of giving evidence may be analysed into a complex impression produced by a number of facts each of which is taken as having a meaning. However long and intricate a piece of reasoning may be, or however rapid and apparently simple a thought may be, its structure consists of nothing but the application of a rule or rules to a case or cases.

This admission that reasoning, or thought, is syllogistic throughout is important in several ways, and we shall best understand its meaning by following out its consequences. In the first place it unifies what used to be regarded as different " kinds of reasoning "—e.g. conditional and categorical (pp. 77—84), induction and deduction (§ 33). Secondly it involves a doctrine about *meaning* which was entirely outside the scope of the old Logic, and which leads to various useful novelties of view. It involves the recognition that every statement gets its meaning from the syllogism *in which it is intended* to perform a function (p. 185) ; or, as we may otherwise say, from its reference to a conclusion. Thus any statement of fact gets whatever meaning it has by bringing the fact under some rule or rules ; while a statement of rule gets whatever meaning

it has by the assumption that such and such facts come
under it. A statement which cannot be regarded as either
a major or a minor premiss is an empty form of words,
a statement devoid of meaning, a sham assertion. The
Laws of Thought, and the Inductive Canons, when interpreted so as to be undeniable, are conspicuous examples
of minor-less and meaningless major premisses.

What this directly contradicts is the old assumption
that meaning is a quality which attaches to a statement by
virtue either of its form or of its internal structure as
composed of terms which possess a similar independent
meaning. For grammatical purposes such assumptions
may suffice, as also for the trivial game of syllogising.
There certainly is a sense in which we can speak of the
average or usual meaning of a sentence, or of a word,
as belonging to it of right ; else grammars and dictionaries
would be useless. Now grammars and dictionaries have an
undoubted use, though it stops short where logic begins.
Their function is that of giving information as to literary
and verbal *custom*, to those who are ignorant of it. So far
as we are unacquainted with literary custom we need a
grammar ; and when we do not know the commonly
accepted meaning of a word we may hope to find it in
a dictionary. What grammars and dictionaries are constitu-
tionally unable to do is to take into account the effect which
a special context, as contrasted with a merely average
context, may have upon a meaning.

What happens when a statement is *used*, in either of
the only two ways in which it can be used,—namely as
major or minor premiss—is that a special interpretation
is put upon it. Such interpretation may agree with the
majority of usual interpretations, or on the other hand it
may depart from the average more or less obviously. Very
obvious departures are rare, and even when they do
occur they are comparatively harmless just because they

are obvious. The logically important kind of departure from the average is that which eludes observation. But whether it happens to deceive us or not, the difference is always there; apart from a particular use a statement has a less determinate meaning than it has *in* that use. The meaning of any statement of a rule consists in its applications, and any particular application determines its meaning for that occasion, whether coinciding or not with its meaning on most other occasions. Similarly with a statement of fact; when we use it—when we connect it with a major premiss —we select, out of all the possible lights that may be thrown upon it, one which is for the time actually intended.

And since statements are composed of words, and get their *primâ facie* meaning from that of the words that enter into them, the determination of their meaning by their use takes effect on the meaning of the words themselves. This consideration is what has made the new view of ambiguity possible, and necessary. Actual ambiguity, like actual meaning, can no longer be regarded as a defect which —like indefiniteness or like "plurality of senses"—attaches to words apart from their use in asserting. It is only *words in statements* that can be ambiguous, as distinct from merely indefinite or merely "equivocal." Ambiguity is related to indefiniteness, and also to plurality of senses, as an actual occurrence is related to the conditions that make the occurrence possible. The conditions of the use of words in asserting are such that every syllogism is *liable* to ambiguity in its middle term, though many actually escape it and many more escape the suspicion of it undeservedly.

Why this is so was explained at length in § 34. In order to serve as a middle term a name must be "descriptive"; and a descriptive term, as such, is never perfectly definite. We are free, if we please, to use the phrase "incompletely descriptive" for "imperfectly definite"; all that matters is that we should recognise that the incompleteness or imperfection *may* be important in regard to the question whether the rule and the case are really or only verbally connected with each other. No name can be descriptive except through being "general" and therefore neglecting individual differences. The description (or conception) of S as a member of the class M intentionally leaves out of sight S's individual difference from the rest of that class ; no one denies that such difference exists, but whenever we say that S is M we *take the risk* of asserting that, though the difference exists, it is negligible (§ 35). And even when the utmost care is taken it is always possible that we have taken this risk in ignorance of some fact which, if known, would have made us hesitate to assume connexion between the case and the rule, and so would have kept us from drawing the conclusion.

It follows that wherever there is a dispute between two people about the truth of a conclusion which seems on the surface to be merely the application of an admitted rule to a case S which comes under it, it is the doubter who sees (or thinks he sees) something in S's individual difference which destroys the real *relevance* of the rule, in spite of its verbal appearance of being relevant. It is the doubter who claims to be setting up facts as against words. On him therefore lies the task of explaining (1) what *is* the overlooked difference, and (2) in what way it is important. The effect of such explanation is not confined to throwing doubts on the particular conclusion which is questioned, but also has a scientific value as leading to a fuller conception of the rule and its exceptions. It is in this way that the discovery of ambiguities—the discovery of individual differences which unexpectedly affect the application of rules—is intimately bound up with all progress in our knowledge of the orderly ways of Nature.

The problem of teaching the new logic seems mainly to

consist in making the student so familiar with this view of ambiguity that his whole conception of the use of language is affected by it. He has to think of "facts" always as *statements of fact* (p. 193), statements which are necessarily descriptive, and which therefore necessarily take a risk and involve a possibility of well-concealed error (pp. 201—3). He has to recognise that what is truth from one point of view may be error from another (pp. 153, 181); and that "point of view" here refers to *purpose*, or the conclusion the statement leads to. And he cannot fully understand this until it has become a second nature with him to recognise that every statement, in order to have a meaning at all, involves a reference to one or more conclusions to which it leads, while its meaning on any particular occasion is determined by the use that is made of it then and there (§ 36).

It comes more naturally to most people to think of rules than of "facts" as possibly needing correction in their statement, because we are well accustomed in the statement of rules to the compromise between conciseness and strict accuracy. We have all, for example, made use of proverbs, and have often seen them misapplied. But for logical purposes we must extend our knowledge of the defect which proverbs commonly suffer from, so as to make it apply even to rules which claim scientific accuracy. Rules about "what causes what" are especially to be treated with suspicion, but no rule is entirely secure against doubts of its interpretation.

An objection is possible here, on the part of those who try to imagine philosophy as a system of truth unrelated to purpose. Are we to assume that *no* rules can be trusted— that the multiplication table, for instance, is a delusion, and that there is no such thing as a trustworthy axiom anywhere? The answer is, in the first place, that the value of *trust* in a rule depends on occasion and purpose. There are occasions on which it is better to trust in a rule which is known to be loose than to have no guide; there are occasions on which an active distrust of a rule would be purposeless, if not worse. And secondly, why should we pretend to know beforehand *which* axioms, if any, can never mislead those who use them? So far as logic is concerned we need do no more than hold ourselves ready to question any interpretation of a rule *if* the occasion should seem to require it, and to allow the same right to other people. In regard to this or that rule—say, the rule that two and two are four—the doubt may never arise. *Only, if it should arise, it cannot be stifled by merely calling the rule an "axiom."* What seems unquestionable to one person often seems questionable to another, and the power of *definitely* challenging—doubting for reasons given—some interpretation of a hitherto accepted rule is essential to progress in knowledge.

The old Logic was quite incapable of recognising the difference between a real and a pretended doubt of a word's interpretation, and also between a doubt based on knowledge and a doubt based on mere ignorance. That leads to a great difference between the old system and the new in regard to the right of requiring further definition. In order to make sure that the rule "All M are P" is interpreted correctly when we apply it to the case of S, we must have in view a definition of "M." On the old assumption that a word normally[1] has only one "correct" definition—that the class M has only one true "essence"—to ask for its definition is either to betray ignorance or to pretend it; and the questioner can be contemptuously referred to a received authority—e.g. to a textbook or a dictionary—for the information, or else treated as a quibbler who is raising a sham difficulty. The advantage this assumption gives to those who do not like their statements criticised is obvious.

[1] I.e. excluding from consideration "equivocal" words in the old sense.

But we have seen (§ 36) how thin and shallow this old conception of the "essence" was. The real doubts of interpretation only begin where the dictionary definition leaves off. They are doubts which do not arise until the accepted definition by *genus* and *differentia* is already known, and their function is to suggest that the *species* thus defined needs further subdivisions—even if for this occasion only. The doubts arise out of the belief that the rule is true in one sense of the word M, and false in another. They rest on the belief that S's individual difference from other cases of M is relevant to the question whether S is M when " M " is interpreted in the sense which allows the rule "All M are P " to be taken as true. The request for further definition therefore is a way of pointedly raising the question whether these *beliefs* are true, and it is only an assertor who feels his position weak and fears exposure who has anything to gain by refusing the offered discussion. When the nature of ambiguity is more widely understood, such an assertor will have to look for some other kind of shelter. But he will not easily find one, and so he may learn to face the doubts and either accept or conquer them.

There is thus room for a good deal of instruction to be given in regard to the nature of definition as a remedy for a discovered ambiguity. In the main this would consist of instruction in the general conditions of the use of language, based upon the discussions in Chap. IX. It is inevitable that in generalising we should express our results in compact formulæ, but the deeper our acquaintance with their application becomes the more we shall learn to think of the doctrines themselves as always needing careful interpretation and as liable to be misapplied. Instead of *doctrines*, therefore, in the sense of truths to be accepted without question, they are better conceived as a convenient way of raising *problems*—problems of application. Given any formula as starting point, what we ought to fix our attention upon are the questions (1) what common opinion does it contradict, and hence what is its value in application ; and (2) how can it mislead us if we interpret it wrongly. Not only the teacher but the examiner would find plenty of material by using this method.

A few examples may help us to see what is here suggested. Take the doctrine that all "fact" is statement of fact (p. 193). What this contradicts is the common assumption that a fact, apart from its statement (or conception), is something that we can recognise. This assumption is supported by the more general assumption that an undeniable axiom of the "A is A" type gives information. It is easy to accept such "truths" as that "facts are facts" and "statements of fact are statements of fact" without reflecting that they tell us nothing. The former, if taken as undeniable, is without application to the only kind of "fact" we ever encounter; and the two taken together have the effect of creating an inapplicable distinction between a fact and its statement.

Now distinctions are never created except to be used, and most distinctions are useful for some purpose (§ 37). But whether the distinction between a fact and its statement has value for any purpose or not, at any rate it is capable of being misapplied. By means of it facts are supposed to have a solidity and a certainty which statements of fact have not; and it is only a short step from this to the notion that some facts *exactly as presented to us* are beyond the reach of criticism. For the most part this belief is not a result of any definite theory about the relation of facts to our recipient minds, but rather of a comfortable absence of theory in the matter, and a hazy remembrance of some convenient metaphorical expressions in common use. Our minds are conceived as "bombarded" by facts, or as "taking them in"; we are supposed to be passive recipients of something that comes to us from outside, something that remains unaltered when it reaches us, though our opinions may be altered by it.

One way of correcting this view is by showing that the distinction between *conceiving* a fact and *describing* it (i.e. stating it) turns upon nothing more important than the question whether we keep the fact to ourselves or try to impart it to someone else. In either case what we call the "fact" is only our *opinion* about the fact. In the absence of doubt it is easy to be unaware of any process of forming such opinion, and the simplest way in which we can become aware of it is through making mistakes and either finding them out or having them pointed out by other people. As this is an experience common to all of us, all that is here needed is a little reflection on our own previous unsuccessful performances in the apprehension of facts.

Conjuring tricks are a useful example of such apprehension, and especially of what is always involved in the acceptance of any fact—namely the unconscious *selection* of some parts of the total fact, and the overlooking of the rest. The conjuror's business is to make us overlook those parts of it that might show us how the trick is done, and wherever he succeeds we have a clear case of "fact" which turns out to be only our opinion about a fact, and an incorrect opinion.

Detective stories are another useful mine of examples of the way in which our minds are always active and selective in the process of apprehending facts, and how every fact as noticed by us is no more than a selected portion of all that is actually presented. Present "the same fact" to a trained and an untrained mind, and it will not be the same; it is already a different "fact" before the process of putting a meaning into it begins. Examples of this kind help us to see another truth about facts—that they are always complex, and that there is no end to the process of analysing them into constituent parts. No fact ever is as simple as it seems; what we regard as the fact is always a selection out of innumerable details; we select what *in our opinion* (however unconsciously formed) is essential, or important.

When explanations of this kind are given, the doctrine that all fact is statement of fact seems fairly safe against misinterpretation. It evidently is not intended to mean "statement" as contrasted with "conception." Nor is it intended to apply to facts which are not composed of smaller details—if such fact-atoms can be imagined as possible. It would be difficult, I think, to find any other ways of misapplying it, but the reader is invited to try.

Closely connected with this doctrine is another: that all statement of fact is descriptive statement. This may be called only another aspect of what we have just been saying. It brings to bear against the common distinction between a plain statement of fact and a coloured (or descriptive) statement, the same criticism as against the distinction between a fact and a statement or opinion. Just as a fact, when recognised, cannot help being an opinion about a fact, so even the simplest and most colourless account of a fact cannot help being descriptive.

But this doctrine takes us a little further, because it involves some account of the process of description, and of the nature of predication, or description of a subject. When we ask how anything, S, is described we find it can only be by comparing S with *something else*. To call a thing *sui generis* is to say that it baffles description—that it is unique, and that therefore we cannot regard it as a member of any class (*genus*) consisting of other members besides itself. But a "class" consisting of one member is not what is ever meant by a class or kind. The whole purpose of making classes is that of grouping together, on the ground of some points of resemblance, things which are *different*, but whose difference is thought to be less important than their resemblance (p. 201).   It is of course possible that what was once a class may dwindle down—as a tontine does, or the Mohican tribe—to a single surviving member ; but then we call him the surviving member, not the *class* itself.   So long as any class can deserve to be called a class it must group together individual cases which are different.

In describing or conceiving anything, then, we necessarily conceive it as a member of a class.   And since anything which is *sui generis* is, as such, not a member of any class, it follows that in describing anything we declare that it is not *sui generis*, not unique.   But then we are confronted with the admitted fact that every individual thing (or person, or case, or event) *is* unique.   Under the old conception of the nature of Truth, therefore, all description is *false*.   S is unique ; when we describe it we say it is not unique ; and there is an end of the matter.

It is at this point that we are saved from a deadlock by the doctrine that *Truth is relative to purpose*.   As soon as we recognise that though S belongs to the class M for one purpose it may be outside that class for another, the fact that the members of a class are all different no longer necessarily destroys the truth of the statement that S is M. That statement no longer denies that S is unique, but it asserts that, for the purpose in hand, its uniqueness—its individual difference—is *irrelevant*.   The particular purpose, it says, is sufficiently served by noting S's resemblance to the other members of the class M, and neglecting the difference.

We are saved in this way from having to admit that all description, or predication, is necessarily *false ;* but on the other hand we are forced to admit that it necessarily involves a *risk of error*.   The opinion that S's individual difference is irrelevant may, like any other opinion, be mistaken.   Its safety against error depends on the extent and accuracy of our knowledge of (1) the individual difference itself, (2) the particular purpose in view, and (3) the relation between them.   Every predication therefore professes to have faced and conquered whatever difficulties there may be in the way of such knowledge; and accordingly all criticism of a predication consists in the suggestion that one or more of these groups of difficulties have been insufficiently disposed of.

These examples may help us to see how closely interwoven the doctrines of logic are. We cannot follow out the consequences of any one of them without being sooner or later led over the same ground that any of the other doctrines, similarly followed, would lead us to.   There are very few main principles at the root of the whole system, and any special logical doctrines that may be formulated, whether about facts, or description, or predication, or about classes and their " essence," or about distinction and definition, or anything else of logical interest, are only different applications of these same few principles.   It is in their applications that we can best understand the meaning of the principles themselves.   Such broad statements as, for instance, " Truth is relative to purpose," or " Every individual case is unique," or "the details in any fact are innumerable," or " the meaning of any statement is determined by the use intended to be made of it on a particular occasion " convey little to us except through the light they throw upon other doctrines of narrower scope; and I would suggest that, both for teaching purposes and for setting questions in an examination, a good method would be to take any list we choose to make of these narrower doctrines and to trace their connexion with each other and their relation to the few main principles themselves.   The following short list, in addition to those already mentioned in the present chapter, may serve for a beginning, and is capable of extension to any desired extent.

" A " is A ; till we know better.

" A " is not not-A ; except when it happens to be so.

A is either " B " or " not-B " ; or both, or neither.

No statement with a meaning is indisputable.

Judgments are never simple.

A major premiss has no Subject, but an antecedent and a consequent clause.

Predication claims the truth of an analogy.

An assertion is the answer to a question with a meaning.

All questions are questions of words, even when they are questions of fact.

All importance is relative to some purpose.

Classes are made by man, not by Nature.

Ambiguity is effective only in a middle term.

The contrast between Induction and Deduction has no logical importance.

There is no distinction except when there is also conjunction.

A mistake of fact always involves a misapplied distinction.

Definition of a species is of no use where the species needs subdivision.

All progress of knowledge involves further discrimination.

Definition, to be effective in removing an ambiguity, must be a postulate, and not a statement of fact.

Proof is never coercive.

[There are few, if any, of these concise doctrines that cannot be misinterpreted, and therefore the problem in expanding them is to guard against this risk.]

The general result of our survey of reasoning and its risks of error is that all the most deceptive kinds of fallacy come under the notion of Ambiguous Middle. But it does not follow that the best way of treating an argument which

seems to us erroneous is expressly to accuse it of containing this technical fallacy.   The use of the notion is chiefly
for our own guidance in conducting the attack, and except
in rare cases it is for several reasons best to avoid direct
reference to verbal difficulties.   We must remember that
at present most people have—thanks to the traditional
Logic—an insufficient notion of what ambiguity is, and
have therefore not begun to understand the difference
between cases where there is a real need for more definition
and those where the demand for it is a tiresome form of
quibbling.   Besides, the actual attack can generally be
managed without the use of any technicalities like "syllogism" or a "middle term," while even enquiries into a
definition are capable of being disguised under other forms
of question, less exasperating and less under suspicion of
wordiness.

Another reason why the notion of ambiguous middle
had better be kept in the background while dealing with
an actual argument is the fact, so often already referred to,
that an argument is now seldom or never put before us in
syllogistic form, and is usually much too complex to be so
expressed as a whole.   We should have to pull it to pieces
before we could discover the various little fragments of
syllogism that compose it.   But there is no need to view
it first as a whole and then in the details of its structure,
because in real life it is the details or fragments that
are usually first presented to us for acceptance or rejection.
What we meet with are alleged facts and their alleged or
assumed "meanings"; and though very often a hint is
given of the general conclusion to which they are all
supposed to point—and though this glimpse of the general
conclusion may be the very thing that makes us strict (or
lenient) in examining the evidence—yet the alleged facts
and the inferences from them claim to be considered on their
own merits, and so the question always takes the form " Is

such and such a fact true, and if so what exactly does it involve "? Actual disputation, except where the objection raised is merely one of inconsistency, always resolves itself sooner or later into the raising of one or both of these two problems.

Now the use of the notion of ambiguous middle is to prevent the enquiries into (1) the truth of the " facts " and (2) the truth of the rules, being kept distinct from each other in cases where the error, though really important, is verbally too fine to be detected except by treating them together. Where an error of fact is gross, or where an absurdly false rule is taken for true, there is no need even to think of ambiguous middle as an explanation. Only where gross and downright errors are absent, or have been corrected, need we begin to use the finer method of criticism. Questions about the truth of " facts " can be kept separate from questions about that of the rules so long as the error itself is not due to such separation.

As we have seen, it is precisely in cases of ambiguous middle that separation of the premisses is the source of the error. A convenient way of expressing the situation without using the technical phrase is by objecting that the fact has been conceived too *simply*, so that its real " meaning " is more complex than the arguer has made it appear. Some important detail in it—some part of its individual difference—has been omitted from the description given of it ; and hence, though the description is true in a sense, it is not true when considered along with the major premiss attached to it. The notion of ambiguous middle here helps the critic to keep in view the reasons why the three special risks noted on p. 240 exhaust all possible criticism of an argument, however obscure the error.

And since obscure error shades off into invisible error, which is indistinguishable from visible truth, we must expect to find these questions often difficult to settle to the satisfaction of both parties. The old assumption was that Logic could by itself decide whether an argument was sound or not, and that everyone must accept its verdict or be convicted of logical ignorance. The new logical method is, by its own principles, forced to be more modest in its claim. It recognises that the only logical criticism of an argument consists in raising difficult questions which may lead us into numerous other difficulties before the parties concerned can agree to consider the original questions settled. There is no coercion or finality anywhere in this method, but only an appeal of the same kind that all progressive science makes to us—namely that before concluding that a piece of reasoning is unsound we should get to understand (to the best of our ability, as fallible men) *how* the error came to be taken for truth.

The suggestion that a fact described simply as " M " is really " M with an important difference" always underlies the request for a definition of " M " in order to remove an ambiguity, and may therefore at any time be substituted for this request. Where M is a familiar word which " everybody knows the meaning of" those who do not understand the nature of ambiguity can hardly be expected to see why this common knowledge of M's meaning should not suffice. To them it naturally seems that the request for a definition is a form of quibbling. But even in their view questions about the details included in this case of so-called M, and about the importance of such details in relation to the conclusion drawn, are questions of *fact*. If they refuse to discuss them they must do so on some other ground than a contempt for verbal hair-splitting, and it is difficult to imagine where they will find one. We may look forward with some confidence to a great increase in the effectiveness of an appeal to facts against the verbalism which springs from uncritical acceptance of the abstract Laws of Thought.

INDEX